Far North Tales

FAR NORTH TALES

Stories from the Peoples of the Arctic Circle

Translated and Retold by Bonnie C. Marshall

Edited by Kira Van Deusen

World Folklore Series

 LIBRARIES UNLIMITED

AN IMPRINT OF ABC-CLIO, LLC
Santa Barbara, California • Denver, Colorado • Oxford, England

Library of Congress Cataloging-in-Publication Data

Marshall, Bonnie C.
   Far north tales : stories from the peoples of the Arctic circle /
translated and retold by Bonnie C. Marshall; edited by Kira Van
Deusen.
    p. cm. — (World folklore series)
  Includes bibliographical references and index.
  ISBN 978-1-59158-761-3 (hardcover : alk. paper) 1. Tales—Arctic
regions. I. Van Deusen, Kira, 1946– II. Title.
  GR390.M37 2011
  398.20911'3—dc22   2010044948

ISBN: 978-1-59158-761-3

15 14 13 12 11   1 2 3 4 5

This book is also available on the World Wide Web as an eBook.
Visit www.abc-clio.com for details.

Libraries Unlimited
An Imprint of ABC-CLIO, LLC

ABC-CLIO, LLC
130 Cremona Drive, P.O. Box 1911
Santa Barbara, California 93116-1911

This book is printed on acid-free paper ∞
Manufactured in the United States of America

Far North Tales: Stories from the Peoples of the Arctic Circle is dedicated to my dear friend and colleague, Alla Vasil'evna Kulagina, Professor of Folklore at Moscow State University, whose passing diminishes both the personal and professional worlds of those who had the happiness of knowing her. May the earth cover her gently.

Kulagina: Alla Vasil'evna Kulagina collecting the repertoire of Fëdor Semënovich Gerasimov in Arkhangel'skaia Oblast' in northern Russia. Courtesy of the Department of Russian Folklore at Moscow State University.

CONTENTS

Part 1: Tales of Daily Life

Part 2: Creation Stories and Myths

Part 3: Tricksters and Fools

Part 4: Legends and *Pourquoi* Tales

Part 5: Stories About Animals and Marriages with Animals

Part 6: Spirits, Shamans, and Shapeshifters

Part 7: Heroes and Heroines

PREFACE

The first time I flew over the Siberian north, I was struck by the immense patterns of waterways. Rivers and streams snaked back and forth, flowed together and apart, and finally emptied into the sea. Their designs reminded me of petroglyphs and embroidery patterns made by indigenous artists. I wondered how people could have known what their land looked like from above, before the days of airplanes. As I listened to Siberian people telling stories, I realized that the shamans could have seen those patterns while on their soul flights and that the patterns are repeated in the microcosm of plant life as well as the macrocosm of landscape.

Years later I flew all over Nunavut. I was recording Inuit elders telling the story of their great shaman Kiviuq. At one point, his way was blocked by a giant seal-oil lamp, and he got across only by jumping from one chunk of fat to another. And now from the plane, the chunks of ice below reminded me of those chunks of fat.

Stories reflect the land and sea, and everything that grows upon and within them. Much of the north is completely devoid of trees, and the ones that do grow are small but hardy. The tundra can feel like a desert, with its broad expanses and deceptive turnings, hills and valleys. Tundra plants grow close to the ground—lichens, berries and flowers that you won't see if you don't pay close attention. The taiga forests stretch enormous distances but are sparser than forests further south.

The vast circumpolar north has been occupied by humans for thousands of years, and the quality of their lives is testimony to their endurance, ingenuity, and spiritual precision. All of this is reflected in their stories.

Bonnie Marshall has gathered an amazing collection of tales from around the northern world. We laugh and cry with the heroes and heroines of indigenous Scandinavia, Russia, Alaska, Canada, and Greenland as they test their wits, fall in love, and journey to other worlds. She has taken the tales from a wide variety of excellent books and archival sources and retold them in her own voice while staying scrupulously close to the originals. She has translated many of the stories from the Russian. Some are published here for the first time in English.

There is magic in these stories, but it always has a solid basis in human common sense. Some stories reflect the cycles of life, and many of them interconnect with each other in interesting ways. For example, we can read the story of the Inuit hero Kiviuq's early life and then find several other stories that are often attributed to Kiviuq but sometimes stand alone, as they do in this collection ("The Fox Wife," "The Man Who Married a Seagull," "The Origin of Fog").

Tricksters can make us laugh until our sides hurt, and then they can be astonishingly cruel. People journey to the huge worlds in the sky and under the water, and in many ways, these worlds turn out to be similar to ours. Some of the tales have the kind of happy ending that we have come to expect from European folktales, but others may end in tragedy or simply stop. Elders explained to me that this is just like life. To them, truth is more important to a good story than a happy resolution is. Clearly, this is not a story-world that stands up to a romantic approach.

Europeans have colonized all these cultures, some for hundreds of years and others only in the twentieth century. Naturally this affects the stories, although the outsiders are rarely mentioned. We can contemplate whether a story that resembles Cinderella traveled north or sprang fresh on the spot.

Hunting is vital to survival in the north, which leads to complex relationships with animals. People need to kill animals to feed and clothe themselves, and yet they observe and interact so closely with them that they have come to understand that the animals have souls. From the tiny mouse to the giant polar bear, all are vitally important, like part of the family. Northern people survive on meat; clothing makes use of the animal skins, which to this day prove more efficient than any fabric humans have devised. We must stay on good terms with animals—and this leads to stories showing how to treat them with fairness and love.

All across the north people live in homes that range from a small igloo made on the spot for spending a single night through portable tents to permanent houses. Tipi-like *chum* and *urasa*, igloos, sod houses, tents, and the more elaborate Chukchi *yaranga*—all are masterworks of adaptation to high winds and very low temperatures. This is where the stories in our book were told generation after generation, to instruct the young and to while away the winter nights. Waldemar Bogoras was a nineteenth-century Russian political exile who spent many years among the Chukchi. He tells us that one storyteller ended his tale by exclaiming, "There! I have killed the wind!" No one felt fear of the storm as long as the story went on.

But for the most part, I did not hear tellers in those dwellings while on my travels in Russia collecting stories from 1992 through 2002. Things have changed radically over the past century and even the past decade. Now most people are living in Soviet-style houses and apartments. In 2004, in Nunavut, Canada, the houses I visited were far better constructed but equally distant from the older way of life; most importantly, all of them were firmly attached to the ground, in permanent communities—a far cry from the portable dwellings and ever-changing locations and social relationships of the past. I cannot emphasize enough the degree to which this settling has altered people's worldview.

One thing that has been lost in many places is the native language. In the Russian north, Chukchi, Yukaghir, Even, and Dolgan are spoken mainly by elders and the very few people who still live nomadically. The lingua franca is Russian. The case with Inuktitut in Canada is complicated. Most young people speak English almost exclusively, although some children are learning Inuktitut in school. They may speak better than the middle generation, who were likely brought up in the residential school system, where speaking the native language was forbidden. In fact, residential schools under Communism in Russia were very similar to those under church and government policy in Canada.

Language is essential to story. Elders insist that certain things cannot be said or implied in a second language, and even those that can be said may come out so awkwardly that the result has nothing to do with the poetry of the original. Languages have also been changed to reflect the syntax of the colonizer's language, with longer sentences. They are losing the verbal economy that was so essential to communicating over long distances outdoors.

And that is to speak only of everyday language. Ancient stories are full of words and phrases known only in story and shamanic work. When we recorded "Kiviuq," elders often used ancient phrases no longer used in ordinary speech, and it took long consultations between elder and interpreter to get an idea of the meaning. For example, "the hole in the environment" (that's the best we could do for *silaup putunga*) refers to the way shamans and, if the situation was urgent enough, even ordinary people could shorten their journeys through spiritual means. They made folds in the earth and passed through long distances quickly or opened a kind of tunnel through air, water, or earth.

Even orthography has been the subject of politics. In early Soviet times, alphabets were devised for most native languages using Roman orthography. A few years later, the powers that be decided that using such an alphabet might connect the minority peoples too strongly with the outside world and shifted the orthography to Cyrillic. Spelling of Inuktitut words has changed as Inuit devise their own systems to better represent their pronunciation.

Understanding of ancient story shifts with the way of life. The forced settling of nomads has destroyed whole worlds and cultures, not only in the north. A hundred years ago, some storytellers knew that their hero Kiviuq, who had wound up stuck in the southern climes after pursuing his goose-wife there, would someday return. But of the forty elders we recorded in 2004, not one believed it anymore. Are they speaking of the demise of their culture, gone to the south along with the hero?

In Russia the parents of an Udeghe story hero killed him because he was bringing back too much game, creating too much work for them. Now the parents are seen as lazy and foolish, whereas in past centuries, it was understood that the son was overhunting, taking more than was needed. He needed a strong lesson—one that could only be administered by the death and rebirth he underwent in the story.

As language is lost, story often goes with it. But stories can live on, in sensitive translation to a new language and a new world, especially in the words of authors like Bonnie Marshall, who is a storyteller herself and thus retains a wonderful sense of orality in her work. Stories have shifted in this way over millennia.

These stories are made to be told (or read) out loud! May you and your listeners enjoy them.

—Kira Van Deusen
Author of *Kiviuq, an Inuit Hero and His Siberian Cousins*

ACKNOWLEDGMENTS

This book was an ambitious project that required the help of many people. It was the suggestion of my Libraries Unlimited editor, Barbara Ittner, to expand a proposed collection of Siberian folktales to include the entire top of the world. Her suggestion spirited me off on an endlessly fascinating journey that I have been reluctant to halt.

One of the friends I found along the way is Kira Van Deusen, Canadian storyteller, who has done fieldwork among the northern peoples of Siberia and Canada. She agreed to become volume editor and contributed the glossary, preface, and several photographs. Her enthusiasm, encouragement, and critical eye have been absolutely essential to the completion of this volume. My thanks to Robert Rodriguez for introducing me to her work.

My friend Daphne Gillispie introduced me to her cousin, Paul Northcott, a talented Canadian photographer. His impressive photographs of the hauntingly beautiful Canadian north grace the pages of this book. Other contributors include Joyce Hill and her friend, Eva Irene Muir, who photographed Alaska. Historical photographs of the Chukchi were donated by my dear friend, Zina Sergeevna Nikitina, who so tragically died before the book manuscript was submitted.

I would like to thank my colleagues at the Department of Russian Folklore at Moscow State University for their help and encouragement and for their hospitality during my summer visit to Moscow. I am grateful to Vasilii Aleksandrovich Kovpik for sending photographs that I selected from Moscow State University's expedition archives and to Professor Vladimir Prokop'evich Anikin, my dissertation mentor during the Soviet era, for the Chukchi numskull joke.

Last, but not least, I would like to thank Susan Brackett, Reference Librarian at the Meredith Public Library, for the many hours she labored obtaining out-of-print books and Arctic classics for me in a world so focused upon technology that it is less receptive to the concept of Interlibrary Loan. It is thanks to Susan's persistence that I was able to obtain the works of Knud Rasmussen and several collections of Alaskan and Canadian stories.

INTRODUCTION

Images of the "last frontier" and the "Land of the Midnight Sun" in reference to the Arctic and bordering Subarctic evoke romantic ideas. Indeed, the frozen beauty of the Far North is striking. Even languages reflect the variety and richness of the land and cultures of the Arctic. There are more than thirty Inuit words for types of snow or snow-related objects and phenomena, more than fifty names related to bears among the Siberian Evenk, and many names connected to reindeer that vary according to the animal's traits among Siberia's reindeer-herding Chukchi.[1] Visions of the Northern Lights, glaciers, expanses of treeless plain called tundra, and miles of boreal forest called taiga come to mind in connection with this part of the world.

But beauty conceals hidden dangers. The climate is unforgiving and makes life difficult for Arctic residents. Traditionally, the indigenous people have had to be hardy and self-sufficient to survive. Illnesses that prevented people from pulling their weight and seasons when there was a lack of game presented daunting challenges. In 1927 in reference to his Fifth Thule Expedition, the Danish Arctic explorer Knud Rasmussen said, "Life is thus an almost uninterrupted struggle for bare existence, and periods of dearth and actual starvation are not infrequent.... It is hardly surprising then to find cannibalism by no means uncommon."[2] Still, the simplicity of life brought moments of joy and a quality of life now lost in the modern world. The stories of these people reflect these conditions and have much to teach us.

The preservation of the stories of the peoples of the Far North is important because many tales are disappearing with diminishing or assimilating indigenous populations. This is especially true of Siberian groups, such as the Enets, the Selkup, the Ket, and the Nganasan people. Perhaps this volume will serve to freeze some of the tales into print so that future generations can enjoy them. Although the Arctic and Subarctic covers a large area indeed, the lifestyles and stories have common features that are reflected in the tales themselves. These common features are discussed throughout this essay.

The World Folklore Series presents stories from the peoples of many regions of the world, photographs of the cultures and areas under scrutiny, and historical and cultural information. *Far North Tales* provides a sampling of stories from many Arctic and bordering Subarctic cultures. The collection provides resource material for students, storytellers, parents reading stories to their children, educators, librarians, and the interested general reader.

In selecting stories, I attempted a combination of well-known and lesser-known tales. Certainly, no collection would be complete without at least some Raven tales, the story of the sea spirit Sedna, and the story of the origin of the narwhal. On the other hand, I selected more obscure but enchanting tales, such as the Deg Hit'an/Ingalik story titled "The Old Woman and the Singing Fish." The interest the tales held for me, the characteristics and values they conveyed, and their lengths were important considerations in their selection.

Choices were somewhat controlled, of course, by the necessity of having multiple sources of the texts in English, unless the texts were in the public domain. In some cases, a story may be found in more than one culture. The people to whom the story belongs are indicated in the table of contents and after the title of each story. It is possible that some stories may be found in more cultures than I have noted, but I have limited my listings to what my research revealed.

Far North Tales is divided into seven sections, each devoted to a story type or theme. The seven parts are "Tales of Daily Life," "Creation Stories and Myths," "Tricksters and Fools," "Legends and *Pourquoi* Tales," "Stories About Animals and Marriages with Animals," "Spirits, Shamans, and Shapeshifters," and "Heroes and Heroines." Other features of this volume include a preface written by distinguished storyteller and researcher Kira Van Deusen. There is a brief cultural history of the Saami, northern Siberian people, Inuit, Yupik, Dene, Alaskan Inupiat, Innu, and northern European Russian groups. Accompanying photographs and a map aid the reader in visualizing the indigenous groups and their territories.

Whether using my own translations, multiple texts in English, texts in transcription, or some combination thereof, I have retold, or restated, the stories in this collection for comprehension and use in our English-speaking culture, a culture vastly different from the culture of the original tales. The retellings are not word-for-word versions of any text. Often, I have combined several texts, selecting appealing features, as I did in "Sedna, the Sea Spirit."

With regard to spelling, the Library of Congress system of transliteration was used with some modification for Russian words. For example, I rendered *iaranga* as *yaranga* in English for ease of pronunciation. In most cases, I added an English *s* to indicate plural, rather than use the Russian plural endings. Names generally known in English are retained in English form for all cultures represented here. With regard to the spelling of Inuit words, I have selected the predominantly used spelling in my original sources, whether or not it coincides with current practice, such as the change from *k* to *q* in recent years.

The Arctic

The Arctic is located north of the tree line.[3] It surrounds the North Pole, and the Arctic Ocean lies in its center. The Arctic includes sections of Alaska, Canada (Yukon, Northwest Territories, and Nunavut), Greenland, Scandinavia (Sweden and Norway), Finland, and Russia.

Arctic winters are long and cold, but summers are short and moderate. Nights become darker until there are twenty-four hours of night, after which days become lighter until there are twenty-four hours of daylight.

The Arctic is dry. The snow swirls around, driven by the winds, causing it to seem like a much greater quantity. Industrialization has affected the fragile ecology of the Arctic. The winds and the ocean currents bring pollutants, such as mercury. These toxins have entered the food chain through the fish and animals that people eat. Nuclear waste is another source of contamination. Other problems include the thinning of the ozone layer and global warming. Rising temperatures have caused carbon dioxide and gas emissions that melt the glaciers and cut off polar bears, caribou, and other animals from their habitat and migratory routes. Meanwhile, the polar ice cap is melting at an unprecedented rate, resulting in erosion, rising sea levels, severe storms, and changing ocean currents. On the positive side, the melting ice makes it possible for people to reach areas previously frozen and inaccessible for the purpose of extracting oil and gas and to mine iron ore, gold, and diamonds.

Fascinating animals live in the Arctic. They include the polar bear, which the Inuit named Nanurluk. The polar bear appears in the stories in this collection titled "Nanurluk, the Polar Bear" and "The Woman Who Adopted a Polar Bear," a tale in which a woman raises a bear cub to be her son. The latter story demonstrates how close the Inuit feel to bears and, by extension, to other Arctic creatures, which include the caribou, foxes, wolves, whales, seals, guillemots, ptarmigan, salmon, and even mosquitoes. These animals appear here in story.

The Subarctic

The Subarctic lies to the south of the Arctic and abuts it. The Canadian Subarctic, for example, includes Nunavik in northern Quebec, Nunatsiavut in Newfoundland and Labrador, and Nitassinan, the ancestral homeland of the Innu on the eastern Labrador Peninsula. Winters are long and can reach –40 degrees, the temperature at which Centigrade and Fahrenheit converge.

There, the tundra's frozen plain gives way to the taiga forest. Life in the Subarctic is not as severe because people, animals, and birds can seek shelter beneath the taiga's tree cover. The taiga is riddled with bogs that remain on its surface because water cannot penetrate the frozen soil. The bogs make a perfect breeding ground for black flies and mosquitoes. Two stories about the origin of these northern pests are "How Mosquitoes Came to Be" and "Two Brothers and a Giant."

The caribou in North America and reindeer in Europe and Siberia are abundant. Their meat has traditionally provided the indigenous people with food and their skins with clothing and shelter. Other animals include moose, European elk, musk ox, and smaller animals, such as the beaver, lynx, mink, ground squirrel, wolverine, muskrat, and many others that appear in these pages. Fish, especially salmon, are an important source of food for Subarctic people.

Peoples of the Arctic and Bordering Subarctic

The Inuit and related people, such as the Aleut of Alaska and the Yupik of Siberia and Alaska, cover a vast territory from Russia's coast to Greenland. The Dene and other Athabaskan-speaking people live near the Inuit in Alaska, the Yukon, the Northwest Territories, and northern British Columbia. On the other side of Canada, in Labrador and northern Quebec, the Algonquian-speaking Innu are neighbors of the Inuit.

Across the Norwegian Sea, Norway, Sweden, and Finland come into view. It is there that the reindeer-herding Saami, once called Laplanders, dwell, as well as on Russia's Kola Peninsula. To the south of the Kola Peninsula the Vep, Karelian, Mansi, and Komi live.

On the east side of Russia's Ural Mountains, a rich variety of indigenous people are spread across Russia's Siberian north: the Nenets, Ket, Dolgan, Nganasan, Evenk, Selkup, Khant, Sahka, Even, Enets, Yukaghir, Koryak, and Chukchi.

The people who inhabit the Arctic and bordering Subarctic represent a myriad of unique cultures, but nevertheless these diverse cultures share some common traits and interests. They have had to adapt to a harsh climate, from which they have had to wrest a subsistence living. Arctic dwellers are traditionally hunters, trappers, gatherers, and fishermen. Sea dwellers hunted sea mammals, such as whales, walrus, and seals. Land dwellers pursued caribou, moose, reindeer, and small mammals. Where available, seaweed, berries, and roots were added to a diet rich in fat and protein.

The social unit was composed of the nuclear family and blood relatives, as well as relations by marriage. The Arctic and Subarctic people lived in tentlike structures, such as igloos, conical bark tents, and cylindrical structures, such as the *yaranga* of Russia's Chukotka Peninsula and Kamchatka. Clothing was made of animal skins, such as those of the caribou, seal, polar bear, rabbit, and other small mammals. Arctic and Subarctic people traveled by foot, skis, boat, and sled. Boats had wooden frames and skin covers. In the Arctic, sealskin-covered kayaks carried one person and the flat-bottomed *umiak* carried supplies and several people. The Dene traveled in a birch-bark or moose-skin-covered canoe. Sleds were pulled by dogs or reindeer.

Religious beliefs were based on animism, a belief that everything has a spirit. Ancestor spirits were of great importance in guiding the individual. Care had to be taken not to offend a spirit and thereby create bad luck. The shaman served as an intermediary who interceded with the spirits on behalf of the people.

Today many people in the Arctic no longer live a nomadic life. They live in modern homes and wear Western dress. They travel by modern conveyances, such as the snow mobile and motorboat. Nevertheless, some maintain or struggle to preserve the old traditional life. These include the reindeer herders of Siberia and Finland. Many of those deprived of their independent traditional lifestyles have had difficulty adjusting to a settled existence and have become involved with alcohol and drugs. Finding employment has been another contemporary problem. Once proud and independent people have become dependent upon government aid. Many people have been granted settlements for the land and rights that were taken from them. Others, such as the Innu of Canada, are still struggling for their rights. Environmental pollution caused by the mining of natural resources, such as gas and oil, present new problems. These are exacerbated by the thinning of the ozone layer and the melting of the polar ice cap.

The stories of these people address many of the issues they have grappled with and reveal their spiritual journey of survival in hostile environments, a survival made possible by their sharing the few material riches that they possessed. The stories are a testament to the joy they found in simple, everyday events.

The Inuit

The Inuit dwell at the top of the world on the frozen tundra. One person is called an Inuk. The Inuit range from Russia's Chukotkan coast to Alaska, Canada, and Greenland. It is 5,000 miles (8,000 kilometers) from the Bering Strait to East Greenland alone, excluding Russia.[4] These hardy people have learned to prosper in extreme conditions. In Alaska, there are 40,000 Inuit, in Canada 30,000, in Greenland 40,000, and in Siberia 1,000.[5]

In times past the Inuit were called Eskimos. In Alaska and Russia, Eskimo is still the preferred designation. The term "Eskimo" encompasses both Alaska's Inupiat and related Yup'ik peoples. However, many aboriginal people found the term "Eskimo" to be offensive because they believed, perhaps mistakenly, that its origins were in a Cree word meaning "eaters of raw meat."[6] In fact, there are other possible meanings attributed to the word, such as "snowshoe netters" and "people who speak a different language" that are based on Innu words.[7] Nevertheless, in 1977 the Inuit Circumpolar Conference adopted "Inuit" as a replacement for "Eskimo."[8] Therefore, in this collection, Inuit will serve as the collective name, except in circumstances in which old sources consulted use the older term, Eskimo, and in reference to the people of Alaska who belong to the Inuit family but prefer to be called either Eskimo or their self-designated name.

The Inuit Family

A geographical division of the Inuit results in additional, more specific naming of the people according to place of habitation. Thus, one group of the Inuit family living in northwest Alaska and the North Slope, as well as the Seward Peninsula, is the Inupiat. The word Inupiat means "real people."[9] The Inupiat are also referred to as Eskimos in Alaska.

The Yup'ik live along the coast of western and southern Alaska and on St. Lawrence Island, as well as along the eastern coast of Chukotka in Russia, where they are called Yupik without the softening of the letter p, which is characteristic in Alaska. The Aleuts, who are related to the Inuit, live on the island chain in south and southwest Alaska.

The Canadian Inuit may be referred to under the umbrella of that single name, although the descendents of the Thule Inuit, who live along Canada's western Arctic coast, prefer the name Inuvialuit. The Caribou Inuit live inland in Canada's heart and range to the western edge of Hudson Bay. They hunt caribou instead of whales, as their name indicates. The Netsilik Inuit live largely in Nunavut. Traditionally, they have subsisted under extreme conditions. The Iglulik Inuit settled in an area from Chesterfield Inlet (Igluligaarjuk) on Hudson Bay to northern Baffin Island in Nunavut. The Baffin Island Inuit in the northeast are their neighbors.

The Inuit of Greenland may be called the Kalaallitt or Greenlanders.

Origin of the Inuit

The general consensus of anthropologists, archeologists, and linguists is that the Inuit, as well as other groups, came to America from Asia. Based on the findings of fossils, it was determined that the ancestors of the Inuit, a Proto-Eskimo-Aleut language–speaking group, came to Alaska 12,000 to 15,000 years ago. The Na Dene–speaking people followed 6,000 years ago. The Eskimo-Aleut family migrated to America around 2,000 years ago.[10]

According to Robert McGhee of the Canadian Museum of Civilization, the Paleo-Eskimo people (5,000 to 3,000 years ago) moved east across Canada, where they hunted caribou, muskoxen, and sea creatures. Their descendants formed the Dorset culture (3,000 to 1,000 years ago) and lived in central and eastern Arctic Canada, where they hunted sea mammals. Inuit legends, in which they are called Tuniit, describe them as gentle giants. When the Arctic climate grew warmer 1,000 years ago and the ice melted, making marine hunting more difficult, the Dorset people disappeared and a new group of Inuit took their place, the Thule Inuit. The Thule people learned to hunt whales from open boats called *umiaks*. The Thule Period extended from 1,000 to 300 years ago. The Thule lived in sod homes built over stones or whalebones. Today's Inuit are their direct descendants.[11]

Inuit Languages

The languages of the Inuit indigenous people belong to the Eskimo-Aleut language family and form a dialect chain that spans the Arctic. According to J. R. Miller, Professor of History at the University of Saskatchewan, the chain includes two branches, an eastern and western branch. The eastern branch stretches from eastern Alaska to Greenland and includes Alaskan Inupiaq, Canadian Inuktitut, and Greenland Kalaallisut. The western branch includes the Yup'ik languages of Central Alaska, the Pacific Gulf and the Russian Far East (Siberian Yupik).[12] Moravian missionaries working in Greenland in the 1760s helped to develop a written language based on the Latin alphabet, which spread westward to Alaska.[13]

A more detailed listing of Inuit languages includes Inuvialuktun, a version of Inuktitut that is spoken by the Inuvialuit (real people) of the Northwest Territories from Alaska's border to Amundsen Gulf, as well as the MacKenzie River Delta, Banks and Victoria Islands, and the Arctic coast.[14] Inuinnaqtun is spoken in western Nunavut and the Northwest Territories.[15] The Alaskan Inupiat people speak Inupiaq. It is divided into Seward Peninsula Inupiaq and Northern Alaskan Inupiaq. No explanation of Inuit languages would be complete without mentioning the splendid work being done to research, develop, and preserve indigenous languages at the Alaska Native Language Center of the University of Alaska at Fairbanks.

In Canada, the United States, and Russia, there is a history of valuing assimilation over preservation of native languages. Early attempts to encourage the use of native languages in Russia were ultimately rejected by the Soviet government. The Alaskan government, too, discouraged use of native languages in favor of English until 1972 when a bill allowing their use passed in Alaska's legislature.[16] In Canada the preservation of indigenous languages, traditions, and stories is encouraged today.

Inuit Culture and Daily Life

Traditionally the Inuit earned a subsistence living hunting, fishing, and gathering. Materials found in nature provided them with food, shelter, clothing, transportation, weapons, and tools. Caribou provided for the inland Inuit, and whales and sea mammals provided for the coastal Inuit. Men did the hunting while women accompanied them on hunting trips, cooked the food brought home, cared for the children, and cleaned and served.[17]

Women were ready for marriage at puberty, and boys were ready when they became successful hunters. Marriages were not always monogamous. A man could have more than one wife, and a woman could have more than one husband. Arctic explorer Knud Rasmussen describes marital arrangements in *Across the Arctic*.[18] He describes customs alien to European cultures, such as the killing of girls at birth unless they had been promised in marriage and therefore provided with a living.[19] Elderly people often committed suicide, rather than be a burden on the community.[20]

Nevertheless, community and family were of the utmost importance to the Inuit. The extended family with its respected leader formed the basic social unit. Several families might pool resources and share a place for the winter.

Transportation was by kayak, a sealskin-covered boat for one person, or by *umiak*, a large boat used to transport people and goods. The dog sled on wooden or whalebone runners also provided transportation. There were snowshoes too, which the Inuit invented and passed on to the rest of the world, along with their kayaks.

Clothing included the parka (*anorak*) and a hood (*amauti*), which women wore and used to carry babies. Boots were referred to as *kamiks* or mukluks.

In the far north, winter houses known as igloos were often made of blocks of snow. Other Inuit groups framed houses that they covered with sod and animal skins. Summer houses resembled tents.

Inuit Beliefs and Traditions

The Inuit believed that all things—humans, animals, and even objects—were endowed with an immortal soul. The Netsilik told Knud Rasmussen that "a soul is life which cannot die."[21] For that reason, rituals surrounded the hunt and proper respect had to be shown the slain animal. If the animal's spirit was offended by some infraction or carelessness, it would return to take revenge and would bring bad luck.

The shaman (*angakok*) was born with a special ability to heal and to communicate with spirits, who imparted special knowledge and advice that the shaman shared with the community. He or she enlisted the help of the spirits for the hunt. Thus, in the tale titled "Sedna, the Sea Spirit," the shaman traveled to Sedna's home at the bottom of the sea to enlist her help in freeing the sea creatures for people's use. Indeed, Sedna, who is also known by other names throughout the Arctic, is the most important Inuit spirit. If she fails to confer favor on the Inuit, they will surely die.

When Knud Rasmussen spent time among the Utkuhikhalingmiut of the Great Fish River area, they explained to him that their religious focus was more on fear than belief.[22] Their religion, then, was one of avoiding disaster by strictly following ritual taboos. Each person had a helping spirit to call upon and to guide him or her through life. If a taboo was broken, the soul of either human or animal could turn into a *to'nraq*, or evil spirit, because the infraction prevented it from moving on and incurred anger against those who had spoiled its afterlife.[23]

With regard to death, the Utkuhikhalingmiut believed people were carried by the moon up to the land of heaven, where they lived on eternal hunting grounds and where their windows were stars.[24] If souls wanted to go on living on earth, they might choose a newborn to live in again. Their new body had special powers and was protected by the soul.[25] This represents a belief in reincarnation.

Rasmussen lists the three most powerful spirits among the Netsilik as Nuliajuk (or Sedna), Nârssuk (or Sila), and Tatqeq (or Aningait).[26] Nuliajuk, the sea spirit, is the most powerful and the most revered of all spirits. Nârssuk (Sila) controls the weather—the wind, snow, and rain. He is an infant, and bad weather comes when he loosens his diaper. If the weather rages too violently, the shaman has to travel to Nârssuk to tighten his diaper so that the bad weather will cease.[27] Tatqeq is the Moon Spirit, who brings luck to the hunter and fertility to women. The moon was a man once. His story is told in "Sister Sun and Brother Moon."

Inuit History

The Saga of the Greenlanders contains a recounting of the colonization of Greenland by Erik the Red (c. 970–1030).[28] Thus, Vikings were the first Europeans to come to the Arctic. They settled along Greenland's coast and found Paleo-Eskimo cultures already living there. Greenland is the world's largest island. Since its interior is covered with ice, the environment was far from hospitable for the Vikings. They disappeared around the fourteenth and fifteenth centuries.[29] In 1576 in search of the Northwest Passage to Asia, Martin Frobisher sailed to what became Frobisher Bay (now Iqaluit) on Baffin Island. Part of his crew mutinied and left.[30]

Other newcomers included Basque fishermen, who established whaling stations in Labrador in the mid-nineteenth century. In the seventeenth century, the Hudson's Bay Company opened trading posts across the Arctic, and by the nineteenth century, the trading company had become Canada's largest private landowner.[31] The Moravian Church began activities in the eighteenth century and provided help and basic tools and materials to the Inuit.

Arctic explorers included Admiral William Edward Parry, who led the British Navel Expedition (1821 and 1823) to the Arctic, where he wintered in Foxe Basin. While there, he documented Inuit life, thereby providing us with valuable information about everyday life among the indigenous people. In 1845, John Franklin conducted an expedition to find the Northwest Passage, and all 129 of his crew died. In the twentieth century, Knud Rasmussen led five Thule Expeditions to the Arctic (1912–1924), during which he collected detailed and valuable information about the Inuit.[32] It was Rasmussen who found the bones of Franklin's men and buried them.[33]

Whalers, fur traders, missionaries (Protestant and Catholic), and the Royal Canadian Mounted Police came to the Arctic and left their mark. Their influence was not always positive. The whalers and traders brought European diseases with them that caused mass deaths, so that by the nineteenth century, the Arctic had lost 90 percent of its population.[34] The Inuit failed to understand or make sense of the laws to which the Canadian police subjected them. Contact with outsiders increased during World War II and the Cold War with the building of roads and with the development of the oil and mining industries. Mistakes were made in the treatment of indigenous people. The Canadian government relocated the Inuit during the 1950s to places where there was a lack of food. Separated from their nomadic way of life, they grappled with unemployment, alcoholism, and drugs. Some young people committed suicide in their despair.

By the 1960s, the government sent Inuit children to boarding schools, where they obtained an education but suffered separation from their families. The students of these schools returned home with new ideas that resulted in the political activism of the 1970s. The Inuit wanted a voice, and thus they began making land claims. Their efforts resulted in the claims settlement of the Inuvialuit Final Agreement (1984) and the formation of the Inuit territories of Nunavut (1999), Nunavik (2003), and Nunatsiavut (2005).

Inuit Tales

It is the stories passed down orally for generations that informed and perpetuated the Inuit belief system. They explain what was created, by whom, and how earth's creatures and the luminaries came into existence. There are tales that explain how the Inuit's food was created. The sea creatures were created from Sedna's hands ("Sedna, the Sea Spirit"), the narwhal morphed from an evil stepmother ("How the Narwhal Came to Be"), and the Mountain Spirit pulled the caribou from the earth ("The Creation of Caribou"). Other stories explain how the sun, moon, stars, and warmth were created ("Raven Steals the Light of the Sun, Moon, and Stars," "Sister Sun and Brother Moon," and "The Star Man"). Raven, who is sometimes referred to as Crow, figures prominently in the creation of the world, just as he does in First Nations' stories.

Pourquoi, or explanatory, tales give information about the origin of creatures, such as birds—the guillemots and ptarmigan in "Guillemots" and "The Origin of the Ptarmigan." They explain how animals and people acquired specific traits—how the raven and the owl got their colors in "Raven and Owl," and why the dog has the habit of following his master when his master leaves in "The Giant Cannibal Dog." Stories explain how fog originated ("The Origin of Fog") and how people's emotions were first discovered ("The First Tears").

Animals take on human qualities in these stories and even marry humans. Two young sisters are kidnapped to become the brides of birds in "The Eagle and Whale Husbands." Inuit men marry a seagull ("The Man Who Married a Seagull") and a fox ("The Fox Wife").

In "Flying to the Moon," the hero is introduced to the Moon Spirit as part of his shamanic initiation rite. Another shamanic journey is described in "The Old Bachelor Who Flew Through the Air in a Kayak." The role of the shaman in saving the community from the dangerous attack of Nanurluk, the fearsome polar bear, is recounted in "Nanurluk, the Polar Bear."

Shapeshifters are featured in "The Jealous Uncle," in which a nephew outwits and escapes his murderous uncle by twisting his eagle bracelet, an amulet that transforms him into a ball of fluffy eagle down. A jealous rage causes an abandoned wife to become a bear in "The Jealous Wife," and a man dissatisfied with his human lot lives for years as a caribou in "The Man Who Became a Caribou."

The best-known Inuit hero is Kiviuq, whose adventures are known throughout the Arctic. Several episodes from his journey are told in "Kiviuq's Eternal Journey." An abused wife named Tayune is a heroine who braves the elements and finds help in the guise of a kind giant in "Tayune and Kinak, the Hill Giant." An abused orphan boy who is thrown about by a man who hooks him by the nostrils may be an unlikely hero, but ultimately he saves his people in "Kagsagsuk, the Boy with Enormous Nostrils."

These stories serve to reflect the words of Igjugarjuk of the Caribou Inuit. "All true wisdom is only to be found far from the dwellings of man in the great solitudes; and it can only be attained through suffering."[35]

Spellings used in the Inuit tales have been kept as they were in the original sources or as they appeared in the majority of sources consulted.

Yupik (Yup'ik) Eskimos

The Yupik, an indigenous people distinct from the Inuit and yet culturally similar, dwell in the "cradle of Eskimo civilization" on the Russian and Alaskan sides of the Bering Sea in an area that has an abundance of fish, birds, and mammals.[36] Siberian Yupik traditionally have lived in the Russian Far East in the Bering District, the Chukchi Autonomous Territory (Chukotka), Magadan Region, and Wrangel Island. Today they are largely concentrated in and around the villages of Naukan, Sireniki, and Chaplino.[37] The majority lives in the United States on St. Lawrence Island and in western and central Alaska. The Alutiiq, or Sugpiaq (Pacific), Yup'ik of southern coastal Alaska, Kodiak Island, and the Kenai Peninsula are not to be confused with their neighbors, the Aleut, despite the similarity in names. The inconsistency in the spelling of their names (Yupik versus Yup'ik) occurs because in the Central Alaskan Yup'ik language, the "p" is elongated so that the name is pronounced Yup'ik.[38]

Yupik (Yup'ik) Languages

Yupik (Yup'ik) means "real people."[39] One person is called a *Yuk*, and *pik* means "real." The Yup'ik of Nunivak Island refer to themselves as Cup'ik.[40] The Yup'ik form the largest of Alaska's Inuit groups.[41] There are 1,700 Yupik on the Russian side of the Bering Strait and approximately 20,000 Yup'ik in Alaska.[42]

There are four Yupik languages. Alutiiq (Sugpiaq) is spoken on the coast of the Gulf of Alaska, Central Alaskan Yup'ik is spoken in Bristol Bay and the Yukon-Kuskokwim Delta, Naukanski is spoken by a few people (70 out of 400 people in 1999) living in Russia's Far Eastern shore of Chukotka, and Siberian Yupik is spoken on the United States' St. Lawrence Island and on the facing shore of Russia's Chukotka.[43]

Yupik (Yup'ik) Culture and Daily Life

Siberian Yupik

Before the Yupik of the Russian Far East came under Soviet influence, they were seminomadic hunters and gatherers who lived in villages by the sea. They hunted sea mammals in kayaks and in flat-bottomed boats called *angiapik*. Although they did not own

---

reindeer, they bartered with the inland Chukchi to obtain reindeer meat to supplement their diet.[44] This bartering continued into modern times. However, today in Sireniki, some Yupik keep a small number of reindeer that they have acquired as a gift from their Chukchi neighbors or through trading, and infrequently through outright purchase.[45] At one time, the Siberian Yupik lived in a *yaranga*, a dome-shaped circular tent covered with reindeer skins, a dwelling they may have borrowed from their enemies, the inland Chukchi, who were able to obtain most of the Yupik lands, leaving only a small strip of coastal land to the Yupik.[46] Today, of course, the Yupik live in more modern housing constructed by the Soviet government when it established state farms. These homes lack indoor plumbing and are drafty and dilapidated in contrast to the modern homes of the Alaskan Yup'ik. The traditional role of women among the Yupik has been to cook, sew, care for the children, and scrape and prepare the hides of sea mammals and reindeer.

Alaskan Yup'ik

The Yup'ik of Alaska hunt and fish most of the year on the coast and inland on the treeless tundra with its many lakes. They hunt on the coast for fish, seal, and walrus. Inland they hunt for caribou, bear, moose, small animals, and birds. Alaskan Yup'ik were seminomadic. Traditionally they spent spring and summer at fish camps in families or groups of families. They returned to their villages for the winter.[47]

The traditional winter housing of Alaska's Yup'ik differed from that of the Siberian Yupik. The men lived in a communal house called *qasgiq,* which served as a kind of community center, where ceremonies, dancing, storytelling, and singing were performed. There, men also taught hunting skills to the boys. Women lived in an *ena* with the children, for whom they cared. They taught the girls sewing, cooking, and crafting skills. Interestingly, boys and girls switched places for a few weeks each winter and learned the skills of the opposite gender.[48] The Alutiiq (also called Pacific Yup'ik or Sugpiaq) live on the southern Alaskan coast. Their traditional housing before the coming of Russian fur traders and missionaries was partially subterranean houses called *barabaras*.[49] Today the Yup'ik live in modern homes and travel on snowmobiles and ATVs. Although Yup'iks still use the traditional walrus-skin boat called the *umiak,* while hunting on they sea, they attach an outboard motor to it.[50]

Yupik (Yup'ik) Beliefs and Traditions

The Yupik believed in the reincarnation of souls. Therefore, a newborn baby would receive the name of a deceased relative.[51] Neither people, nor animals, really died. The Alaskan Yup'ik conducted a winter celebration of the life cycle during the five-day Bladder Festival. In the belief that the soul of the seals they had killed migrated to their bladders, the Yup'ik collected the seals' bladders during the hunting season. The bladders were inflated and hung in the *qasgiq* to dry. In winter, they were pushed through the ice to return to the sea in the belief that they would be reborn and continue the life cycle.[52]

Shamans were thought to have the power to heal and to intercede with the spirits on behalf of their people. Their role was to keep evil at bay and to maintain a working relationship with hunted animals.

Raven (who created the world), the wolf, and the orca (killer whale) are sacred animals in Yupik mythology and cannot be killed. The wolf and the orca are thought to be two aspects of the same creature. In winter, the creature appears as a wolf and in summer as an orca. The orca was said to help sea hunters, who threw tobacco into the sea as a sacrifice to the killer whale to persuade it to help in hunting walruses. Only people chosen by the sea spirit could kill whales. Once the whale was killed, it had to be treated with respect and regaled like a guest so that it would not become sad. Eventually, the slain whale was sent back to the sea in hopes that it would return to future hunters.[53]

History of the Russian Yupik and Alaskan Yup'ik

Tsarist political exiles became interested in promoting the traditions and culture of Siberia's indigenous people. Because of their activism and influence, the Soviet government established the Committee for the Assistance of the Peoples of the Northern Borderlands, which was shortened to the Committee of the North.[54] The committee's goal was to support the native people and protect them from exploitation. As time passed, the focus became centered more on educating the native people to political and ideological awareness. And so Lenin sent idealistic young people out to cultural bases with mobile Red Tents to educate the indigenous people about communism. Chukotka's first base was established in 1928.[55] In the same year, the Central Committee made an addition to the criminal code titled "Crimes That Constitute Survivals of Tribalism." By the 1930s, when Stalin forced the native people onto collective farms thereby annihilating their nomadic lifestyle, native traditions became criminal. Well-to-do people and shamans, as religious leaders, were exterminated. Children were forcibly taken from their families and placed in boarding schools. After the collapse of the Soviet Union in 1991, supplies to villages distant from Moscow and European Russia ended. The Yupik, who had forgotten how to live off the land, had to survive once again on fishing and hunting in a land compromised by industrial pollution, making survival more difficult than it was for their ancestors.[56] Because the Soviet Union had a centralized system of government, this policy extended to all of the Siberian indigenous people, regardless of their location.

The Alaskan Yup'ik were untouched by outside influences until the coming of Russian fur traders and Russian Orthodox missionaries in the 1800s. They accepted only those aspects of Russian Orthodoxy that fit in well with their traditional beliefs, thereby retaining their language and their emphasis on family life.[57] Even when faced with diseases brought by the newcomers, the Yup'ik remained strong and resilient.[58] In some regards, the experience of the Alaskan Yup'ik echoes that of their Siberian counterparts. Their children, too, were placed in government schools that prevented them from using their native tongue, thus alienating them from their culture and traditional values. It was not until 1972 that the Alaska Legislature passed a bill giving children the right to speak their native language in school.[59]

Yupik (Yup'ik) Tales

Tsarist political exiles served as early ethnographers and gathered information about Siberia's native people. Vladimir (Waldemar) Bogoraz (variant Bogoras), Vladimir Jochelson, and Leo Sternberg were three Russian scholars who played an important role in pioneering ethnological research in Siberia. They were arrested in the 1880s and exiled for joining the People's Will (*Narodnaia Volia*) revolutionary movement. They participated in the Jessup North Pacific Expedition, which was planned and executed by Franz Boas.[60] Vladimir Bogoraz (Waldemar Bogoras) did research on the Yupik Eskimos that resulted in the publication of a collection of tales titled *The Eskimo of Siberia*.[61]

This collection includes several Yupik stories involving animals. "The Teals and the Fox" is a trickster tale with an unexpected twist. The fox plays the role of sly boots and trickster in many cultures, but here he is the one duped by a flock of teals. The teals create a precariously constructed boat to ride Fox out to sea, where they drop him. In "Who Shall I Be?" a bear cub decides to change his identity. When he attempts to become a ground squirrel, a deer, and then a duck, he ends up embarrassing himself and learns that it is better to remain as he was born.

The legend titled "The Little Warrior Mouse" offers an explanation for the presence of a mountain named in Mouse's honor, but the story's emphasis is to demonstrate how diligently Mouse was willing to work to become famous and not be forgotten in story and song. "The Stolen Song" is a *pourquoi* tale in which Raven, who is trickster as well as creator, snatches a lullaby from Snow Bunting's throat, taking her song by force. Father Snow Bunting retrieves the song, and Raven is left with the ugly "caw," so characteristic of his voice.

The Alaskan Yup'ik story titled "The Evil Old Woman with Long Nails" contains many fairy-tale elements. A young boy breaks a prohibition and crosses the river in defiance of his grandmother's command. This act leads him into danger. He meets an old woman who resembles the witches of European folktales. A ptarmigan acts as the boy's helper and causes the old woman to drown, thereby rescuing the boy, who has learned a difficult lesson.

First Nations People of the Northwest

Hunting and gathering First Nations people of northwestern North America live in Alaska, the Yukon, and the Northwest Territories. They speak one of the Northern Athabaskan languages and traditionally have been called Athabaskans. Today, they prefer to be called by their own name for themselves, the Dene, which means "people."[62]

Origin of the First Nations People of the Northwest

Scholars speculate that the ancestors of the Dene walked across the frozen Bering Strait or traveled in boats to this continent after the Ice Age.[63] The MacKenzie River Slavey story titled "How the Seasons Were Created," in which Bear steals warmth and keeps it in a bag, seems to support this theory because it tells of a time of extreme cold. Around AD 750, a volcano erupted in the Yukon, causing some of the people to leave the area and travel south.[64] For this reason, Athabaskan-speaking people are found today on the Pacific coast and even in the southern part of the United States, where the Apache form another branch of the Athabaskan-speaking family.

First Nations' Languages in the Northwest

In Alaska, there are eleven Dene groups. They are the Ahtna, Han, Deg Hit'an/Ingalik, Gwitchen, Holikachuk, Koyukon, Tanacross, Tanaina/ Dena'ina, Upper Kuskokwim, and Upper and Lower Tanana.[65] There are twenty Athabaskan or Na-Dene speaking groups in Canada.[66] Groups in the northwestern area of Canada's Yukon and Northwest Territories include the Tahltan-Tagish-Kaska and related Tlingit subgroup and the Slavey-Hare subgroup.[67] The Yukon Native Language Centre in Whitchorse, Yukon, is working to preserve and disseminate information about First Nations languages.

First Nations' Culture and Daily Life

The northwestern Dene traditionally have hunted, trapped, fished, and gathered plants and herbs to subsist. They lived in small matrilineal groups and moved through the areas where they might find game. Some groups were always on the move, while others, such as the Deg Hit'an/Ingalik and Tanaina/Dena'ina moved seasonally.[68] In the coniferous northern forests, they sought caribou, moose, bear, and smaller animals, such as rabbit, ground squirrel, fox, wolf, mink, wolverine, and muskrat. The pelts of these animals could be traded. Birds and fish, especially salmon, were caught, too.

They have adapted to the areas in which they live. For example, the Deg Hit'an/Ingalik living along the Yukon and Kuskokwin Rivers have adopted some of the traditions of their Yup'ik neighbors, relying more on salmon than animals, although other Dene groups hunted caribou in the fall. Caribou were trapped when they were corralled into a prepared space or driven into a body of water.

The Dene lived in winter villages and spring fish camps. At the fish camp, they caught salmon and other fish with nets, poles, and spears. The fish were smoked, dried, and stored in caches as food for the long winter. In winter, the Dene lived in houses that were partly subterranean or in log cabins with sod roofs. Some lived in domed tentlike structures covered with animal skins and birch bark. In summer they lived in temporary branch dwellings.

Travel was by foot, by birch bark or moose hide canoe, and by raft down waterways that served as highways to trading partners. Snowshoes and toboggans were used in winter.

Clothing was made of animal hides, especially caribou, and in winter consisted of pants, a belted coat, often hooded, mittens, and moccasins. Clever decorations—fringes, shells, beads, porcupine quills, and feathers—were added.

Dene celebrated after successful hunting seasons. They held a weeklong ceremony honoring the dead, and they socialized during trade meetings. These occasions inspired games, songs, dances, storytelling, and feasting. They provided a respite from a difficult life.

Survival was particularly difficult in winter after food supplies ran out. The Dene were required to move on to find sustenance. It was then that people sometimes starved.[69]

Not all of the Dene groups are represented by stories in this collection. It would require a multivolume work to do so. However, a closer look at the groups represented by stories is in order. The Deg Hit'an, which means "people from here," selected their own appellation in lieu of the pejorative Ingalik, which means "having lice eggs."[70] Their home in Alaska is along the Yukon, Innoko, and Kuskokwim Rivers. At present, they number only somewhat more than 500, but in 1830, before falling victim to European diseases, they numbered between 1,500 and 2,000 people.[71] The major part of their diet was fish, although they hunted larger animals, such as caribou and bear. Influenced by the Inuit, they adopted Inuit clothing styles and weapons and participated in potlatches, during which the wealthy gave to the poorer as a validation of their wealth. The Deg Hit'an bury the dead in the ground and very rarely cremate them. They observed their passing with a potlatch.[72]

The Tlingit speak a language that may have split from the Athabaskan language 5,000 years ago.[73] They are considered a Northwest Coast people, but one of the four Tlingit groups, the Inland Tlingit, is not coastal and has mixed with other peoples, such as the Kaska.

The Kaska live in the southeast Yukon and northern British Columbia in one of the last regions explored by the Hudson's Bay Company. They are related to the Tahltan and Tagish, and indeed these three groups were once known collectively as the Nahani.[74] The Kaska hunted caribou and lived traditionally in sod-covered lodges and conical tents made of poles and brush. Today most of the Kaska live on reserves.[75] Their two clan designations are Crow (Raven) and Wolf.[76] The Kaska, like other native groups, were reduced in number by influenza around 1920. Their community, reachable by road today, benefited by jobs provided during World War II and by the construction of the Alaska Highway.[77]

The Tahltan live in northern British Columbia by the Stikine, Nass, and Skeena Rivers, the area where according to Tahltan belief the earth was created.[78] Traditionally they were hunters and trappers who preferred meat to the fish in their river waters.[79] Their two clans are the Raven and the Wolf clans. Today the Tahltan First Nation is embroiled in a battle to preserve the sacred headwaters of the rivers against the encroachment of Royal Dutch Shell, which plans a mining project there.[80]

The Slavey-Hare language–speaking group of the Great Slave Lake and Lesser Slave Lake areas extends into British Columbia and Alberta. The North Slavey language is spoken by the Sahtu people of the middle Mackenzie River, Mackenzie Mountains, Great Bear Lake, and Great Slave Lake areas of the Northwest Territories.[81] The name "Slavey," or "Slave," was given to these people by the Cree, who robbed and enslaved them. The region that they occupy has been inhabited since 3,000 BC).[82] The seminomadic Slavey (Sahtu Dene) relied on fish as their staple food. In summer they congregated in large fish camps to net and dry fish. In winter they fished on lakes in family groups. In addition, they snared small animals and hunted bear and moose, which they lured by rubbing an antler against a tree in imitation of the male moose.

Today the Slavey number approximately 5,000.[83] They live in towns in modern homes supplied by the government, but they have not lost their traditional ways. The Slavey have suffered due to Canada's taking part in the Manhattan Project. Radium ore deposits that went into the construction of the first atomic bombs were carried in cloth sacks by the Slavey. Many of them suffered radiation poisoning.[84]

The Koyukon Dene live in northern Alaska along the Yukon and Koyukuk rivers. Their name represents a combination of the rivers' names. Traditionally, they survived by hunting and trapping animals. Russian traders came up the Yukon River in 1838, but the Koyukon lived without further infiltration until the Yukon Gold Rush in 1888.[85]

The Ahtna dwell in Alaska's Copper River basin, surrounded by the Chugash and St. Elias and Wrangell mountains. The Ahtna were hunters and gatherers, as well as fishermen. In fact, salmon were their major source of food. They spoke three separate dialects, and each group had a chief and shaman. They lived in wooden houses that were partially subterranean. They numbered 500 people in the eighteenth century and 300 in 1980.[86] Apparently, their numbers eventually became stable because the Alaska Native Language Center gives 500 as the approximate modern-day population.[87] Like the Koyukon, their first contact was with Russians, who arrived in the eighteenth century. Their next encounter with outsiders occurred during the Gold Rush. Author John Smelcer states that the Ahtna were perhaps the last First Nations group discovered in North America and that they lived isolated from the outside world until the coming of Lieutenant Henry Allen in 1885.[88] Smelcer speaks with regret about the loss within the past fifty years of Ahtna traditions and language.

First Nations' Beliefs and Traditions

The Dene believed that animals, plants, people, and even inanimate objects had spirits. There was a time when the line dividing people and animals was blurred so that animals could become people and people could become animals, shifting forms at will. People and animals were brothers, and therefore animals had to be treated with respect. If they were treated well, they would help the Dene and lend them their power.

The shaman was the most powerful because he could influence the outcome of the hunt by enlisting the aid of his spirit helpers. In addition, he could cure diseases with incantations and herbs.

Like the Inuit, the Dene believed that the universe was composed of multiple worlds. The Deg Hit'an/Ingalik, for example, believed that the universe consisted of four levels—one above the earth and two below it.[89] The shaman was able to travel between all of the levels.

The Dene had specific beliefs about death. Groups such as the Kaska believed in reincarnation and recognized the traits of deceased relatives in children and young people.[90] Although the dead are buried today, originally the Yukon Dene cremated them and built spirit houses as a home for the ashes. Spirit houses are still erected over graves today.[91] The Slavey thought that when people died, they lost their "shadow." They placed the dead in trees or buried them.[92]

First Nations' History

Europeans first explored Nunavut and the Northwest Territories in search of the Northwest Passage. Explorers included Henry Hudson (died c. 1611), discoverer of Hudson Bay; Sir Martin Frobisher (c. 1535–1595), for whom Frobisher Bay was named; Samuel Hearne (1745–1792), who went down the Coppermine River in 1771; fur trader and explorer Alexander MacKenzie (c. 1763–1820), who reached the mouth of the MacKenzie River in 1789, thereby becoming the first European to cross the Pacific Ocean; and Sir John Franklin (1786–1847), whose expedition ended tragically with the death of everyone aboard. Knud Rasmussen (1879–1933) recounted his adventures in *Across the Arctic* and was the first to cross the Northwest Passage by dogsled.[93]

The area now in Nunavut, the Yukon, and the Northwest Territories was owned by the trading company known as the Hudson's Bay Company and was sold to Canada in 1870.[94] In 1992, the Northwest Territories was divided so that the Inuit dwelled in the east and the Dene in the west. Nunavut, largely Inuit, came into existence in 1999.[95]

The first visitors to Alaska and the Northwest Territories were Russians. In 1741, Captain Vitus Jonasen Bering of the Russian navy explored Alaska's coast. His tales of the existence of abundant fur-bearing animals in the area resulted in a lively fur-trading venture. Inuit and First Nations people traded the furs for goods such as weapons, beads, and metal. The Tlingit acted as middlemen between the indigenous people and the Russian, and later British and American, traders. The Hudson's Bay Company set up trading posts at strategic points along bodies of water. The trading company did not always receive a warm welcome. For example, in 1872, the Tlingit attacked Fort Selkirk and drove the Hudson's Bay Company out of the southern Yukon.[96]

Missionaries followed. Fur traders introduced the Russian Orthodox religion in the mid-1700s. Catholic and Protestant Anglican missionaries, whose claims to colonize North America's west coast dated back to the papal bull of 1493, came with the Spanish and the British, whose Captain James Cook discovered Cook Inlet in 1778 and brought the influences of their cultures to the area. In the mid-1880s, American whalers whaled off the waters of the Arctic coast and traded. The United States purchased Alaska for $7,200,000 in 1867, an unpopular acquirement referred to as "Seward's Folly," so named after Secretary of State William Seward who approved the purchase.[97]

The impact of European and American incursions on the First Nations peoples differed little from the impact they had on the Inuit. They brought diseases with them, such as smallpox, that decimated entire native populations because the native people had no immunity against them. The indigenous people lost their independence and self-sufficiency and began relying on the products and goods that the newcomers brought with them to trade. In addition, the indigenous people became easily addicted to alcohol, of which they had no prior knowledge or resistance.

In 1896, gold was discovered in the Yukon Klondike. By 1899, gold was found in Nome, Alaska. Prospectors rushed to these areas, and the population of places like Dawson City swelled. For a period, some native peoples found work, bringing supplies to the miners by river, but the Gold Rush stopped as abruptly as it had started when the gold was depleted in the early 1900s. The devastation left in its wake had a negative impact on the local people, now deprived of their hunting grounds, which had been burned, and consequently of their daily food.[98]

World War II brought disruption to Alaska's Aleutian Islands, when Attu Island was invaded and occupied in 1942 by the Japanese. Aleuts were evacuated and resettled to another island. The year 1942 also marked the completion of the Alaska-Canada Military Highway that ran from Great Falls, Montana, to Fairbanks, Alaska. The highway made the area more accessible to outsiders.

The discovery of oil in Prudhoe Bay in 1968 brought even more people into the area and resulted in the building of the Alaska pipeline, completed in 1977, between North

Slope and Valdez. The building of the pipeline disrupted the migration routes of caribou, which had an impact on the native peoples, who relied upon caribou for food, and resulted in the uniting of indigenous groups in an attempt to gain back the lands that were taken from them. Although they have been successful in their endeavors, there are still a few outstanding land claims in arbitration.

Canadian governmental policy with regard to their First Nations has evolved from an attempt to force assimilation to a policy in support of independence and preservation of traditional culture. In Alaska, indigenous peoples have been given a voice in the governance through the creation of native village corporations.[99]

First Nations Tales

Much like the Inuit, the Dene have two basic types of stories.[100] There are stories set in Myth Time, or Distant Time, that pertain to the creation of the world, the spirit, and the sacred. The second type of story is set in more recent times with references to specific locations. Some of these stories might be called "memorates." These two genres are valued greatly by the Dene and provide them with guidance. Dene writer Bren Kolson states: "Stories are our culture. They express beliefs and values that teach people how to live a good life in harmony with the Earth and all its creatures."[101]

The most important character, the absolute star of Dene tales, is Raven, sometimes called Crow. Raven created the world. Without him, there would be no earth, no people, and no animals. Raven is complex because although he does much good and is sometimes helpful to humans, he can also act in a selfish, ridiculous manner in his role as trickster. In "Raven Steals the Light of the Sun, Moon, and Stars," Raven retrieves light; in "How the Seasons Were Created," he obtains warmth for all creatures. On the other hand, Raven can be trifling, as he was when he tried to trick fishermen out of their catch and as a result got his beak broken ("Why Raven's Beak Is Crooked").

Other creators include the Kaska man who created whales by carving them out of wood ("The Kaska Man Who Made Whales"); the Upper Yukon version of "Wolverine and Mink Create Earth," in which it is Man and Muskrat who create earth; and the Camp Robber who creates the caribou in the Dene version of "The Creation of Caribou."

Legends and *pourquoi* tales are a logical extension of creation myths. Raven figures as a character here, too, when he and Owl paint one another ("Raven and Owl"), with disastrous results for Raven. Both Tlingit and Kaska stories give an explanation concerning how mankind became saddled with the nuisance of mosquitoes in "How Mosquitoes Came to Be" and "Two Brothers and a Giant," respectively. Often *pourquoi*, or explanatory, tales give the reason for the existence of a very small detail of nature. For example, in the story titled "Beaver and Porcupine," the reader learns why tree bark has a shaggy appearance.

Human emotions are the topic of "The Jealous Wife" and of the poignant tale about the old woman suffering from loneliness and disappointment entitled "The Old Woman and the Singing Fish." A jealous rage transforms a woman into a bear in "The Jealous Wife," and jealousy leads an uncle to kill his nephews in "The Jealous Uncle," two tales the Dene share with the Inuit. These instructive stories demonstrate how not to live. Jealousy leads to self-destruction and living in isolation apart from the group leads to despair.

The Innu of Eastern Quebec and Labrador

The Innu live in approximately twelve communities on the Ungava Peninsula in Eastern Quebec and Labrador. They call their ancestral homeland, where they have lived for 2,000 or more years, Nitassinan. Nitassinan is home to an estimated 10,000 to 20,000 Innu, depending on the source consulted.[102]

Origin of the Innu

The Innu were present when the Vikings arrived at the end of the tenth century. Their ancestors are thought to be the Maritime Archaic Indians (c. 7000 BC) and the more recent Point Revenge Indians, who survived into the sixteenth century, but there is much speculation and not a great deal of evidence regarding their origins.[103]

The Innu were falsely divided into two groups, one called the Montagnais and another group called the Naskapi. However, they are the same people with slight variations in their language and culture.[104] The French called the Innu Montagnais, which means "mountain people." The Montagnais Innu lived along the north shore of the Gulf of St. Lawrence. Further north near Labrador's Ungava Bay, and therefore beyond the reach of Christian missionary influence, a smaller band, the Naskapi, lived. Their name means "people beyond the horizon."[105] Today's Montagnais and Naskapi in Labrador belong to the Innu Nation, and the Quebec Montagnais belong to the Mamuitun or Mammit Innuat First Nation. There is yet a third splinter group of Innu, called the Mushuau Innuat. This band broke away from the Naskapi in the twentieth century. The name Innu, which is preferred by the people themselves means "human being." The Innu are an Algonquin-speaking people, and the language that they speak is called Innu-aimun.[106]

Innu Culture and Daily Life

The Innu have been hunters and gatherers until recent years. They began relinquishing their family-based hunting culture in the 1960s.[107] The loss of their preferred lifestyle has created problems of adjustment and subsistence for the Innu. Traditionally, the Innu hunted caribou, moose, seal, porcupine, and bear. The women snared small game.

The Innu lived in conical wigwams made of birch bark in the south and covered with caribou hide in the north. Today's Innu live in Western-style houses and drive snowmobiles, but their adjustment to a modern, industrial society has been difficult and runs counter to their traditions of respect for the land and for all living creatures.

Innu Beliefs and Traditions

Caribou were the animals most important to the Innu as a source both of physical and of spiritual nourishment. Caribou Spirit (*Kanipinikassikeu*) is the most important spirit in the Innu belief system. Caribou Spirit is master of the caribou, as well as master of all the other animals.[108]

The Innu communicated with the animal spirits through the shaking tent, which is set up for the shaman. Once inside, the shaman speaks to the spirits with the help of the *Mishtapeu*, who are kind giants who live in the Other World, *Tshishtashkamuku*. The Other World is connected to this world by a bridge. The voices of the spirits that emanate from the tent, its shaking, and the drama associated with this ritual were amusing and awe inspiring. Despite the disapproval of the Catholic Church, this tradition lingered into the 1870s.[109]

History of the Innu

In 1668, King Charles II granted the Hudson's Bay Company land around the Hudson Bay and Labrador. The Hudson's Bay Company enlisted Innu expertise in trapping, but the demands of commercial trapping disrupted the Innu lifestyle. Their inability and reluctance to comply with company demands were interpreted by company managers as laziness. The company relocated the Innu without regard to their needs and lifestyle. Eventually, the number of caribou dwindled. Hudson's Bay managers even withheld ammunition when production was not up to expectations, thereby contributing to the starvation of the Innu.[110] Contact with Europeans brought disease. For the first time, the Innu encountered smallpox, flu, tuberculosis, and whooping cough. With no immunity to these diseases, they died in great numbers. Relocations created problems of survival and adjustment to a foreign non-nomadic lifestyle.[111]

The building of mining towns, such as the iron ore mining towns of Wabash and Labrador City and the nickel mines at Voisey's Bay, have ravaged the land inhabited both by the Innu and by their traditional enemies, the Inuit. Snowmobile trails cut through hunting grounds and disturb the animals with their noise. A hydroelectric plant was built on the Churchill River. Innu lands were flooded when the Smallwood Reservoir was created in 1970. The noise made by NATO low-level flights at the military base at Goose Bay in Labrador affected both humans and animals.[112]

European influences have brought a near cultural collapse for the Innu.[113] Attempts to force Western civilization onto the nomadic Innu, to make them into trappers dependent on European trade items, and to convert them to Christian religions have been destructive to their economic independence and to their sense of self-worth. John Gimlette, author of *Theatre of Fish,* describes today's Labrador Innu settlements at Goose Bay, Sheshatshu, and Natuashish (Davis Inlet) in unflattering terms and states that the Innu regard Sheshatshu as a concentration camp.[114] Elizabeth Penashue and Rose Gregorie expressed the Innu reaction to European influence and culture succinctly. "To keep us in one place, in a village, they have tried to separate us from everything that gives our life as a people meaning; it has also meant that we have been changed in only a few years from one of the most self-reliant, independent peoples in the world to one of the most dependent."[115]

Throughout all of these hardships and cultural adjustments, the Innu retain a feeling of stewardship toward the land. "To the Innu, the land is their history, their culture, and their future."[116] The Innu never signed away the claim to their homeland, and they are working today to regain control of it.

Innu Tales

The Innu refer to two types of tales, *atanukana* and *tipatshimuna*.[117] *Atanukana* are best described as myths. Included among these tales are creation stories. Less than forty years ago, the older generation of Innu still considered these stories to be literally true. *Tipatshimuna*, on the other hand, are similar to memorates. They are accounts of incidents told by the person who experienced them or by someone the narrator knew. They include tales of encounters with spirits. "Wolverine (*Kuekuatsheu*) and Mink Create Earth," then, is an *atanukan,* whereas "Toadman (*Anikunapeu*) Takes a Wife," which describes a young girl's encounter with the master spirit of frogs and toads, is a *tipatshimun*.

The most important and most powerful spirit in the Innu religious pantheon is *Kanipinikassikueu,* Caribou Spirit. He is the supreme ruler of animal spirits and has been bested by only one. On that occasion Fart Man (*Matshishkapeu*) caused Caribou Spirit to release the caribou against his will. This story is told in "Fart Man (*Matshishkapeu*)." As a mythic character, Fart Man is a source of great amusement to the Innu, who find humor in the concept of flatulence. It should be noted that there are many ribald Innu tales with scatological overtones, which is characteristic of many indigenous cultures. They are related frankly and with unashamed humor.

Other popular characters include the brave but foolhardy folk hero *Tshakapesh* (Moon Spirit), and *Kuekuatsheu* (Wolverine), the cunning hero of the Innu trickster cycle. Wolverine falls into the tradition of Raven in Siberia and the northwest of North America. Wolverine is both foolish and wise, destructive and creative. Gluttonous and childish, he lies, acts outrageously, and is always in trouble. In "Wolverine (*Kuekuatsheu*) and the Brant," Wolverine fails to heed the advice of the brants and falls to his death, only to offend people with his putrid smell.

As popular as the *Kuekuatsheu* cycle of myths is, the cycle about *Tshakapesh*, the Moon Spirit, figures importantly, too. *Tshakapesh*'s miraculous birth, as told in "Tshakapesh, the Moon Spirit," was typical of a super hero's birth—he grew by leaps and bounds, had the strength of several men, and was born a warrior. The Mammoth present in the story indicates how ancient the tale is since mammoths have long been extinct.

The Saami

The Saami are the original inhabitants of northern Scandinavia (Norway and Sweden), Finland, and Russia. They live mainly in the Arctic Circle on the mountains and tundra, the Arctic treeless plain. The southern section of their habitat is forested.[118]

The Saami were once called "Lapps," and the area they inhabited was called Lapland. This area is not a separate country but rather it is located within the borders of the countries mentioned above. The name "Lapp" was introduced by Swedish Vikings in the ninth and tenth centuries and was a translation loan word from the Saami meaning "a group of fishermen and hunters" or "a patch of cloth."[119] Because of the latter meaning, which can be construed to mean that Lapps wear patched clothing, the Saami call themselves Sámit (Saami or Sami). They call the area that they inhabit Sápmi, rather than Lapland.[120]

Origin of the Saami

The origin of the Saami is shrouded in mystery, and theories regarding their origin differ because they have no genetic resemblance to other people. Some scholars believe that the Saami came from Central Asia. They refer to their Mongoloid features as evidence.[121] Other sources make the claim that the Saami are a subgroup of Europeans, descended from hunting and gathering people.[122]

The same mystery surrounds their numbers. Wikipedia gives an estimation of a population ranging anywhere from 80,000 to 135,000, a considerable margin for error.[123] *The Columbia Encyclopedia* places the population at 80,000, and Elina Helander, Director of the Nordic Sami Institute, places the total population somewhere between 60,000 and 100,000.[124] The reason for these discrepancies lies in the difficulty of getting a true count of people who are spread over a wide territory that is located within the borders of not one but four countries. The logistics of coordinating a census is staggering and may never be properly done. Another difficulty involves developing criteria for defining people of Saami descent.

The Saami Language

The Saami language is a Finno-Ugric language and is part of the Uralic family of languages. There are fifty dialects that fall into three language categories (East, Central, and South Saami).[125] Scholars disagree regarding whether to refer to these groups as dialects or languages, perhaps because the dialects, or languages, are not mutually intelligible.[126]

Saami Culture and Daily Life

The Saami are well known as seminomadic reindeer herders. Traditionally, they have been involved in hunting, fishing, and trapping. At the turn of the twentieth century, the *Catholic Encyclopedia* divided the Saami, then referred to as Lapps, into three groups: mountain, forest, and fisher Lapps. Mountain Lapps lived in a portable conical tent called a *kata* in Swedish, *vezha* in Russian, or *lavvu* in Saami, which was used in reindeer herding. Forest Lapps, the most comfortable of the three groups, lived in permanent dwellings that were log cabins. Fisher Lapps were the most impoverished of the three categories.[127] Wikipedia uses another scheme that divides the Saami into Mountain Saami, who hunt and herd reindeer and who today represent only 10 percent of all Saami, and Sea Saami, who settled on waterways and the coast and who combine fishing with farming.[128] The Mountain Saami started taming reindeer around AD 1500, and it is thought that it was women who began domesticating the reindeer.[129] Today herding, rather than hunting reindeer in the wild, is prevalent. Dwellings are modern homes, rather than the *kata* of yesteryear.

Traditionally, groups of Saami families lived together in a *siida*, whereas today they live in nuclear families.[130] The traditional role of men has been hunting, constructing sleds and boats, and maintaining tools and equipment. Women, on the other hand, have had the responsibility of caring for the household, cooking, and sewing.

The traditional food of the Saami is, of course, reindeer meat. Fish and berries, particularly the cloudberry, figure into their diet, too. The evening meal is the main meal of the day. Before the refrigerator came into use, Saami stored food in storage sheds, called *njalla*, that were raised above the ground.

The traditional Saami costume sports bright hues of red, blue, and yellow. Strips of color border tunics and skirts, and women wear fringed scarves. Shoes are pointed at the toe, and the point turns up. The reindeer skin coat provides warmth in winter.[131]

Crafts are inspired by the reindeer and the herding life. Today many Saami supplement their income with their carvings and objects made of reindeer antlers, bone, and silver.

The *yoik*, a slow song sung *a cappella* and deep in the throat, represents an ancient musical tradition. Another addition to music attributed to the Saami is the invention of a small reed pipe.[132] Yet another invention that the Saami gave the world was skis. Byzantine historian Procopius (c. 490–562) wrote about the "skiing Finns" (i.e., Saami) early in the Christian era.[133]

Saami Beliefs and Traditions

A matchmaker or person speaking on behalf of the prospective groom arranged traditional Saami marriages. It was the custom for the suitor and matchmaker to visit the prospective bride's family. The suitor asked to make coffee for the family. If the parents of the young woman agreed to his making coffee, it was a sign that they approved of the young man. If the young woman unharnessed the visitor's reindeer, it was an indication that she approved of the suitor. Reindeer were given to the couple as wedding gifts because the number of reindeer a family had was indicative of their wealth and status.[134]

When a couple had children, the children were given the names of relatives who had died. It was not customary to have a surname, and the Saami resisted bearing surnames for many years.[135] The ancient nomadic Saami had no cemeteries; rather, they buried their dead near the place they had died. The dead were interred often in a sledge above ground, in the crevice of a rock, or in a shallow grave. Care was taken to keep the body intact and safe from animals because it was believed that the soul would be destroyed along with the skeleton. Loss of one's soul meant that it could not find a new body to inhabit, nor could it experience an afterlife. The shell-less soul might haunt others. In such cases, the dead were considered to be a threat, but on the other hand, they also protected relatives.[136]

Russian and Scandinavian missionaries converted reluctant Saamis to Christianity during the eighteenth century.[137] Today the Saami in northern Scandinavia are Lutherans, and the Kola Peninsula Saami in Russia are Russian Orthodox.

Originally, Saami beliefs were animistic. They thought that living and inanimate objects had souls and that spirits were associated with the dead and with places. The shaman served as an intermediary between earth and other worlds, with which he connected when he chanted or sang the *yoik*, when he drummed, and when he went into a trance.

The cosmos, according to ancient Saami belief, had four levels: the world above the sky, the world in the sky, earth, and the underworld. Gods, or spirits, were associated with all four levels.[138] Foremost in importance was the Sky God (*Radien*), who lived above the sky and kept order in the universe.

The sky was the abode of several gods. The Sun, associated with fertility and the origin of reindeer, and the Moon, protector of reindeer, inhabited the sky. The God of Winds was associated with hunting and herding reindeer. The God of Thunder was very powerful and associated with weather. He was both feared and revered because he had a dual nature. He might help the Saami by protecting the reindeer and destroying evil spirits, but he might also wreak havoc and thus had to be appeased.

The Father of Man was an ancestor god. His wife, the Mother of Man, dwelled with the earth gods. Although the Mother of Man had no daughters in North Saami tradition, she had three in South Saami tradition. They were the Creative Old Woman, goddess of pregnancy and birth; Old Woman of the Bow, who protected women giving birth and who was associated with hunting; and Old Woman of the Door, who watched over babies. These goddesses lived beneath the Saami home and were worshipped by women. Other earth gods included a God of Hunting and the Goddess of plants and vegetation, *Rananeid*, who was responsible for creating the green pastures on which the reindeer fed.

The Underworld resembled the world above and, unlike the Christian hell, was a happy place. The Ruler of the Underworld was *Jabmiidahkka*, a female deity. The God of Pestilence (*Ruto*), enemy of gods, men, and shamans, also dwelled in the Underworld.

Saami History

The Roman historian Cornelius Tacitus referred to a people he called "Fenni" in AD 98 in his "De origine et situ Germanorum." His is the first known written work about the Saami.[139] He describes the "Fenni" in an uncomplimentary manner as living in barbaric misery and poverty in their twig hovels and relying upon the vagaries of hunting luck to subsist. Documents of the Christian era, too, such as Adam of Bremen's *Gesta Hammaburgensis ecclesiae pontificum* (c. 1070) and the Christian law codes *Eidsivathingslag* and *Borgarthingslag* (c. 1120), as well as *Historia Norvegiae* (AD 1190) refer to the presence of Finns or Scrithifinns. It was not until sometime between AD 1100 and 1230 that the Saami were referred to as Lapps in the *Saga of the Orkneyislanders*. By the thirteenth century, the name Saami appears.[140] In these writings, the Saami are referred to as pagans.

Christian missionaries, Roman Catholic in the thirteenth century and Protestant later, undertook conversion attempts, but the Saami were reluctant to give up their shamanistic beliefs and kept them into the eighteenth century. The Pietist Thomas von Westen, for example, preached against shamanism in Norway from 1716 to 1727. To von Westen's credit, he encouraged the use of the Saami language, as did Niels Vibe Stockfleth, who managed to institute a Saami studies program at the University of Oslo in the eighteenth century.[141]

Similar attempts at Christianization were being made in other areas where the Saami lived. On Russia's Kola Peninsula, for example, it was Russian Orthodox missionaries, such as the Monk Trifon in the sixteenth century, who did the converting, often with the ulterior motive of gaining new lands and collecting tribute from the natives.[142] Throughout Saami territory, they had to pay tribute to Swedes, Norwegians, Finns, Karelians, Muscovites, and Novgorodians, and sometimes they paid tribute to more than one nation at the same time. In later years, it was the state that replaced the church in exploiting the Saami.

In Scandinavia, colonization of Saami lands began in the 1600s and 1700s. In Russia, colonization began in earnest after the abolition of serfdom in 1861. Saami were plied with alcohol to cheat them out of their goods, and exorbitant prices were charged for imported goods that the indigenous people needed, such as flour and sugar. In Russia, the new settlers did not have to pay taxes and were exempt from military service as an inducement for them to settle among the Saami.

Saami culture was discouraged in favor of the culture of the relocated settlers. From 1900 to 1940, Norway, for example, put a great deal of money and effort into pressuring the Saami to become Norwegian in culture and language. Swedish and Finnish governments were less insistent.[143] In Russia, the attempt at Russification was even more intense than in Norway. By 1924, the Kola Peninsula Saami felt the long arm of the Soviet government. They were forced into kolkhozes (collective farms), a lifestyle alien to their nomadic one. Uncooperative Saami were sent to the Solovets Concentration Camp. Communist ideology was taught in schools, and many children were sent to boarding schools away from the influence of their parents and traditional Saami lifestyle.

After World War II, Scandinavian governmental policies regarding the Saami became more liberal. Today the governments of Norway, Finland, and Sweden are attempting to preserve and promote Saami culture. Norway's Sami Act of 1987 is an assurance of that intent. The law gives the Saami special rights, for example, with regard to reindeer herding. There are Saami Parliaments in Norway (established 1989), Sweden (established 1993), and Finland (established 1995) protecting Saami interests. The idea of creating a Saami nation emerged in the 1970s. Today the Saami have a flag, a national song, and a national day.

The Russian Saami, on the other hand, were resettled in the 1960s to a collective named Lovozero in the center of the Kola Peninsula. This change disrupted their natural lifestyle on the tundra and led to dependency on the Soviet government, unemployment, and alcoholism. In a December 21, 2006, BBC news article titled "Russia's Sami Fight for Their Lives," a picture of desperation is described. Driven from their coastal fishing areas and forced off the grazing land of the tundra, jobless Saami live bored, with only vodka to comfort them, in cramped substandard apartments. Mining activities have caused heavy metal pollution, and nuclear waste, too, pollutes the area. Consequently, population numbers are down, and the future seems bleak.[144]

Saami Tales

Saami folktales have been influenced by Christian and Scandinavian traditions. Frequently, it was missionaries who gathered the stories and changed them to accommodate Christian ideology and to fit into the Scandinavian worldview.[145]

The collection of Saami legends began with Pehr Högström in his *Beskrifning öfwerde til Sweriges Krona lydande Lapmarker* (1747). The first collector of folktales was Jonas A. Nensén. Jacob à Fellman collected Saami tales in Finland. And Saami clergyman Lars Levi à Laestadius (1800–1861), founder of the Apostolic Lutheran Church, was active in collecting among the Swedish Saami.[146] The lost manuscript titled *Fragments of Lappish Mythology*, Laestadius's collection of Saami mythology and beliefs, although collected and written by him between 1838 and 1845, was never published until after its 1959 discovery in the archives of Yale University. The work was published in Swedish in 1997 and in Finnish in 2000. An English version was published in 2002. Just Knud Qvigstad (1853–1957) collected a great many legends and folktales, a thousand of which were published in *Lap-*

pisk eventyr og sagn (Saami Fairy Tales and Legends). Qvigstad also classified Saami legends and folktales in *Lappischa Märchen und Sagenvarianten* (1925). In Russia, Vasilii Ivanovich Nemirovich-Danchenko (1845–1936), traveler, war correspondent, and brother of the cofounder of the Moscow Art Theater, did pioneering work.[147]

In "Legends and Folktales" (*The Encyclopaedia of Saami Culture*), Hans-Herman Bartens places Saami traditional stories into two categories: legends and folktales. He associates legends with religious beliefs and worldview and folktales with entertaining narratives. Although the reduction of a body of oral tradition to two categories may seem simplistic, the Saami themselves fail to make even this distinction and refer to legends and folktales with the same word—*mainnas* in northern and eastern regions and *cuvccas* in western regions.[148]

Saami stories are peopled by the *stallos*, cannibal giants; shamans who defend and heal their people and take magic journeys on their behalf; gods, such as the Sun and Moon; shapeshifters; clever and silly animals; heroes who save their people; little folk who live underground; and inept humans whose actions are laughable.

Reindeer are important to Saami economy and are treated with respect. A white deer was considered to bring good luck. How much greater then, is the luck that a deer with golden antlers brings? In "Oleshek, the Deer with the Golden Antlers," the reindeer Oleshek saves all of the people swallowed by the insatiable clay man.

Reindeer feature, too, as the Sun god's servants, and they draw his sledge across the sky in the afternoon and evening. Sky gods are the subject of the story titled "Daughter of the Moon and Son of the Sun." The tale recounts the vain attempts of the Sun god and his son Peival'ke (Sun Ray) to arrange a marriage for Peival'ke with the Moon goddess's daughter, Niekiia, who is in turn in love with Nainas (Northern Lights). The behavior of the gods is very like the behavior of mortals. Peival'ke suffers unrequited love, and the Sun rages in a fit of temper. Niekiia and Nainas are forever separated in this tale that has features of both myth and etiological legend explaining why there is a face on the moon.

Chakhkli are tiny earth spirits who live in another level of the Saami cosmos—the Underworld. The Saami display a dual attitude toward the *chakhkli*. On one hand, the *chakhkli* are helpful and devoted to the Saami, often serving as their protectors, just as the boy Yarashka did in the story titled "The Chakhkli." On the other hand, *chakhkli* can be a nuisance, just as Yarashka was when he tore his adopted mother's fishing nets and thought it was funny. This negative and mischievous aspect of the *chakhkli* personality often surfaces when they believe someone has not behaved properly toward them. Yarashka reacted badly to his adopted mother's anger and desire to be rid of him. Nevertheless, Yarashka's loyalty to his adopted family is steady, as he proves when he risks his life to save them from an attack by Chuds (Karelians, Veps, or Finns).

The story titled "Sergevan', the Hunter" demonstrates Saami respect for ancestors. Sergevan' has no luck hunting until he meets an old woman in the forest, an ancestress and the betrothed of his great-great-great grandfather. She teaches Sergevan' the proper way to hunt. The union of Sergevan's strength and his ancestor's wisdom makes an unbeatable combination.

The People of Northern Russia

Russia's vast Arctic and bordering Subarctic stretches from its border with Finland in the west to the Bering Strait in the East. It sprawls across two continents—Europe and Asia. The Ural Mountains mark the division between the continents.

Beyond the Ural Mountains lies Siberia, known simultaneously as an enormous prison camp to which both tsars and Soviets sent their miscreants and political prisoners and as a mysterious wonderland of winter beauty—rich in gold, diamonds, oil, and gas. Traditionally, the area of Siberia that lies closest to the Bering Sea, the Sea of Okhotsk, and the Sea of Japan has been called the Russian Far East. Siberian rivers run north and drain into the Arctic Ocean. The main rivers are long and appear as vertical lines on the map. They include the Ob, Yenisei, and Lena. The name "Siberia" is said to have originated variously from the word for a Turkish tribe, a famous shaman, and the Turkish word meaning "sleeping land."[149] Indeed, Siberia is a sleeping giant, rich in resources and having great potential.

The soil of the Arctic tundra is permanently frozen and stretches from the Kola Peninsula in Europe eastward to the Chukotka Peninsula in the Russian Far East. Below the barren area of permafrost, where the Siberian larch is the only tree able to survive, the forested taiga, which is greater in the northwest, stretches across Russia. Summer north of the Arctic Circle lasts only one month. The lowest recorded temperature is –96.1° F (–71.2° C) in the Sakha (Yakut) Republic, the coldest area of Siberia.[150]

Origin of the People of Northern Russia

People lived in Siberia as long ago as 45,000 to 40,000 BC.[151] The migrations to present-day northern European Russia and northern Siberia were long and complicated. Much remains either speculative or shrouded in mystery.

Finno-Ugric groups have lived in northern European and Central Russia since prehistoric times. There is archeological evidence dating from the twelfth to the fourteenth centuries that testifies to the existence of Russians, as well as to Finnic groups that were ancestors of the Komi, and Ugric groups that were ancestors of the Khants and Mansi.[152]

Russians moved into northern areas from their home in the Kiev-Novgorod-Moscow area. The Russians of the Kola Peninsula were called Pomory. Their ancestors were twelfth century explorers from ancient Novgorod.[153] The Saami, also Kola Peninsula people, are discussed in a separate section.

Karelians, Veps, and Komi also inhabit Russia's European north. Karelians are members of an original Baltic-Finnic group that lived between Lakes Ladoga and Onega in Russia, as well as in Finland. They used to be called Izhorians. The Veps, too, are a Finnic people. In historical writings, they are sometimes called Chuds. The Komi, who referred to themselves as Zyrians, have ancestors of Finno-Urgric origin. Their history begins in the seventh century.[154]

In the Ural Mountains area and continuing eastward across the northern West Siberian Plain and Central Siberian Plateau dwell the Mansi, Khant, Enets, Nenets, Selkup, Ket, Evenk, Nganasan, Dolgan, Even, and Sakha/Yakut. The Mansi were first mentioned in 1396 in the Russian chronicles.[155] At that time, they were called Voguls. They lived west of the Urals and migrated to areas of the rivers Irtysh and Ob. The Ob-Ugric group to which they belonged separated from the Hungarians around the thirteenth century. The Khant, once called Ostyaks, had the same Ob-Ugric ancestors as the Mansi, but they separated from the Mansi in the thirteenth century and presumably migrated eastward across the River Ob.

The Enets, who now inhabit the east bank of the Yenisey River, used to be called the Yenisey Samoyeds. They are a Uralic people whose Samoyedic ancestors separated from the Finno-Ugric group, migrating north between the eleventh and thirteenth centuries. They are the smallest of the Samoyedic groups.

The Nenets and Selkup are Uralic people, too. The Nenets, who live in the polar regions of northern European Russia and northwestern Siberia, are the largest group of Samoyedic people. They divided from the Southern Samoyeds during the first millennium AD and migrated northeast and northwest of the Ural Mountains. Today the Selkup live by the River Taz. According to one theory, they separated from their Samoyedic ancestors in the first millennium BC. According to another theory, they were already living in their present location at that early date.

Another of the Samoyedic people is the Nganasan, who live on the Taimyr Peninsula. In the past, they were called Tavgi Samoyed, and they dwell the farthest north of all the Samoyedic groups. They are a Uralic people. It is thought that their ancestors moved north from the vicinity of the Altai and Sayan Mountains.

The Ket, once known as the Yenisey-Ostyaks because they live in the Yenisey River basin, belong to the Mongoloid North Asian people, although they have some Uralic features. It is speculated that their ancestors migrated from the south, perhaps from the Sayan Mountains area, and were driven northward by "mountain people."

The Evenk, once called the Tungus, range through an enormous area from the River Ob to the Sea of Okhotsk and from the Arctic Ocean to Manchuria. They are Paleo-Siberians whose original home is thought to be Lake Baikal. They migrated up to the tundra and across the steppes, Siberian grasslands, perhaps driven away by Turkish groups.

The Dolgan, who live today on the southern part of the Taimyr Peninsula and on the northern Yenisey River, belong to the Mongolian North Asiatic group. They formed as a mixture of several groups including Sakha/Yakut, Russian settlers, and Tungus clans.

The Even, who are widely spread over an area from the Verkhoyansk Mountain Range to the northern Russian Far East, belong to the Paleo-Siberian group. It is thought that they are the result of the mixing of Tungus and Yukaghir peoples.

The Sakha, until very recently called Yakut, originated in the Lake Baikal area and were formed as a mixture of the Turkish tribes from the steppes and Altai Mountains with the indigenous Siberians, especially the Even and Evenk.[156]

The Russian Far East lies in Russia's eastern extremity. There, the reindeer-herding Koryak dwell in the northern part of the Kamchatka Peninsula and on the nearby mainland. They are natives of Kamchatka and belong to the Mongolian North Asian people. They are thought to be descendants of Neolithic people.

North of the Koryak, the Yukaghir live in the Sakha Republic, much diminished in number and territory in comparison to their seventeenth-century presence. They belong to the Baikal group of North Asians and are regarded as indigenous Siberians.

The Yupik Eskimos, another Far Eastern group, live in the Chukchi Autonomous Region, as well as the Magadan area and Wrangel Island. They have been discussed in another section. The Chukchi live over a much wider area in the Chukchi Autonomous Region, the Sakha/Yakut Republic, and the Koryak Autonomous Region. They belong to the North Asian people and are one of Siberia's aboriginal people.

Languages of the People of Northern Russia

There are four ethno-linguistic groups represented among Russia's northern people.[157] They are Indo-European, Uralic, Altaic, and Paleo-Asiatic. Russian belongs to the Slavic branch of the Indo-European group. It is the most widely spoken of the Slavic languages.[158] Russian is the official language of the country, and many native languages are in danger of being displaced by it, thereby becoming lost to future generations.

The Uralic ethno-linguistic group has Finno-Ugric and Samoyedic sub-branches. The Karelians, Komi, Saami, and Vep of northern European Russia belong to the Finnic sub-branch. Karelian is so closely related to Finnish that some scholars consider it to be an eastern dialect. Komi, also known as Zyrian, has two dialects, one spoken in the Komi Republic and the other spoken in Perm. The language of the Vep exists in northern, central, and southern dialects.

The Khant and Mansi people belong to the Ugric branch of the Finno-Ugric group. The language of the Khants separated from the Ob-Ugric language in the thirteenth century.

The Nenets, Nganasan, Selkup, and Enets languages belong to the Samoyedic branch of Uralic languages. The Enets have two dialects, Tundra Enets and Wood Enets. The Nenets, too, have Tundra and Taiga dialects. Like the Inuit, they have many words related to snow and words describing nature. Nganasan has western and eastern dialects. There is a strong influence of Evenk, Dolgan, and Nenets in their loan words, but Russian is the predominant language among the Nganasan today. The Selkup best represent the southern Samoyedic group. They have northern, central, and southern dialects.

The Altaic ethno-linguistic group is divided into Tungus-Manchu and Turkic branches. The Even and Evenk belong to the Tungus-Manchu branch. The language of the Even has eastern and western dialects and has common features with that of the Evenk. The Evenk represent the largest of the northern Tungus-Manchu group. Their vocabulary has similarities to Turkic and Mongolian languages.

The Sakha/Yakut and Dolgan languages belong to the Turkic branch of the Altaic ethno-linguistic group. Sakha is a Turkic language that is used as a second language in the Sakha Republic. Russian is the official language. The Dolgan speak a dialect of the Sakha/Yakut language with a strong Evenk influence.

The Chukchi, Ket, Koryak, and Yukaghir belong to the Paleo-Asiatic ethno-linguistic group. The Ket are the only people of the western Paleo-Asiatic group. Their language is an isolate, the origin of which is unknown. The Chukchi belong to the Chukchi-Kamchatkan sub-group. Their language is closely related to Koryak and has coastal and tundra dialects. The language of the Koryaks is understood by the Chukchi and displays a heavy influence of Russian. Yukaghir is an isolated language that may have separated from the Uralic languages more than 8,000 years ago. It has Forest and Tundra dialects. The vocabulary is of unknown origin.

Culture and Daily Life of the People of Northern Russia

The Russians, Karelians, Veps, and Komi of northwestern European Russia traditionally lived in tribal groups and subsisted by fishing, hunting, herding reindeer, cutting timber, and cultivating crops. Until the last half of the nineteenth century, the Karelians lived in large groups of twenty-five to thirty families.[159] The Karelians are the most urbanized of the indigenous people of the Barents Region of Russia.[160] Their population is rapidly decreasing. The Komi, who are surrounded by forests, engage in cattle breeding, hunting, woodworking, and reindeer herding. Like the Russians, the traditional garb of the women was a *sarafan,* a long pinafore-type dress. When Stalin, the Soviet leader, industrialized the Soviet Union, the Komi were engaged in the oil, coal, and wood industries, which were developed by labor camp prisoners. In the 1990s, the wood and coal industries were shut down. People left the area, and today the Republic of Komi is peppered with ghost towns. Roads to this area are passable only in winter.[161]

Reindeer figure importantly in the lives of the Mansi, Khant, Nenets, Selkup, Ket, Dolgan, Nganasan, Evenk, and Enets of the West Siberian Plain and Central Siberia. The Even, Yukaghir, Koryak, and Chukchi of Russia's Far East also are engaged in reindeer husbandry and hunting. These groups could be called "reindeer people" because traditionally they have hunted or domesticated reindeer.[162] These were nomadic or seminomadic people, and in some cases, they still are. In summer, they migrated with the reindeer to the Arctic tundra and in autumn they returned to the forest tundra area. Many still follow the ancient way of life, although the Soviet government forced these nomadic people to settle in villages and to work in brigades, rather than in their traditional family or clan groups.[163] The Nganasan led an independent way of life hunting wild reindeer to the end of the nineteenth century.[164]

The traditional dwelling was an easily transportable conical tent covered with tree bark or animal skins. These dwellings resemble a tipi, but Russians refer to them as *chums.*

Reindeer provided food, clothing, and in many cases transportation, although dogs pulled sleds, too, and helped to herd reindeer. The reindeer were used as a decoy to lure unsuspecting wild reindeer during the hunt.[165]

The Sakha/Yakut, Yukaghir, Even, Koryak, and Chukchi live in the north in Russia's Far East. The Sakha Republic, once called Yakutia, is the largest republic in the Russian Federation. It is rich in gold, coal, and gas. In the 1950s, diamonds were discovered. The Sakha came originally from the south and brought with them the knowledge of horse and cattle breeding, an occupation that they continue to engage in. Additionally, they fish, hunt, and herd reindeer.[166]

The other people of Russia's northern Far East are also involved in hunting, fishing, and reindeer husbandry. Until the eighteenth century, hunting reindeer was the main occupation of the Yukaghir of the Upper Kolyma Valley. With the coming of the Soviets, the Yukaghir were placed on state farms, where, like the Sakha, they raised reindeer, cattle, and horses.

The root of the name for the Koryak means "reindeer." They, too, are reindeer people living on the Kamchatka Peninsula and nearby mainland, where they have fished and tended reindeer for many years. The economy of their Even neighbors, too, is based on reindeer.

The Chukchi, who live between the Chukchi and Bering Seas are divided into coastal and inland dwellers. Their self-designations mean "coastal people" and "reindeer people." The coastal Chukchi hunt seals, whales, walruses, and fish. The "reindeer people" herd reindeer. Traditionally, the two groups have traded with one another—reindeer skins for fish, oil, and sea mammals.

Of course, today there are many changes. People, such as the Ket, live in Russian-style houses in settlements. They have access to schools, clinics, and stores. Many dress like Russians and eat commercial foods. Nevertheless, a significant number of people keep the old nomadic ways and continue to hunt, fish, and gather.

Beliefs and Traditions of the People of Northern Russia

During the tsarist regime in Russia, the indigenous peoples of the north were converted, often forcibly, to Russian Orthodoxy. Therefore, the so-called conversion was quite superficial, and many of the ancient pagan beliefs survived. Generally speaking, the beliefs were animistic. The Komi, for instance, believed in guardian spirits or shadow souls. They thought, as did the ancient Russians and other people of northern European Russia, that there were spirits of the forest, the water, the bathhouse, the field, and so on.

The shaman was an important figure who played an intermediary role between people and the spirit worlds. He or she requested help of the spirits in curing illnesses, bringing on a successful hunt, and in predicting the future. Indeed, the word "shaman" was borrowed from the Evenk language.[167] Shamans had the ability to go into a trance and travel to other worlds.

Earth was typically one level of a multilayered reality in the indigenous cosmology. In many cases, there were three worlds—an upper, middle, and lower world as the Mansi and Sakha believed.[168] The Nenets and others, however, thought the universe had seven layers.[169] If a shaman was not available, which was the case among Koryak and Chukchi groups, a family member was able to perform some of the duties of the shaman. [170] Shamans had protector spirits and special clothing and equipment, such as the shaman drum, to help him or her on a spiritual journey. To get to other worlds, the shaman might climb the world tree as was done in Evenk ritual, perhaps to retrieve the soul of the sick person, which evil spirits had stolen.[171]

Amulets, or charms, protected people from evil spirits and from misfortune. Today it is the older generation that maintains the ancient beliefs.

The Nganasan are a special group, in that they were not subjected to Christianization.[172] As a result, shamans existed among them for a very long time. The last Nganasan shaman died in 1989.[173] The Nganasan worshiped, among others, Great Mother Sun, Moon, Earth, Water, and Fire. Traditionally, they placed the dead in a sleigh above the earth with food and possessions for the journey.

History of the People of Northern Russia

The year AD 862 generally marks the beginning of the Russian state.[174] Non-Slavic groups were already living on the land, such as the Finno-Ugrian people of what became northern European Russia and the various indigenous people of what became Siberia. There were constant waves of invasions. The first were the Cimmerians (1000 to 700 BC), then nomadic Iranian-speaking Scythians (seventh to the end of third century BC), and later Sarmatians (third century BC to third century AD). The Turkic speaking Huns from Central Asia invaded in AD 370, and the Asiatic Avars came in AD 558. A Turkic people called the Bulgars and the seminomadic Khazars from Asia (seventh century AD), who were more cosmopolitan than previous invaders, followed.[175]

The Mongols, also referred to as the Tatars, from Mongolia, Manchuria, and Siberia, defeated Kievan Russia in 1240. Known as the Golden Horde, they ruled for two centuries.[176] The remnants of the Golden Horde populated Siberia. Many of the local tribes congregated in the Khanate of Sibir and offered resistance to the Russians. In 1579, under the Russian Tsar Ivan IV (the Terrible), the wealthy Stroganovs sent an expedition led by the Cossack Yermak against the Khanate. Yermak defeated Khan Kuchum in 1582. By 1598, the Russians were in control of western Siberia, and the way was paved for Russian expansion into Siberia.[177]

Representatives of the Russian tsar, most frequently Cossacks and adventurers, waged a military campaign across Siberia, building forts and trading posts and subduing the indigenous people in order to do so. By 1640, these mercenaries reached the Pacific Ocean. Siberia became a colony managed by an office in faraway Moscow, and later in St. Petersburg, by people distantly removed from the everyday reality that was experienced by the indigenous people. The mercenaries exacted tributes of fur, slaves, and natural resources.[178] Corrupt military governors cared little about the lives of the people they found in the north. They were interested only in extracting wealth. Sometimes more than one official demanded tribute, or a dishonest official demanded tribute more than once in the same year. Some people ended up paying multiple times so that future generations had to pay off their grandfathers' debts.

The tactics used were brutal. If someone failed to pay, the head of the family was thrown into the fortress prison. When the officials finally came to understand that a prisoner was unlikely to be able to pay off his debt, they began imprisoning hostage women and children in an attempt to force payment.[179] The idea was to buy cheap and sell dear. The mercenaries traded tea, sugar, tobacco, and other products for astronomical numbers of furs. They plied the natives with vodka to cheat them out of a profit. The indigenous people were unused to drinking and so easily became addicted. The invaders brought disease with them, just as newcomers did in other parts of the Arctic.

The natives were forcibly converted to Russian Orthodoxy. Shamans were persecuted, executed, and imprisoned so that shamanism was either wiped out or forced underground. According to Kira Van Deusen, "The persecution of shamans was so strong that most were gone or not practicing by 1990 and the ancient beliefs were held most strongly by older people who had not gone to the residential schools, who spoke the native languages, and had lived the older nomadic lifestyle. In the post-Soviet period as those elders were dying off, and with new cultural freedom, there has been a revival of shamanism among many Siberian peoples. This continues to the present day as people are facing difficult problems with the economy and with the breakdown of the health system, which is accompanied by health problems caused by industrial pollution and other causes."[180]

By the eighteenth century, the fur trade declined, and mining became the chief economic activity. The Russian Empire and a few wealthy families were involved in mining silver, lead, copper, and later gold. From the seventeenth century on, Siberia was used as a penal colony to which prisoners were exiled. Prisoners, often political dissenters who were members of the Intelligentsia, were forced to work in mines, the lumber industry, and other enterprises.

The policy of exploitation continued under the Soviet regime. The prison camp system expanded, especially under Joseph Stalin (1922–1953).[181] Under Stalin, Siberia's indigenous people were forced to settle on collective farms, thereby losing ownership of their reindeer.[182] Children were taken to boarding schools, where they had to speak Russian, although in the early years of Soviet power, the use of native languages was encouraged.

There was little concern about the impact of industry on the native people or on the environment. Acid rains caused heavy metals to enter the food chain via the reindeer, which eat contaminated moss and are in turn eaten by people. These metals have had an impact on people's health. Oil and gas spills have destroyed the earth, polluted the waters, and destroyed the migratory routes of the reindeer, the population of which is decreasing, as is the population of the indigenous peoples themselves. Radioactive contamination of food due to the nuclear testing of the 1950s and 1960s has destroyed the health of the Koryak and Chukchi, who suffer now from cancer, a disease previously unheard of.

The native people have suffered discrimination on the job and unemployment, and they are belittled for their identity.[183] The Chukchi, in particular, are a popular butt of numskull jokes. Jokes about the Chukchi resemble Polish jokes in Western culture. Here is one in which the Chukchi man may be presented as a numskull, but he is nobody's fool.

A Chukchi man was riding in a Moscow taxi. When he reached his destination, the taxi driver said, "That will be 200 rubles."
The Chukchi man gave the driver 100 rubles.
"Why did you give me only 100 rubles?" the taxi cab driver asked.
"What do you mean 'why'? You rode in the taxi, too, didn't you?"[184]

Tales of the People of Northern Russia

Folktales of the people of northern European Russia resemble Russian and European folktales to a far greater degree than do the stories of people living east of the Ural Mountains. Thus, the Karelian Cinderella story titled "The Black Ewe and the Blue Reindeer," in which the evil witch Siuoiatar turns the heroine into an ewe, and the Komi "Yoma and the Two Sisters," in which a girl is abused by her stepmother, can be classified as fairy tales. The Russian "Shapshifter," in which the mother turns into a pig, is a memorate (*bylichka*), a tale told by the person who experienced it or who learned it from a friend or relative. The Vep story of "Twelve Clever Brothers," who get lost because of their stupidity, is a numskull tale.

Once across the Ural Mountains and into Siberia, it is more difficult to give stories a Western classification. There are, of course, *pourquoi*, or explanatory tales, a genre familiar to the western reader. The Nenets and Ket story titled "The Cuckoo," for example, explains why the cuckoo fails to take care of its young. The Even tale about why the dog befriends people ("Dog in Search of a Friend") and the self-explanatory Mansi tale titled "Why the Rabbit Has Long Ears" have much in common with Western *pourquoi* tales. "The Forest Spirit," a Khant story, might be classified as a memorate.

Tales about animals, too, have their European counterparts, although different in composition and told from a different point of view. The fox, for example, makes an appearance in the Chukchi tale "The Ingrates" and the rabbit in "Hare Rescues the Sun." Raven, trickster and creator in Alaskan tales, figures importantly in Siberia too, as in the Koryak "Kuikynniaku, the Raven." The woodpecker appears in the Evenk story of the justice rendering bird in "The Woodpecker's Reward," and the wolf makes a fool of himself in the Chukchi "Raven and Wolf."

Often the lines between human and animal are blurred, as they are in the Khant story "Machenkat" in which a young woman offends her sister-in-law by throwing hot ashes into her face when she is in the form of a bear.

Siberian tales in which the reader enters a spirit world are very different from Western fare. These stories are peopled by deified luminaries, such as the Moon in the Chukchi "The Girl and the Moon Spirit" and the Nganasan "The Shaman in the Moon." There are personified constellations, too, in the Sakha story titled "The Crane's Feather." The elements are deified in the Ket "Whirlwind's Sister." Earth Spirit and Fire Spirit are present in the Nganasan "How the Reindeer Reconciled Tui-Niamy, the Fire Spirit, and Mou-Niamy, the Earth Spirit." Fire Spirit appears in the Selkup story of the same name, in which Fire appears as a silvery, smoky, shimmering tiny creature.

Overall, the stories in this collection represent the wealth that the northern peoples possess. Populations have grown smaller in number in some cases or have been assimilated to such a degree that there is a danger that the spiritual legacy may disappear with the folk. It would be a loss too painful to contemplate. My words are not identical to those of the original tellers, but hopefully the spirit is still evident and the tales have been rendered enjoyable to the English-speaking world. Libraries Unlimited is to be commended for keeping story traditions alive in its World Folklore Series.

Bonnie C. Marshall

MAP OF ARCTIC REGION

From the Perry-Castañeda Library Map Collection, the University of Texas at Austin. Produced by the CIA. Courtesy of *The World Factbook 2009*. Washington, DC: Central Intelligence Agency, 2009.

PART 1

TALES OF DAILY LIFE

GRANNY CHACHAKAN-CHACHAKAN

(Sakha/Yakut)

*G*ranny Chachakan-Chachakan lived in a little village. One winter she went to the river to fetch some water, as was her custom. She went up to the ice hole and noticed that the hole was covered with a thick layer of ice.

Granny beat a hole through the ice and threw aside big chunks until she could see the water again. Then, she scooped up a bucket full of water. She set the bucket down and filled a second bucket. Granny's buckets were good ones. They were made of birch bark and were decorated with designs on the edge.

After filling the second bucket, Granny held both buckets, one in each hand, and headed home. But suddenly she slipped on the smooth ice and fell down beside the ice hole. All of the water poured out of her buckets.

It was a frosty morning. While Granny groaned and grunted and attempted to get up, the hem of her skirt became stuck to the ice. No matter how hard she tried, Granny could not get up.

She looked around to see if there was anyone nearby to help her. She glanced at the sun, which had just risen, and asked, "Sun, oh, Sun, aren't you the strongest being in the world?"

"I am very strong, Granny," Sun answered, "but because a black cloud can cover me, Storm Cloud is stronger."

Granny spoke to Storm Cloud. "Storm Cloud, oh Storm Cloud, aren't you the strongest being in the world?"

"Well, yes, Granny, I am very strong. But the wind can blow me away, so Wind is stronger."

Granny spoke to Wind. "Wind, oh Wind, aren't you the strongest being in the world?"

"Well, yes, Granny, I am very strong," said Wind, "but Mountain can block my path."

Granny looked up at the huge mountain of stone in front of her and asked, "Mountain, oh Mountain, aren't you the strongest being in the world?"

"Well, yes, Granny. I am very strong, but a human being can smash me to smithereens, so Man is stronger."

Granny turned to a man passing by. "Man, oh Man, aren't you the strongest being in the world?" she asked.

"Yes, indeed, I am very strong, Granny. But I am afraid of fire, so Fire is stronger than I am."

Granny spoke to Fire. "Fire, oh Fire, aren't you the strongest being in the world?"

"Yes, Granny, I am very strong. But if water is thrown over me, I die, so Water is stronger."

Granny spoke to the water flowing in the river. "Water, oh Water, aren't you the strongest being in the world?"

"Yes, Granny, it's true that I am very strong, but Earth can drink me up until I'm gone."

Granny spoke to Earth. "Earth, oh Earth, aren't you the strongest being in the world?"

"Yes, Granny, I'm probably the strongest being in the world," said Earth.

Then Granny lost her temper. "Then let go of my skirt! Why are you holding onto it?"

She tugged at her dress. By then the ice had already melted. Granny Chachakan-Chachakan stood on her feet and took the buckets in her hands. She scooped out some water once again and went home.

When she got back home, her grandsons had already put the water on for tea, and it was boiling. They all sat down to tea—with rolls and sugar.

THE OLD MAN

(Yukaghir)

*A*n old Yukaghir man was wandering through the taiga, Siberia's coniferous forest that lies just south of the tundra. As he was walking, he caught sight of a small *urasa,* a nomad's tent that was covered with animal skins and birch bark. The *urasa* was very clean on the outside. The skins had been fitted closely to the poles. There was good order everywhere.

"A young, beautiful woman probably lives here," the old man thought.

He hid in the bushes, waiting for the moment when the woman of the house would come out. No one came out, however, so the old man decided that the young woman who was living in the *urasa* was afraid to come out.

Evening came. The old man decided to crawl onto the top of the *urasa* and peep into the smoke hole to see who lived inside. The old man climbed up, looked into the opening, and saw a very well-dressed woman sitting by the fire. The woman was sewing something.

The old man wanted very much to see the woman's face. He began to stretch the skins around the opening of the hole to enlarge it. The old man's face was dirty. He had not washed up even once since he had been born. The hair on his head was long, greasy, and dirty. Dirt even fell from his eyelashes. The old man tried to open his eyes as wide as possible to have a good look at the woman below. When he did so, flakes of dirt from his hair and eyelashes sprinkled down onto the woman.

The woman let out a scream. She took fright and decided that an evil monster was sitting on top of her home. She took the thread made of sinew, with which she had been sewing, and tied the thread to a pole. She held the pole over the fire so that the threads began burning. She hoped that she might smoke out the monster with the bad smell of burning sinew.

The fire made the burning threads scatter in all directions. They twisted into ringlets, contracted, and turned black. The pungent smell rose and caused the old man to sneeze. The woman raised her face and looked up to see who was there.

The old man saw the woman's old, ugly face. He took fright and slid quickly down off the *urasa* crying, "Burn the threads, Grandma, and smoke the monster out!" Fearing that she would follow him, he ran off wherever his nose led him.

Meanwhile, the old woman was so terrified that she could not move from the spot. The threads had burned up. Her work had fallen into the fire and burned up, too. Then, the fire died down and night came. With the night came peace and quiet.

The old woman came to her senses and started the fire again. She looked up into the smoke hole. No monster was there now. Everything was as it had been before.

She went out of her home and looked around. She saw footprints going away from the *urasa,* and she followed them. They led her far into the taiga. The old woman understood that the burning threads had frightened the monster and had caused him to run away into the forest.

The old woman returned home. She blew on the fire to make it burn more brightly. She boiled some water for tea, drank her fill, and then she went to bed.

SERGEVAN', THE HUNTER

(Saami)

*O*ne day Sergevan' went hunting. Sergevan' was the son of Sergei, the grandson of Andrei, the great grandson of Matvei, the great-great grandson of Even, and the great-great-great grandson of Peur. He was following the trails of his old father, grandfather, great grandfather, and great-great grandfather. He walked for one day, two days, and three days. He had eaten all of the food that he had brought on his journey, but still he had not killed a single animal.

Sergevan' became angry. "I heard from Grandfather and from Father that there were many wild deer in the area if only you had enough arrows to shoot them. Now only trampled down trails are left."

Then Sergevan' noticed another trail. No one had walked down that trail for a long time. It was overgrown with grass. Sergevan' turned onto the grass-grown trail. He walked along the trail until he came to a little cottage overgrown with moss. An old woman was sitting on a stone beside the cottage. The old woman was very old. Indeed, she was ancient.

When the old woman caught sight of the hunter, she said, "The trail has led you to me, Sergevan'."

Sergevan' was surprised that the old woman knew his name. "Hello, Grandmother," he said. "I've never seen you and don't know who you are."

"You don't know me, Sergevan', but I know you," the old woman answered. "I am your great-great-great grandfather's betrothed."

Sergevan' saw that the old woman was quite thin. She was literally skin and bones. Perhaps she had not eaten anything for a long time. Perhaps she was hungry. He rummaged around in the leather bag hanging on his shoulder. He felt a dry crust on the bottom and gave it to the old woman.

The old woman took the crust and began sucking on it. The crust was dry, and she had no teeth.

"You must have been very beautiful when you were young," Sergevan' said.

"I don't know whether I was beautiful or ugly, but I certainly was young once."

"Why didn't you marry my great-great-great grandfather?"

"I just didn't. I would say 'cold,' and he would say 'hot.' I would say 'snow,' and he would reply 'rain.' I would say 'go right,' and he would go left. Oh, Peur, Peur, how wonderful our life would have been if only you had let me have my way just once!"

After uttering these words, the old woman burst into tears. She wept so bitterly and plaintively that Sergevan' could not restrain himself from weeping, too.

Then, the old woman laughed and said, "Why are you crying about something that happened a century ago? Look! The crows are listening. They'll spread rumors over the entire tundra, and everyone who has a mouth will ridicule you."

Thus they chatted, laughed, wept, wept some more, smiled, and finally went to bed.

In the morning, Sergevan' said, "I must go hunting, but there's not a single wild animal in the tundra. The deer have moved away and left."

"There are animals in the tundra. The deer haven't moved away," said the old woman.

"What are you talking about?" Sergevan' asked, becoming angry. "I have been walking for three days and looking everywhere. I haven't killed one animal."

"You didn't walk down the right trails or look in the right places," the old woman insisted. "Your great-great-great grandfather, my great-great-great betrothed, tried to lure the deer with songs. And when he crept up to an animal, he approached from the windward side so that the wind was blowing at his back. That's why your great-great-great grandfather...."

Sergevan' did not hear the old woman out. Instead, he grabbed his bow and arrow and ran out of the cottage.

Sergevan' wandered until noon down trails and through places where there were no trails. He kept singing songs to lure the deer. Finally, he grew weary of singing and became silent. It was then that he caught sight of a deer. He approached the deer from the windward side. But as soon as he had crept close to the deer, it waved its tail and skipped away.

A very angry Sergevan' returned to Grandmother's. "Everything that you told me is wrong!" he scolded.

Grandmother laughed. "Great-great-great grandson, you are just like your great-great-great grandfather, my betrothed. I tell a story, and he comes to another conclusion. You didn't hear me out this morning, Sergevan', so hear me out this evening. I'll begin the story from the point where you ran out of the cottage. Your great-great-great grandfather's songs didn't lure the animals to him; they frightened the animals away. He approached the animals from the windward side, and that is why he didn't bag any game. When the wind blows at a person's back, it carries man's smell to the animal. Instead, you have to creep up to the animal quietly and let the wind blow in your face, so that the wind carries your smell away from the animal."

Sergevan' burst out laughing, so happy was he. "Well, I'll go hunting again right away. I'll do it your way."

"Oh, Sergevan', Sergevan', great-great-great grandson of your great-great-great grandfather, where do you plan to go at night? You're supposed to go to bed at night and go hunting in the morning."

This time Sergevan' listened to Grandmother and went to bed. As soon as dawn came, he set out to hunt. He went quietly. He did not walk, but rather crept. In the distance, he noticed first a deer, then a fox. He approached from the side, so that the wind was blowing in his face. He crept closer. Without rushing, he drew the bow and released an arrow.

Toward evening he returned to Grandmother with a big bag of game. He and the old woman ate the marrow, which was a delicacy, from the deer bone.

"What do you say, great-great-great betrothed of my great-great-great grandfather," Sergevan' proposed. "I have no mother or grandmother. Come live with me. You'll be a mother and grandmother to me."

The old woman shook her head. "No, Sergevan', I have lived here an entire century. The trees here grew before my very eyes, and over the years I watched moss cover the stones. You know yourself that every bird longs for its own nest and every animal runs to its own burrow. I wouldn't leave this place to go anywhere."

"Well, then," said Sergevan', "we can do it another way. If you won't come to live with me, I could come live with you. Let me be your great-great-great grandson."

That is exactly what they decided to do. Sergevan' went to live with the old woman. Her old and wise mind and his youthful strength were a perfect combination. They lived in harmony and sang songs until the end of their days.

THE OLD WOMAN AND THE DWARFS

(Netsilik Inuit)

There once was an old woman whose neighbors had gone hunting. She was at home alone.

One day some dwarfs, a man and his wife, visited her. The old woman invited them in, and the dwarfs took their possessions and some meat into a side room of the old woman's house, and there they stayed. They ate their meal and went to sleep without offering the old woman a scrap of food, even though it was the custom to share one's food with others.

In the morning, the stingy couple began taking their things out, preparing to leave. Finally, everything was outside, except the hindquarters of a caribou. Still, they had not made a single present of meat to the old woman.

While the dwarf and his wife were outside, the old woman seized the opportunity to spit on the caribou meat, which caused the meat to freeze to the snow house. The dwarf's wife pried and struck the meat to loosen it, but it held fast.

After struggling with the meat for a long time, the tiny woman shouted to her husband outside. "Come get the meat. I can't get it loose."

"If you can't get it loose, just leave it," the dwarf's husband answered.

Reluctantly, the dwarf's wife gave up her attempts to loosen the meat and went outside. After a while, the dwarf couple went away.

As soon as they left, the old woman rushed to the caribou hind legs in anticipation of enjoying a feast. When she went over to the caribou legs to prepare them for her dinner, she saw nothing but the hindquarters of a small long-tailed duck in their place.

TWO BROTHERS

(Enets)

A chum,* which is a tent covered with reindeer hides, stood at the fork of a river. A woman with two little sons lived in the *chum*.

One day the woman left to get something for the family to eat. However, she did not return. No one knows what had happened to her. Perhaps a bear mauled her to death, or perhaps she drowned in the river. At any rate, her two little boys were left alone.

At first they kept crying and calling for their mother. Then, they got used to being alone. They gathered mushrooms and berries, and they fished in the nearby river. Thus, they lived and little by little grew into young men.

How many years, how many winters passed, it is impossible to say because they did not know how to count. One day one brother said to the other, "Why are we living alone? Remember that Mother told us there are other people in the world. Let's go look for them."

"And how will we do that?" asked the other brother.

"Like this—you walk on the left bank of the river in the direction of the current, and your name will be Left Bank. I'll walk on the right bank of the river in the direction of the current, and my name will be Right Bank. We'll find other people and see how they live. Then, we'll come back and meet in our *chum*."

They agreed on this plan and set out. Right Bank walked all day long. Toward evening he made a hut of branches and lay down to sleep. As he was lying there, he thought, "Left Bank has probably made a hut, too. I hope he has made it well, so that he won't get wet if it rains."

In the morning, he got up and walked on. He walked for many days.

The river led him to a lake, which was the source of the river. The lake was big, and its shores were low lying and boggy, going both to the left and to the right.

Right Bank stopped to consider what to do. "How will my brother, Left Bank, get across a lake like this? He's probably standing this very moment on a low-lying bank like I am and probably, like me, he doesn't know what to do."

---

* Pronounced "choom."

Then, Right Bank caught sight of a gnarled log standing with one end stuck on shore and its top swaying in the water. Right Bank hopped onto the log and pushed it away from shore. He began sailing, rowing with his hands.

"And has Left Bank found a log like this one? He must have. If I found one, he, too, found a log and is sailing on it," thought Right Bank.

He steered the log across the lake. He wanted to land when suddenly an animal jumped from the shore into the water. Right Bank was so startled that he almost fell off the log. Then, he guessed that it was only an otter and laughed at his fear.

"My brother, Left Bank, is silly. What will he do when he sees the otter?"

Right Bank saw a path leading away from the lake, just like the path that he and his brother had followed from their *chum* to the river. "Perhaps people live here," thought Right Bank.

He walked on and, sure enough—he met a girl. She was gathering cloudberries. When the girl saw Right Bank, she gave him some berries to eat.

"My brother, Left Bank, likes berries, too," said Right Bank as he put a fistful of berries into his mouth.

The girl was surprised. "Where is your brother?" she asked. "I don't begrudge him some berries, too."

"He set out on the other side of the river in search of other people."

"So you're looking for other people," the girl said. "Come to our village. The Tau* (Nganasan) people are in our village."

Right Bank grew pensive. "Did my brother, Left Bank, follow a girl, too? He probably did. After all, we left our *chum* to find people. I think I'll go with the girl!"

They came to a village with many *chums*. People were walking about among the *chums*. Men, women, and children were running about.

"Oh, my goodness, it seems that there are many people in the world!" exclaimed Right Bank. "Actually there are two times as many as there are here because my brother, Left Bank, must have come to a village like this one. He, too, has seen many people."

The girl led Right Bank to her *chum,* to her mother and father. Right Bank began living with them. But people cannot live or exist without working. So the girl's father said to Right Bank, "You will take the reindeer to pasture."

"How can one take reindeer to pasture?" asked Right Bank. "The reindeer run about freely wherever they want. If only I could ask my brother, Left Bank, about it. We never saw reindeer in the forest even once."

It turned out that it is possible to take reindeer to pasture after all. One can even ride on reindeer. The domestic deer liked Right Bank. He began taking them to pasture, and they say that he did a good job.

* Tau is the Enets word for the Nganasan.

Right Bank learned a great deal from the village people. He learned to count. He calculated that he had lived in the village of the Tau (Nganasan) people for seven years.

"How many years I've been here!" he thought. "It would be interesting to find out how many years my brother, Left Bank, has lived in his village—more years or less years. It must be the same number of years. After all, we set out from our *chum* on the same day."

Seven years is a long time. In that time, Right Bank had grown into a man. The little girl who had given him cloudberries to eat had also grown up. She had become a beautiful young woman, and Right Bank married her.

The young woman's father gave them some reindeer. Right Bank was happy. "Now Left Bank and I can take our reindeer to pasture together," he thought. "Together we'll have a good sized herd."

He thought for a moment and then said to his wife, "It's time to set out on a journey. My brother, Left Bank, must already be in our old *chum* with his wife and reindeer. We can't be late!"

They set out. It was winter. The reindeer traveled quickly, much faster than a person could travel on foot. Then, too, the lake was frozen. Right Bank drove the reindeer easily across the lake.

Right Bank caught sight of his *chum,* which stood at the fork of the river. He hurried to his home, urging on his reindeer.

He saw a herd of harnessed reindeer moving in a line along the other bank of the river. A man was sitting in the front sled, urging the reindeer on. A woman, apparently his wife, was sitting in the second sled.

"Look, my brother, Left Bank, is coming. We're not too late," Right Bank told his wife.

The reindeer herds came together. Right Bank hopped out of his sled, and the other man hopped out of his sled. The two men looked at one another. Right Bank looked and saw not his brother, Left Bank, but a total stranger.

Right Bank became angry. "What are you doing here?" he asked. "Why have you come here?"

"I've come home to my own *chum,*" the stranger answered. "I've come home to meet my brother."

"If you want to be called my brother, tell me how you lived and what happened to you," said Right Bank. "Then we'll see whether or not this is your *chum* and whether or not you are my brother."

The stranger began telling his story. "I walked along the left bank of the river, as my name dictated. I don't know how many days I walked because at that time I didn't know how to count...."

"He must be my brother," Right Bank thought, "because that is how I set out."

"Then, I came to a high bank overlooking a lake. I was frightened by a crane as it flew up out of the reeds…."

"He's not my brother," Right Bank thought bitterly. "The shore of the lake was low lying. And it wasn't a crane, but an otter, that frightened me."

"I sailed across the lake on a gnarled log…."

"That's exactly how it was!" Right Bank thought in delight.

"After sailing across the lake, I met a girl. She was gathering bilberries and gave me some to eat."

"You've forgotten!" cried Right Bank. "It wasn't bilberries, but cloudberries."

"What? Did the girl give you cloudberries?" asked the traveler. "That means you aren't my brother, Right Bank."

"I am your brother, Right Bank. It's you who aren't my brother, Left Bank! Well, go on. Tell me some more."

"The girl turned out to be from a camp of the Somatu[*] (tundra Enets) people."

"She was from the Tau (Nganasan) people. Again, it isn't turning out right!"

"She took me to her parents. I lived there for seven years. I went hunting with her father…."

"And why didn't you take reindeer to pasture?" Right Bank asked angrily.

The other man did not listen to him and went on telling his story. "I became a good hunter. I caught many sables and polar foxes. Later, I married the old folks' daughter. I exchanged the animal pelts for reindeer and came here."

"Well, that's it!" exclaimed Right Bank. "You aren't my brother. My wife's father gave me the reindeer."

The other man said, "Maybe you're not my brother, but I plan to live here. This is my *chum*."

"What do you mean? How do you know it's your *chum*? What proof do you have?"

"When I left this place, I hid some white stones near the left side of the *chum*."

"That's right!" Right Bank joined in. "And I hid some black stones near the right side. Let's see if they are there."

They went into the *chum* and looked around. Sure enough, the white and black stones were lying just where they said they were.

"It turns out that we are brothers, after all," said Right Bank.

The two men hugged and then called their wives. They began living together in friendship. Right Bank took the reindeer to pasture, and Left Bank went hunting. They lived their lives well. They raised their children and lived to see their grandchildren.

---

[*] Somatu is the Enets word for the Enets people who live in the tundra.

OLESHEK, THE DEER WITH THE GOLDEN ANTLERS

(Saami)

*A*n old man formed a man of clay. After making him, the old man placed him beneath the window and went back into the house.

The old man went to his wife and said, "Come look at the Clay Man I made."

As the old woman looked out the window, the Clay Man came alive. The woman got scared and said, "What have you done, old man? Now the Clay Man will come in and eat us up."

Suddenly, they heard "tromp, tromp, tromp" coming from the other side of the window. The Clay Man was walking clumsily.

The door opened, and the Clay Man came into the cottage. He looked here and there and all around. The old man was sitting in a corner tying a new fishing net. The old woman was repairing a net.

The Clay Man grabbed the old man and the old woman and gobbled them up. He ate both of them at once—hands, feet, and even the net. After gobbling them up, he went out onto the street.

Two girls were walking down the street to the village well to fetch water, one with two buckets and another with a yoke for carrying the buckets. Well, didn't the Clay Man eat up both of them—buckets, yoke, and all!

The Clay Man walked on. He met three old women carrying baskets of berries. He ate up the old women—berries, baskets, and all.

Once again, the Clay Man walked on. He came upon three fishermen repairing their boat beside the sea. He gobbled up all three of them, together with their boat, and plodded on.

The Clay Man walked on and came to three men chopping wood. He ate up all three of them—axes and all.

Again, he went on. He walked until he came to a mountain. A young deer was grazing on top of the mountain.

The Clay Man looked at the deer. "I'm going to eat you up," he announced.

Oleshek, the Deer, said, "Clay Man, oh Clay Man, why climb the mountain to eat me up? Stand at the foot of the mountain and open your mouth wide. I'll jump down from the mountain straight into your mouth, so that it will be easier for you to eat me."

The Clay Man was happy. "He, he, he," he giggled.

The Clay Man stood at the foot of the mountain and opened his mouth as wide as he could. He watched as Oleshek, the Deer, jumped toward his mouth.

Oleshek jumped from atop the mountain and bang—he thrust his antlers into the Clay Man's stomach!

The Clay Man broke into hundreds of pieces that scattered everywhere. The people whom he had eaten came tumbling out of his belly.

They ran to their homes. The old man and the old woman ran dragging their net. The girls ran carrying the buckets and yoke. The old women ran off with their baskets of berries. The woodcutters ran away with their axes, and the fishermen sailed off in their boat. Oleshek, the Deer, followed them.

The grateful girls brought some gold to Oleshek. The men gilded Oleshek's antlers with the gold that the girls had brought. From that day on, Oleshek became known as the Deer with the Golden Antlers.

THE OLD WOMAN AND THE SINGING FISH

(Deg Hit'an/Ingalik)

*T*here was an old woman who lived alone beside a lake. She always worked by herself. In summer, she set nets and caught many fish, which she cleaned and hung up to dry. After the fish had dried, she put them in her food cache. She had a grass cache where she stored plenty of food. It made her happy to have plenty of food and no worries about where her next meal was coming from.

When winter came, she cooked the fish. Although she had plenty of food, she cooked only bones because of her fear of being without something to eat. "I might run short of food in winter," she thought. Sometimes, as a treat, she made "Indian ice cream" (*sxusem*)* by mixing berries and fat, and she ate that.

Every evening at dusk the old woman climbed up onto the roof and opened the curtain over the smoke hole. She made a fire, put on a pot, and prepared her modest meal. She dished up her food and ate. After she had finished eating, she thought, "That's enough. I'll close the curtain now and go to bed."

The old woman put dirt on the fire to extinguish it and went outside. She climbed up onto the roof and closed the curtain over the smoke hole.

She went back to the doorway and stood there listening. She listened attentively as if waiting for something to happen or someone to come. She stuck her fingers in her ears and twirled them around. It was then that she heard something. Could it be? She thought she heard someone singing. Was someone coming?

Excited, she ran inside and grabbed the washbasin from under the shelf. She filled the basin with water and washed her face. She combed her hair hastily, but carefully. Then, she reached down and got her workbag. She took some clothing out of the workbag. It was a handsome fish skin parka, which she put on quickly in anticipation of greeting her guest.

Then, the old woman went back out of her house and waited. After some time had passed, she heard someone singing again. She went back into the house and sat on the bench. She stayed there, spinning sinew.

After a short time had passed, she went out again and listened. Yes, there it was again—someone was singing! "I wonder if it's a man," the old woman thought.

* *Sxusem*, traditionally referred to as "Indian ice cream," is a dessert made by native peoples of Pacific North America.

She walked down below the house and looked around on the shore of the lake. There she saw a little fish, singing as it swam. The old woman picked up a stick and struck the water with the stick angrily.

Then, the old woman went back home. She went inside. She sat there for a short while and went back out again. Now it was quiet. "It must have been a man," she thought.

Saddened, the old woman went back into the house and ate some "Indian ice cream" (*sxusem*). She got lonely and began to cry. Finally, the old woman ran off into the woods crying.

And that is the end of the story.

PART 2

CREATION STORIES AND MYTHS

SEDNA, THE SEA SPIRIT

(Inuit—Arctic)

Sedna is the most important Inuit deity because she controls and rules the sea creatures that the Inuit depend on to sustain life. Sedna's sad story is known throughout the Arctic in different versions. Her name varies. The Netsilik Eskimos, or Inuit, call her Nuliajuk, for example, and the Utkuhikjalingmiut call her Putilik.[1] Other names include Nerrivik, Siarnaq, Takanakapsaluk, and Arnakuaqsak (or Arnarquagssaq).[2]

The sea spirit, Sedna, lives in Adlivun, the Inuit Underworld, with the souls of the dead and with her father, Anguta, who brings the dead to Adlivun, where they must sleep for a year before passing on to Quidlivun, the Land of the Moon.[3] In 2003, an asteroid discovered on the outer edge of our solar system was named Sedna in honor of the spirit.

The story that follows includes elements from several versions of the widely known Arctic tale.

*S*edna was a beautiful Inuit girl with thick, long hair. Many suitors came to her father, Anguta, to beg for her hand in marriage. Unimpressed by all of them, Sedna refused to leave home.

Anguta worried about what would happen to Sedna when he grew too old to hunt. "Who will provide for my daughter?" he wondered.

One day there appeared an unknown hunter dressed in fancy furs and wearing Arctic glasses made of walrus tusk with a slit through which the wearer peered in order to protect his eyes from the blinding sun reflected off the snow. What a fine figure he cut! He wooed Sedna with a bewitching song, in which he promised her a home covered in the finest skins, a bed made of the softest furs, and plenty of tasty meat to eat. Seduced by the young man's sweet song, Sedna agreed to marry him.

Sedna left her father for her new home. She and her husband journeyed long over the sea until they reached a barren island with high cliffs.

To Sedna's disappointment, her life was not all that her husband had promised. Instead of a home covered in fine skins, she had to live in a drafty nest of twigs. There was nowhere to get warm. The wind blew through the moss and twigs, and Sedna lay in the nest shivering. Her handsome hunter brought only fish, fish, and more fish to eat. There was never a scrap of meat as he had promised. Miserable, hungry, and cold, Sedna wept.

One day the walrus tusk glasses slipped from the eyes of Sedna's husband, and she saw that his eyes were ugly. "How horrid you look with those bird's eyes of yours," she cried out in surprise.

Her husband laughed at her discomfort. He took off his clothing and revealed that he was not human at all. He was a grey seabird known as a fulmar. The fulmar strutted about, looking very much like a seagull.

Sedna was in despair. "Aja, aja! What a terrible mistake I've made," she wailed. "How can I go on living in squalor with a wretched fulmar as a husband? I want to go home."

Sedna's cries were so loud that they were carried across the water, borne on the Arctic winds, and reached her father's ears. Anguta hopped into his boat and sailed in the direction of his daughter's voice.

When Anguta arrived, the fulmar husband was away searching for fish. Sedna was waiting for her father on the seashore. She got into the boat quickly, and father and daughter paddled away.

They had not gone far before Anguta spotted a gray speck on the horizon. The speck grew larger. Soon, it became apparent that it was Sedna's fulmar husband in hot pursuit.

"Give me back my wife!" the bird shrieked.

"Never!" Anguta replied.

His refusal angered the fulmar, who spread wide his wings and flapped them until the sea became dark and agitated. With the flapping of his wings, the fulmar created a violent storm that alternately tossed the boat up onto the waves and then plunged it down into the abyss.

Fear gripped Anguta's heart. Finally, in desperation he grabbed Sedna and threw her into the raging water. "Take your wife back, but leave me alone," he cried out to the fulmar.

Sedna was stunned by her father's betrayal. For a moment, she froze in the icy Arctic water. Then, her instinct for survival took over, and Sedna began fighting for her life. She grabbed the side of her father's boat and held on for dear life. Afraid for his own life, Anguta tried to disengage his daughter's fingers from the boat. When that failed, he took an axe and chopped off Sedna's fingers to the first joint. The fingers fell into the water and turned into seals.

Still, Sedna clung to the side of the boat. Anguta chopped off her fingers to the second joint. Sedna's fingers sank into the water and became walruses.

With the stumps of her hands, Sedna persisted in clinging to the side of the boat. Her father chopped off her hands, which turned into whales, and gave her a final shove with the oar. Sedna sank slowly down into the sea.

A frozen Sedna descended to Adlivun, the Underworld, where she became mistress of the sea and ruler of the sea creatures. It is she who decides when to give the sea creatures to man to be hunted.

She has never stopped being angry for being treated badly. When her anger rages, so does the sea. During her fits of temper, she creates storms and withholds food from the Inuit hunters, who must respect her and try to placate her so that she will release the sea creatures for their use. If hunters fail to treat a slain animal properly and fail to respect its spirit, Sedna becomes offended. Her hair gets soiled with the dirt of men's sins.

When Sedna stays angry for long periods of time and makes the sea creatures disappear, a shaman must intercede on behalf of the hunters. The shaman becomes a fish and descends to the bottom of the sea to ask for Sedna's help and good will.[4] The shaman must swim through a wheel of ice that turns round and round. Then, he has to avoid getting caught in a cauldron of boiling seals that blocks his way. Finally, he must slip past a vicious dog that guards the passageway to Sedna's home. Only the most accomplished of shamans can slip by the dog unnoticed.

When at the end of his journey to the bottom of the sea the shaman comes face to face with Sedna, he asks her what the hunters have done wrong and promises that they will never again offend the spirit if she returns the sea creatures to them.

The shaman calms Sedna by combing the tangles from her hair, thereby combing out the dirt of men's sins. He makes two long braids. Sedna has no fingers with which to comb and braid her hair, so she is very grateful to the shaman for grooming her.

As a reward to him, Sedna releases the sea creatures to the hunters. Once again, the Inuit are blessed with meat and with skins to be used as clothing, bedding, rugs, and as covering for their boats and homes.

HOW THE NARWHAL CAME TO BE

(Inuit and North American First Nations)

The narwhal (Monodon monoceros) is at the top of the endangered species list of Arctic creatures. The polar bear ranks second. There are currently 50,000 to 80,000 narwhals in the Arctic.[1] This mysterious and unique whale has an upper left incisor tooth that grows into a long, spiraled tusk on the male, and on a few females, of the species. This tusk is reminiscent of the legendary unicorn's horn and was once believed to have magical power. It was in demand as an antidote to poison. Queen Elizabeth I (1533–1603) paid 10,000 pounds, the price of a castle, for a narwhal tooth.[2] The story of the narwhal's origin is known in Alaska, Canada, and Greenland.

A blind boy lived with his loving sister and mean stepmother. The family frequently went hungry because they had no hunter in the family to bring them food. The boy had been born blind, so he could not hunt. Sometimes his sister was able to snare small animals, such as rabbits, but most of the time, they went without meat.

One hungry winter, an enormous bear in search of a meal frightened them by peering into the window of their sod house. After her initial fright, the stepmother said to the boy, "Quick, a bear is at the window. I'll aim the arrow, and you draw the bow."

The arrow reached its mark, and the bear fell backward onto the snow, dead.

"Tough luck, boy. Can't you do anything right?" asked the stepmother, pretending that the boy had missed the bear.

Then she turned to the girl and whispered, "Don't let on to your brother that he killed the bear. That way we'll have to divide the meat only two ways." The stepmother skinned the bear and hid the meat.

The girl told her brother in secret that he had killed the bear and was a good hunter. While the stepmother and girl ate bear meat, the boy was given old fish to eat. He didn't get a taste of the meat of the animal he had slain. However, when the stepmother was not around, the sister, who loved her brother dearly, always put aside a bit of meat and gave it to him secretly. Since the bear was large, its meat lasted for many meals.

Shortly after the killing of the bear, an old man came to visit. During his stay, he noticed how badly the stepmother treated her stepson. He took the children aside. "Watch for a friendly loon that will come to you from across the water," he told the children. "When the loon is nearby, grab him by the neck, boy, and he'll cure your blindness."

In the spring, as brother and sister were walking on the shore, a loon did indeed swim up to them. The loon told the boy to grab his neck and to hold his breath. After the boy had a firm hold on the loon's neck, the loon dove to the bottom of the water. The boy held his breath until he thought he would burst. When they emerged, the loon asked, "Can you see, boy?"

"No, I can't," the boy replied, so the loon dove again, this time deeper. It was even more difficult for the boy to hold his breath.

"Can you see now?" asked the loon after they had emerged.

"I can see a faint light," the boy replied, gasping for breath.

The bird dove four times in all before the breathless boy received sight. Overjoyed and staring in wonder at the world he had never known, except through the words of his sister, he embraced the loon in gratitude.

"Don't say anything to your stepmother about being able to see," advised the loon. "In summer I will send you a pod of whales to harpoon and to add to your supply of food."

It happened just as the loon had promised. One summer's day, a pod of whales approached. The boy grabbed his harpoon and tied the line to his sister's waist so that she could hold the harpooned animal.

The stepmother noticed what the children were doing. She ran up to the water and pushed the girl aside. "No, no, tie the line around my waist, instead," she demanded. She knew that she would have a right to part of the whale meat if she participated in the hunt.

"Very well," the boy said, and he twisted the line securely around the woman's waist.

Nervous, the stepmother ordered, "Harpoon the smallest whale, boy."

But the boy looked for the largest whale and threw the harpoon. It struck the enormous mammal. The whale pulled away and swam far out to sea, dragging the evil stepmother along.

The whale dove to the bottom of the sea. As the stepmother sank with the whale, she spun round and round at the end of the line. Her long hair twisted into a tusk, and she became the first narwhal. To this day the narwhal sports a long, spiraled tusk that protrudes from its head.

RAVEN STEALS THE LIGHT OF THE SUN, MOON, AND STARS

(Inuit and Dene)

*I*n Distant Time there was darkness everywhere. It was never light. Raven was the most powerful of all creatures during those times.

One day Raven heard that a wealthy chief living on the banks of a river had possession of the sun, moon, and stars and that he kept them in an ornately carved box. Because he kept the sun, moon, and stars locked up, the world was dark all the time. No one could hunt or fish. People crawled about on the ground in search of firewood. Those were hard times, indeed.

The chief had a beautiful daughter. He and his people guarded well both his daughter and the box of luminaries.

Raven decided to go to the chief and take back the sun, moon, and the stars. "People are living in darkness. They can't find food and are hungry. Give the light back to them," Raven begged.

The chief refused to comply with Raven's request. It was then that Raven knew he would have to trick the man and his people in order to steal their treasure. After all, Raven has a reputation for being a good trickster. He flew to the top of a tree near the chief's lodge and observed what was going on. He noticed that every morning the chief's daughter went to the river to fetch water.

One morning Raven hid in a pine tree that hung over the water. He changed into a pine needle and waited for the beautiful daughter to come with her bucket to fetch water.

The girl came and filled her bucket with water. Then she dipped her drinking cup into the water to take a drink. Raven, in the form of a pine needle, jumped into the drinking cup. The thirsty girl drank the water, and with the water she swallowed the pine needle.

Now inside the belly of the chief's daughter, Raven turned into a baby so that the girl became pregnant.

"Who is the father?" the chief asked his daughter.

"I don't know," the girl replied. "I have never known a man."

The baby grew by leaps and bounds. Soon the daughter gave birth to a son, who was, in reality, Raven.

The chief loved his grandson very much and spoiled him by giving him everything he asked for. One day the boy looked at an ornate box and began crying.

"What's the matter, grandson?" asked the chief.

Raven, disguised as the baby boy, pointed to the box and blubbered. He cried until his grandfather gave in and gave the boy the box to play with.

The grandson opened the box and took out the stars and the moon. He rolled the stars and the moon around on the ground and suddenly grabbed them and threw them through the smoke hole up into the sky.

The unhappy grandfather took the box away from the boy, but he did not have the heart to punish his dearly loved grandson.

Soon Raven, disguised as the baby boy, began pointing at the box and crying again. He wailed so long and so loud that he almost made himself sick. He wailed until his indulgent grandfather gave in and let him play with the box again.

The boy played with the box for a long time, rolling the sun on the ground. Suddenly, Raven turned back into a bird. He scooped up the box and flew up through the smoke hole. He found the stars and the moon hanging outside the chief's lodge, and he put them back into the box. Now his box contained the sun, the moon, and the stars.

Then, Raven took the box to the people, who were huddling together in the darkness. "Would you like to have light?" he asked them.

The people laughed at him and thought he was lying or playing a trick.

Raven opened the box, and the stars and moon came tumbling out. Raven let one of the sun's rays shine from the box to prove that he was not lying. Although it was just one ray, it blinded the people, who were accustomed to darkness. Raven opened the box wider, and the sun popped out. Sun, moon, and stars rose into the sky, where they have been to this day, driving the darkness away.

THE KASKA MAN WHO MADE WHALES

(Kaska and Tlingit)

A Kaska man married to a Tlingit woman lived by the sea. The man's sister was married to his wife's brother, and they lived in the same village. The village people could see an island of ice, a glacier, out in the sea. No one had ever been able to climb to the top of the island of ice.

One day the man was with his Tlingit relatives, and they were hunting seals near the island of ice in a large canoe. "The Kaska are an inland people, and they are good climbers," the Kaska man's father-in-law said. "I would like to see my son-in-law climb to the top of the island of ice."

"I'll try," the Kaska man said. He put on his snowshoes and the spurs that he attached to his snowshoes when he went walking on ice. He took his walking stick with the sharp end. Then he steered his canoe toward the island and landed.

The Kaska man had no problem climbing the ice to the very top of the island. The Tlingit were angry and jealous when they saw how easily he had reached the top of the island. They began shouting at him. Then they turned their canoe away from him and paddled away, leaving the Kaska man stranded there.

The Kaska man's brother-in-law, a mere boy, felt sorry for him and paddled in the opposite direction because he didn't want to desert his relative.

The Kaska man grieved when he was abandoned. Finally, he lay down on the ice and fell asleep. It seemed as if he was dreaming that his relatives had abandoned him so cruelly, but indeed it was all too real.

Suddenly, he heard a voice speaking. "Come down here in the water with us."

The Kaska man obeyed the voice and swam beneath the sea. He came to a house that belonged to the Seal People.

"How did you happen to be sleeping on the ice above?" they asked. He told them the story of how his cruel relatives had abandoned him.

A Seal Man was lying in bed sick in the underwater house. He had been speared by a Tlingit. The harpoon was still embedded in his body. The shamans of the Seal People could

---

not understand what was wrong with him and what they could do to make him feel better. They had tried many cures, but all of them had failed.

"Stranger, will you try to cure him?" the Seal People asked.

The Kaska man knew why the Seal Man was ill. He blew on the wound and pulled out the harpoon's head. Without the harpoon stuck in his body, the Seal Man began to feel better.

The Seal People were happy. "Do you want to go home?" they asked the Kaska man.

"Yes, I would like to go home now," he replied.

The Seal People put the Kaska man in a seal bladder that had been blown up to accommodate him. They tied the neck of the bladder securely and set it afloat on the sea. The Kaska man drifted on the sea as if encased in a big bubble.

"Now you must think only of your home," the Seal People instructed. "If you think of anything else, you will return to us. When you hit the sand and hear the sound of the waves breaking on the shore, you will know that you are home. Then, you may open the bladder and get out."

The Kaska man floated halfway home. He tried not to think of the Seal people. However, he began thinking of the place he had just left, and he found himself back under the sea again with the Seal People.

Once again the Seal People placed him in the bladder and warned him to think only of home. They set him adrift. This happened several times before the Kaska man managed to focus his thoughts long enough to reach home. He sent the bladder back to the Seal People after he arrived home. He told no one, except his wife, of his adventures.

The next day he went into the bush near the seashore and began carving pieces of wood into the shape of whales. He threw them into the water, but they were too light and quickly bounced to the surface. He tried different types of wood, but all of them bobbed up out of the water too soon. Finally, the Kaska man found a hard, heavy wood, which he carved into whales. When he threw the carved whales into the water, this time they went deep down into the water and came to the surface a long way away. The Kaska man turned his pieces of wood into real whales and sent them off to catch seals.

After the whales had brought him several seals, he called them back. "Now go meet the big canoe with the seal hunters," he said. "Push it over and smash it, but spare the boy who steered his canoe in the opposite direction and refused to take part when my relatives abandoned me and mocked me. Leave the boy a piece of canoe to float home on."

The whales did as the Kaska man ordered. They drowned all the seal hunters, except the boy.

Then, the Kaska man called the whales back. "From now on you will be real whales. Go into the sea. You will push canoes over sometimes, and you will eat seals. You will be the biggest and the strongest of all the ocean animals."

To this day the Tlingit say that it was a Kaska man who made the whales.

WOLVERINE AND MINK
CREATE EARTH

(Innu, Eastern Cree, and Upper Yukon Dene)

The sly wolverine is a secretive animal that avoids contact with humans. It is very muscular and strong and can weigh up to forty-five pounds. The wolverine can become vicious when provoked.[1] Both men and animals give the wolverine a wide berth. Lucien Turner reports that the indigenous people of Labrador and Quebec believed the wolverine was possessed by an evil spirit, and they treated the animal badly when they captured it.[2] Today the wolverine is no longer seen in Innu territory. The wolverine has disappeared, but its legacy lives on in myth. The culture hero, Wolverine (Kuekuatsheu), is credited with creating the earth. This is how it happened.

Many long years ago, a heavy rain flooded the land. Wolverine saw the water getting higher and built a raft for the animals. When there was no more land to stand upon, Wolverine told the animals to climb onto the raft so that they would not drown. Wolverine also gathered different varieties of plants and put them on board the raft.

Then Wolverine asked the animals to help him create earth in those vast waters. First, he went to Otter. "Swim to the bottom of the water, Otter, and bring back some mud."

Otter dove down, but he was not able to get a paw full of mud. He could not make it to the bottom.

"All right, then, you go, Beaver," said Wolverine.

Beaver, too, was unable to reach the bottom. Beaver emerged, gasping for breath.

"You give it a try, Muskrat," said Wolverine.

Muskrat was able to swim deeper, but still he could not touch the bottom. He did get a glimpse of some vegetation down there.

"Come here, Seal. You should be able to reach the bottom," said Wolverine.

He was right. Seal swam straight to the bottom, but he could not gather any mud in his flippers. He just flopped his flippers and stirred up the mud until the bottom became cloudy.

"Mink, it's your turn," commanded Wolverine.

Wolverine tied a strip of hide around Mink's leg, and Mink dove to the bottom. She was there for a long time, and Wolverine began to think that she had drowned.

Just when Wolverine had given up hope, Mink emerged, more dead than alive. Mink had scooped mud and tiny stones into her tiny paws.

Wolverine took the mud and stones and mixed them together. The mixture grew and grew into an enormous island. This island is the world upon which we and the animals live today.[3]

HOW THE SEASONS WERE CREATED

(MacKenzie River Slavey)

*I*n the beginning, before there were humans, animals walked the earth. The animals of old had the ability to change into whatever form they pleased. They were shapeshifters. There was a time, too, when all of the creatures suffered because it was a long, long winter. For three years it snowed without stopping. The rivers and lakes were frozen over so that the animals could not get a drink of water, nor could they fish. The trees and plants never bloomed in the unbearable cold, and the animals huddled together for warmth.

Finally, unable to stand it any longer, the animals gathered for a big council to decide what they should do. Creatures from land and sea were invited. After a discussion, the animals decided that it was the absence of warmth that made the winter go on perpetually. Without heat, the animals would continue to suffer, so they resolved to find out where the heat had gone and bring it back.

As each creature gave its opinion, everyone realized that an important animal was missing. Bear was not at the council, and in fact, Bear had not been seen by anyone for three years.

"Perhaps Bear is responsible for our lack of warmth and our eternal winter," suggested wily Wolverine. "Perhaps the bears are keeping all the heat to themselves."

"Well, let's find out," the animals replied in a chorus.

The creatures voted to go in search of Bear. They chose Wolf, Fox, Wolverine, Lynx, Mouse, Dogfish, and Pike as the search party. The search party traveled all over the earth in their quest for Bear. However, in those days Bear did not live on earth. He dwelled in the upper world up in the sky.

Finally, the search party happened upon a hole in the sky that led to the upper world. The creatures climbed through the hole and emerged in the upper world, which seemed to be an exact copy of earth. In their explorations, the animals found that everything looked like it did on earth.

They came to a lake, like any earthly lake. Beside the lake was a tipi with a campfire burning in front of it. They looked inside the tipi and found two bear cubs lying together. "Where is your mother?" the search party asked.

"She's gone hunting," the cubs replied.

The search party looked around inside the tipi and saw several big bags hanging from poles. "What's in this bag?" asked wily Wolverine.

"Our mother keeps rain in that bag," the cubs answered.

"And what's in this bag?"

"She keeps the winds in that bag," the cubs explained.

"And what about this bag?"

"Mother keeps fog in that one," declared the cubs.

"What does she keep in this bag over here?" asked Wolverine.

"It's a secret. Mother told us not to tell anyone what is in that bag."

"Oh, don't be scared," Fox said persuasively. "You can tell us what is in the bag. We won't tell anyone else."

"No, no, Mother will spank us if we tell."

"But your mother will never find out that you've told us," said Lynx.

"Oh, all right," the cubs agreed reluctantly. "Mother keeps heat in that bag."

"So-o-o," said the creatures, and they went outside to hold a council. They decided to leave as quickly as possible in case Bear should return unexpectedly. They went to a safer place and hid there.

"How can we steal the bag that holds heat from Bear?" asked Wolverine.

"Somehow, we must distract Mother Bear," said Fox. "But how?"

"I've got it!" said Lynx. "I'll change into a caribou, and I'll go to the other side of the lake. Mother Bear will follow me."

"Very clever, Lynx," said Wolverine. "Bear will see that you are across the lake, and she'll paddle across the lake in her canoe to hunt you down. Meanwhile, we'll sneak into her tipi and steal the bag holding heat."

"I can help, too," Mouse piped up. "I'll gnaw through Bear's paddle so that it will break before she gets to the other side of the lake. That will buy us some more time."

Lynx hurried to the other side of the lake and shifted his shape. Lynx became a caribou. Mouse hopped into Bear's canoe and gnawed almost completely through Bear's paddle. The other creatures hid behind Bear's tipi.

Mother Bear came home to her cubs. Suddenly, one of the cubs caught sight of Lynx disguised as a caribou on the other side of the lake. "Oh, look, there's a caribou across the lake!" the cub cried.

Bear jumped into her canoe in hot pursuit. Caribou-Lynx strolled along the shore, pretending not to see Bear, in order to lure Bear closer. As Bear got halfway across the lake, Caribou-Lynx bolted away. Bear began paddling furiously, placing her entire weight on the paddle. Suddenly, the paddle snapped where Mouse had chewed it. Because Bear was leaning on the paddle with all of her weight, she fell into the water, and the canoe turned over.

Meanwhile, Lynx turned back into his true shape and hurried to the other side of the lake. "Be quick!" he shouted to the other animals. "Soon Bear will be after us."

The search party ran into the tipi and pulled the bag holding heat off the pole. Tugging at the bag, they rushed to the hole in the sky that led to their world below. However, the bag was big and very heavy. They took turns dragging the bag, but they made slow progress. Bear was snapping at their heels.

Just as the animals were completely exhausted and Mother Bear had almost overtaken them, they caught sight of the hole in the sky that led to their world below. Only Dogfish and Pike had not yet taken their turn at dragging the bag. Dogfish seized the bag and managed to move it a few inches to the edge of the hole in the sky. Then, Pike gave the bag a slap with her tail and tipped the bag just enough to cause it to drop into the hole to the lower world. One by one, the animals jumped down the hole after the bag just in the nick of time.

As soon as the bag of heat hit the ground, it burst open. Heat rushed out, spreading over the entire earth. Warmth spread everywhere, melting the ice and snow and causing the sun to shine again. The cold and darkness were banished.

The melting snow and ice caused floodwaters to cover the earth. Now the creatures of earth had a new problem. They were afraid that they might drown.

To save themselves, the creatures of earth climbed up the world tree, a giant tree that grew almost to the sky above. "Help us!" they screamed from the world tree's highest branches.

Suddenly, a giant fish appeared. It drank the waters and grew larger with every gulp. Finally, it became an enormous mountain that looked like a fish.

After the flood, the sun shone and soaked up the excess water. The trees and plants that had been covered with ice in their deathly sleep came to life and blossomed with leaves and flowers. The animals were joyful because it was summer.

From that time on, earth experienced a warm season coming after a cold season. And thus winter eventually turns into summer to this very day.

TOY PEOPLE

(Chukchi)

*T*here once lived an old woman and an old man. They had a daughter, whom they named Kèlena. One day the old man said to Kèlena, "In the morning, dress in your best clothes. Your bridegroom is coming to get you."

Kèlena knew whom her father had in mind, and she despised her prospective husband. "I won't marry him," said Kèlena. "He is greedy. He won't even throw his leftover bones to the dogs."

"So you won't marry," said her father. "Then leave us. I hope we never see you again. Get out!"

That night Kèlena got up quietly. She put on her fur jacket and reindeer fur boots. Then, she took a sack down from the shelf. She untied it and took out three little bags made of reindeer hide.

One little bag contained seal and walrus teeth. The second little bag contained reindeer teeth. The third little bag contained mice skins. These were Kèlena's toys, with which she played when she was a very little girl. "This is all I need," said Kèlena.

She took the big sack and put a whalebone and the three little bags with her toys into it. Kèlena glanced out of the *yaranga*, the tent made of reindeer hide that she had called home. It was quiet. The moon was shining so that every blade of grass was as visible as it was in daytime.

"What nice weather," said Kèlena. "No wind is blowing." And she went down to the seashore.

Kèlena walked all night long. Toward morning she came to the Utensk region. "This is a good place," the girl thought. "I think I'll stay here."

She untied the sack and took out the little reindeer hide bag with the seal and walrus teeth. Kèlena went to the seashore. She threw all of the seal teeth into the water and said, "When I wake up tomorrow, there will be many seals in the sea."

Then, she took the walrus teeth and threw them onto the sand and said, "And these will become walruses!"

She threw the whalebone far out to sea. "This bone will make many whales," said Kèlena. "Now I have populated the sea."

Kèlena went into the Utensk tundra. She untied the little bag with the reindeer teeth and scattered them onto the white moss. "There will be many reindeer here," said the girl.

Then, she untied the little bag with the mice skins, threw them onto the earth, and said, "These will become polar foxes."

Kèlena broke off willow twigs and built little *yarangas* with them on the seashore. "These will be homes for people," said Kèlena.

Kèlena took two small stones and said, "You will be a boy, and you will be a girl."

She made grown people with large stones—hunters, fishermen, deer herders.

Then, Kèlena went up a hill and looked around at the sea, the tundra, and the sandy shore. "Come to life!" she cried.

All at once seals began splashing in the sea. Walruses began roaring on the sand. Whales struck the water with their tails. Polar foxes began running along the seashore. Reindeer began stamping their hooves.

Kèlena sat on the seashore and said, "Oh, how tired I am!"

Little girls and boys ran out of the *yarangas* and surrounded Kèlena. "Hello, Grandmother," they said. "Let's go home."

"I've already become an old woman," thought Kèlena. "I have very little strength left."

The people of Utensk placed Kèlena on a soft skin in the midst of the *yarangas*. "Who is it who cries 'gy-gy-gy-gy-gy' so loudly?" they asked.

"The walruses are crying," said Kèlena.

She broke a willow branch and gave half of the branch to a hunter. "Take this harpoon," she said. "Go to the sea and throw this harpoon into a walrus. The walrus will be your food."

The hunter went to the sea and killed a walrus. The people boiled the walrus meat. They gave the best piece to Grandmother Kèlena on a wooden plate.

Kèlena ate the walrus meat and thought, "It doesn't matter that I've grown old. After I am dead, the people of Utensk will remember me."

A fire burned in the *yaranga*. Hunters and their wives and children warmed themselves by the fire. They looked at old Kèlena and said, "We have a wise grandmother. She forgot nothing. She created everything that we need."

THE CREATION OF CARIBOU

(Netsilik and Caribou Inuit and Upper Yukon Dene)

*B*efore all of the animals were on earth, and at a time when men could become animals and animals could become men, there lived a mountain spirit. A beautiful Arctic fox took the Mountain Spirit's fancy, and he married her.

The Mountain Spirit never went hunting with the foxes. Instead, he sat at home with his wife and never caught anything. His wife's brothers made fun of their sister's husband because, unlike them, he was a bad hunter who contributed nothing of value to the household. "What a lazy n'er-do-well your husband is," they would complain to their sister.

Shamed by his brothers-in-law, the Mountain Spirit walked out into the countryside and struck a hole in the ground the way a fisherman would strike a hole in the ice to fish. Then the Mountain Spirit hung a long cord down into the earth the way a fisherman would drop a fishing line into the water.

Out of the ground the Mountain Spirit pulled one piece after another of delicious dried caribou meat. He took the meat home and showed it to his brothers-in-law. There was great feasting and rejoicing.

The foxes were sorry that they had made fun of their sister's husband. "Thank goodness that we didn't drive away the Mountain Spirit," they said, "because he is a good provider."

Indeed, thereafter, live caribou came pouring out of the hole in the earth that the Mountain Spirit had made. The caribou jumped out of the hole until the earth was covered with them. When the Mountain Spirit thought there were enough caribou on earth, he closed up the hole again.

Yes, at one time there were no caribou until the Mountain Spirit released them. They came from inside the earth for man's benefit.

THE INGRATES

(Chukchi)

en brothers lived together in a *yaranga,* a portable tent covered with walrus skins and supported by whalebones. Every morning the brothers left their tent to go into the tundra to hunt.

Soon the brothers noticed that when they were not at home, someone was coming to the *yaranga* and was sewing fur clothing—fur jackets, sealskin boots, and deerskin leggings—for them. Dressed in the clothing, the brothers could track animals easily because the clothing kept them warm, even in a hard frost.

"Who is coming to our *yaranga?*" the brothers asked in surprise.

They began taking turns standing guard. They lay in wait for ten days outside their home, but no one came.

Then, the brothers filled an old jacket with dry moss and made a scarecrow. The oldest brother remained in the *yaranga* while the nine other brothers went hunting, taking the scarecrow with them. From a distance it seemed as if all ten brothers had gone hunting.

Meanwhile, the oldest brother stood guard behind the bed curtain in the *yaranga.* Soon, he saw Fox enter the *yaranga.* She took needle and thread and started sewing. The oldest brother came out from behind the bed curtain and grabbed her.

"Release me," Fox said timidly.

The oldest boy let Fox go and ran off to catch up with his brothers.

"Well," said his brother, "did you find out who stays in our *yaranga* when we are gone?"

"It's Fox!" the oldest boy replied.

"That's good. Now we have a homemaker while we are gone," the brothers said.

While the brothers were hunting, Fox stayed in the *yaranga* and sewed ten dolls, one doll for each brother. Then she said to the dolls, "Arise and come alive! Now you are no longer dolls. You are women. Go meet your husbands."

Suddenly, the dolls turned into living women. They went outside to meet the brothers. The doll women lit a fire, brewed tea, and sat on deerskins beside the young men.

"These are your wives," said Fox.

"You have brought happiness to our *yaranga*," the brothers said to Fox as they drank tea. "Stay with us. We will love you like a mother."

Suddenly, the youngest and merriest of the wives looked at her fingers and began laughing, "Ha, ha, ha! Ha, ha, ha!"

Then, all of the young women looked at their fingers and began laughing. "Ha, ha, ha! Ha, ha, ha!"

The brothers looked at their wives' hands and started laughing, too. They laughed because there were no fingernails on their wives' fingers. Fox had completely forgotten about the nails when she had made the dolls.

Everyone was laughing at Fox. Fox took offense and said, "You are very ungrateful people. Yes, indeed, you are ingrates!"

Then, Fox ran out of the *yaranga*. No one ever saw her again.

The young women turned back into dolls. The brothers remained alone, as they had been before Fox came. They lived alone all their lives until one day they were too old to think about marrying or to think about wives anymore.

YES', THE SKY GOD

(Ket)

*O*ld man Yes' lived with his old wife, Khosiadam, way up above the sky. They had a son.

One day the boy said, "I'm going hunting."

"It's cold outside. Be sure to put on your fur coat," his mother admonished.

"I don't need a fur coat," the young man replied, and he went outdoors dressed improperly. He walked on and on and traveled a great distance.

"I'm going to give the boy a scare," his father decided. "I'll let a cold wind blow from the West."

Yes' released a cold wind. The boy felt the cold and began rushing home. He ran and ran until he fell down. The son of Yes' froze on the spot.

The boy's father knew all about what had happened to his son because Yes' was a shaman. "Oh, my son has frozen," he declared.

His old wife, Khosiadam, began scolding her husband. Old man Yes' began scolding his wife in turn. They had a bad quarrel.

"Why have you frozen my son?" old Khosiadam asked.

Irritated, Yes' gave Khosiadam a kick, and she fell down-down-down out of the sky and landed on earth.

Khosiadam picked herself up and shouted these words. "From now on, old man, I will stay down here and be Mother Earth. You will stay up there, old man, and be the Sky God."

DAWN

(Dolgan)

There once lived three wealthy brothers. They lived in nice, warm *chums,*[*] which are tents covered with reindeer hides. They had many reindeer. When they gathered all of their reindeer into a single herd, the herd was so enormous that it could not fit altogether on the large moss-covered spit of land,[**] where they were living.

Near the rich brothers' *chums* stood the tumbledown *chum* of their uncle. Their uncle was an old man. He could not work much. He did not have any reindeer, so he had no reindeer hides from which to sew fine clothes. The old man lived in poverty, barely saving himself from dying of hunger. His old wife lived with him. They had a son whom they were feeding and raising.

One winter the old folks had nothing to eat. They sent their son to their wealthy nephews to ask them for some meat. The boy went to fetch the meat. Instead of meat, the wealthy brothers gave the boy the membrane that lines the deer's belly.

"Eat this belly membrane," they told the boy. "We'll give you some reindeer intestines. Eat the intestines. We'll give you the lungs, too. Now go home."

The old woman cooked the deer's belly and fed the old man and their son. She, herself, ate the leftovers.

Night passed. In the morning the old man went out of the *chum* and took fright. Neither *chums* nor deer were in the camp. His wealthy nephews had taken their possessions and had moved in the middle of the night. They had quietly driven their reindeer away, too.

Saddened, the old man returned to his *chum*. "We will die, old woman," he said. "Our wealthy nephews have abandoned us. We'll never catch up with them. Where could we go on foot in such a frost? Now we'll just have to wait for death."

The old woman felt sorry for her son. She burst into tears. The old man cried, too. They grieved and grieved. Then, all three of them got into a single sleeping bag, huddling together for warmth. They wrapped themselves in deer hide and went to sleep hungry.

The old man awoke first. He got out of the sleeping bag and could not believe how warm it was. Where could such warmth come from in a tumbledown *chum* in winter?

[*] Pronounced "chooms."

[**] A spit is a narrow point of land extending into a body of water.

The old man wanted to go out. He lifted the door flap and dropped it at once in terror. He woke the old woman and said quietly, "A giant caterpillar with many legs has surrounded our *chum*. She has come to us to get a tribute.* What shall we give her? We don't have anything. So now she won't let us out of the *chum,* and she'll eat us up."

The caterpillar lay quietly, as if she were dead, but she heard everything they were whispering about in the *chum*.

The old man grabbed a spear that was used to kill bears. He gave the spear to his son and folded back the tent flap. The caterpillar opened her eyes.

"I know that you came for a tribute," the old man said. "But I have nothing to give you. My wife and I have only one little son and a spear for killing bears. If you want, take them."

The caterpillar grabbed the boy in her mouth and flew into the sky with him. The old people were left alone. They sat in their *chum* and grieved for their son.

The caterpillar flew for a long time. Finally, she flew to the edge of the sky and alighted. She spit out the boy, who was holding his father's spear firmly. The boy saw before him the same kind of forests, mountains, and swamps that he had known on earth.

Thus, the boy began living with the giant caterpillar. The caterpillar gave him food and drink. The boy noticed, however, that the caterpillar was very sad and seemed always to be thinking about something. The boy did not understand anything. He just noticed that when the caterpillar lay on her stomach, it was night. When she turned onto her side, it became dawn. When she lay on her back with her belly turned up, it became as light as day. The caterpillar's belly was red and glittered like fire.

One day when it was daylight, another enormous caterpillar came flying toward the bright caterpillar. The other caterpillar was black as night. When she alighted, it became dark. The black caterpillar seized hold of the bright caterpillar and began strangling her.

The two caterpillars began fighting. They wrapped their bodies around a tree and tore it up by the roots. They snaked their bodies around a hill and razed it to the ground. They surrounded a stone and crushed the stone into sand.

While the caterpillars fought, the boy stood watching. Light and darkness, day and night, flashed before his eyes. The black caterpillar was conquering the caterpillar with the fiery belly.

Then, the boy thought, "Why am I standing here with a spear, instead of helping my own bright caterpillar with her battle. I'm going to try to help her. I'll perish anyway, no matter what I do."

The boy ran up to the black caterpillar and pierced her heart with his spear. Immediately, it became as light as day.

The caterpillar with the fiery belly grabbed the boy and flew back to earth with him. She flew up to the *chum* and released the boy.

---

* Russians exacted tribute from the indigenous people of Siberia on behalf of the tsar. Frequently, a good share of the tribute went into the collectors' pockets.

Part 2: Creation Stories and Myths

"Take your son," she said to the old people. "He helped me kill the black caterpillar who wanted to eat me up because I give people light every morning. She wanted eternal night to be on earth. Now it won't happen. I'm going back to the sky. I'm going to lie down at the edge of the sky, and I'll turn my body around slowly. When my back is to you, it will be night. When I turn onto my side, you will see the dawning light. When I lie on my back and open my belly, there will be daylight on earth."

The caterpillar with the fiery belly created some reindeer for the boy. Then she flew away high up into the sky.

SISTER SUN AND BROTHER MOON

(Inuit, Aleut, and Deg Hit'an/Ingalik)

The movement of the sun and moon, the waxing and waning of the moon, and solar eclipses are explained in the following tale, which is widespread throughout the Arctic.

In the old days, a beautiful young woman and her brother lived in a big village. The village had a dance house. Every night the young people sang and danced and enjoyed one another's company in the dance house.

One night when the lamps were out, a man entered the dance house. He lay down with the beautiful young woman and kissed her.[1] The young woman did not like being kissed. She did not know who had kissed her because she could not see her violator's face.

The next night she was ready for the intruder. She blackened her mouth with soot from the oil lamps. When the man kissed her, his lips were blackened, too.[2]

The next day, the young woman looked for the man with sooty lips and was shocked to find that it was her brother who had kissed and violated her. She grew red with shame and hot with rage. "You have done a terrible thing to me," she screamed.

She was so angry that she sharpened her knife and cut off her breasts, which she presented to her brother. "Since you enjoy me so much, eat these," she said.

Then, she grabbed a torch and fled into the dark night. "We must never see one another again," she said.

Her brother grabbed another torch and ran after her. In his haste, he stumbled and fell in the snow so that his torch flickered and almost went out. Even with the faint glow of his torch he was able to see his sister's bloody footprints in the snow and follow them.

Sister and brother ran so fast that they rose on the wind into the sky. The sister with her bright light became the sun, and the brother with his dim light became the moon. The sparks from their torches became stars.

Brother Moon continues to chase Sister Sun to this day. But Sister Sun hides from Brother Moon and appears only after he has gone. Whenever Brother Moon catches up to Sister Sun, there is a solar eclipse.

In Alaska Brother Moon is known as Igaluk, and in Greenland he is called Anningan. Sister Sun is known as Malina in the myths of Greenland.

Brother Moon still loves his sister so much that he forgets to eat. He gets thinner and thinner with each passing day. Eventually, he becomes so hungry and thin that he has to disappear for three days each month so that he can eat. After he has eaten and is full once again, he returns to chase his sister through the sky.

HARE RESCUES THE SUN

(Chukchi)

*L*ong ago the earth was dark because evil spirits called the *kelet** had stolen the sun. They took the sun away to their house and played ball with it, throwing it from one *kele* to another.

When Hare found out that the *kelet* had stolen the sun, he said, "I'll get the sun back and chase the darkness away. How will we see without the sun? How will anything grow without the sun?"

Hare climbed onto the *kelet*'s *yaranga,* or tent home, and looked down the smoke hole. The *kelet* family was playing ball with the sun. Hare dropped down into the *yaranga* from the vent hole on top.

"Look, a fat hare!" cried a *kele.*

"Don't hurt me," said Hare, "and I'll give you plenty of oil."

"Oh, my, will you? How many kettles do you have?"

"Two kettles," Hare replied, and he kicked the sun so hard that it nearly jumped out of the vent hole. Then Hare gave a hop and almost jumped high enough to reach the vent hole. But he did not quite make it and instead fell to earth.

"Look, a fat hare!" the *kelet* cried again, in a chorus this time.

"Don't hurt me, and I'll fill you up with oil," Hare promised again.

"Oh, my, will you? How many kettles do you have?"

"Three kettles," Hare replied, and he kicked the sun again. This time the sun bounded up and out of the vent hole. It shot into the air and stuck to the sky. Then Hare gave a hop and flew through the vent hole, too. He bounded away as fast as his legs could hop.

One of the *kelet* flew after him.

Little Hare met Eagle. "Please hide me, Eagle," Hare said. "A *kele* is chasing me."

"All right," Eagle said, and Eagle hid Hare under his right wing.

The *kele* saw Eagle, too, and approached him. "Have you seen Hare?"

* The *kelet* (plural) are evil earth spirits. People wore amulets to protect themselves against the *kelet.* In Chukchi mythology, the moon is the sun of the *kelet.*

Part 2: Creation Stories and Myths

"Yes, I saw him," Eagle replied. "He climbed high up into the sky."

"Oh, dear, how can I follow him there?" asked the *kele*.

"Get on my back, and I'll take you up to the sky."

The *kele* obeyed, and Eagle carried him high up into the sky. After some time had passed, Eagle said, "*Kele*, look down to earth and tell me what size it appears to be."

"About the size of a big lake," the *kele* said.

"Then, we'd better fly higher," said Eagle.

They flew on. After some time had passed, Eagle said, "Look down again. What is the size of the earth now?"

"It's the size of a small lake," the *kele* replied.

"Then, let's go higher. Now look down at the earth. What size is it now?"

"It's the size of the piece of seal hide that covers our *yaranga*."

"Oh, we have to go higher. What size is the earth now?"

"It's the size of a small seal hide."

"Oh, we must go higher. Now what size is the earth?"

"It's the size of a boot sole made of seal hide."

"We're getting closer," Eagle declared, and he soared on. "What size is the earth now?"

"It's the size of a patch on the boot sole."

"We're almost there!" declared Eagle. "What size is the earth now?"

"It's the size of a worm hole in a reindeer skin. No, now earth has completely disappeared. I don't see it anymore at all," said the *kele*.

"Oh, I'm tired," said Eagle. "I've lost my strength, and I think I've sprained my back."

Eagle dropped the *kele*. The *kele* fell down and kept falling for a long time. At last, the *kele* reached earth and fell head first into the ground up to his waist.

Eagle called to Hare. "Your tormenter can't get you now. Don't be afraid. Go have a look."

Hare made a stone hammer and hurried over to the *kele,* whose legs were sticking up out of the ground. Hare struck the soles of the *kele*'s shoes with his hammer. He hammered until the *kele* disappeared altogether into the earth.

Since that time, the *kelet* have continued to live underground.

HOW REINDEER RECONCILED TUI-NIAMY, MOTHER FIRE, AND MOU-NIAMY, MOTHER EARTH

(Nganasan)

*A*fter the Earth was born, two mothers began quarreling. They were Tui-Nia-my, Mother Fire, and Mou-Niamy, Mother Earth.

"I am the most important one," said Tui-Niamy. "I give people warmth, and I provide the fire on which they cook fish."

"No, I am the most important one," countered Mou-Niamy. "Without me, there would be no place for people to set up their *chum*s.* There would be no place for reindeer moss to grow, which the reindeer eat, and all of the reindeer would die of hunger."

"Why argue?" asked Tui-Niamy, Mother Fire, growing angrier by the minute. "I'm just going to up and burn the *chum*s and all the trees in the forest and the moss on the tun-dra."

Mou-Niamy, Mother Earth, grew even angrier. "And I shall make a gap in the tundra so that Mother Water will drown you, Fire, and everything around you."

Tui-Niamy raged. Mou-Niamy shook. Everyone was in trouble.

Reindeer came running from the tundra. He scattered the conflagration across the ground with his hooves. Tui-Niamy, Mother Fire, calmed down and abated. Then Reindeer stamped a path from the *chum* to lower ground, where water flowed.

From that day on, Tui-Niamy, Mother Fire, began living in the *chum*. Mou-Niamy Mother Earth settled inside the ground. Now, reindeer warm themselves by the Fire, Tui-Niamy. When they nibble on reindeer moss, they converse with Earth, Mou-Niamy, so that she won't get bored.

---

* Pronounced "choom." A reindeer-hide tent.

DAUGHTER OF THE MOON AND SON OF THE SUN

(Saami)

*A*ll day long the Sun rides across the azure sky in his single-runner sledge and surveys his lands. In the morning the Bear pulls his sledge, in the afternoon the Reindeer Stag pulls it, and in the evening gloaming the Reindeer Doe pulls the Sun's sledge. The Sun has a great deal of business to attend to. He must give life to everything growing. He must help the trees, reindeer moss, and grass to grow. And he must give light and warmth to animals, people, and birds so that they can grow and multiply, thereby increasing the Sun's wealth. By evening the Sun tires and sinks wearily into the sea. By then he wants only to rest, to sleep.

One day, as the Sun was resting, his son Peival'ke—Sun Ray—began bothering him. "Father, it's time for me to marry!" said Peival'ke.

"Well, that's right. It is high time. Do you have a bride in mind?"

"No. I tried my golden boots on all the maidens on earth, but my boots didn't fit even one of them. Their feet are heavy. They won't be able to get off the ground, and I must fly through the sky."

"You aren't looking for a bride in the right place, Peival'ke," said the Sun. "I'll ask the Moon on your behalf. It is rumored that she has given birth to a daughter. Of course, the Moon is poorer than we are, but like us she rides across the sky so that her daughter would make a suitable bride."

The Sun waited until the Moon was still in the morning sky just as the Sun was rising. The Sun rolled closer to the Moon and said, "Tell me, neighbor, is it true that you have a beautiful daughter? I have a bridegroom for her, my son Peival'ke—Sun Ray."

"The Moon began hiding in mist. "My child is still too young. I can't even feel her weight in my arms as I hold her. Her light is still dim. She barely shines. How can you even speak of marriage?"

"It doesn't matter," replied the Sun. "My home is a wealthy one. We'll feed her well. We'll fatten her up. Just let Peival'ke look at her."

"Oh, no," cried the terrified Moon, and she covered her child with a cloud. "He will burn her, your Peival'ke. To tell you the truth, she is already promised to Nainas, the Northern Lights. There he is, walking over the sea."

"So, that's how it is then!" the Sun exclaimed angrily. "You refuse us for some ragged patches of color. You seem to have forgotten, neighbor, that I give life to everyone. I have both wealth and strength."

"Your strength is only half the strength possible," said the Moon. "Where are you when dusk comes? And where are you at night? Where is your strength all through the long winter? But Nainas—Northern Lights—shines in winter and gives light at night."

These words infuriated the Sun still more. He hurled fiery arrows and seethed with anger. "I'll marry my son to your daughter all the same," he shouted.

Thunder began roaring; the winds howled; the sea waters rose; and the mountains rumbled. Everything on earth shook and trembled. The reindeer herds huddled together, and the Saami people hid in their *vezha*s, their tents covered with twigs and moss.

The Moon hurried away into the night darkness. "Apparently, I'm going to have to hide my child safely from the Sun's eyes," she thought.

The Moon looked down and saw a lake with an island floating in it, where an old man and his wife, kind people, lived. "I can entrust my daughter to them," she said.

The Sun grew tired of raging. The thunder grew quiet, and the winds died down. The old couple went to the forest to strip birch bark from the birch trees. It was there that they saw a silver cradle hanging from the branch of a fir tree.

They heard a tiny, child's voice saying, "Niekiia—I'm not here!"

When they looked into the silver cradle, they saw a child like any other, except that she gleamed with moonlight.

The old couple carried the cradle home, rejoicing that now they had a daughter. They began raising the girl. She obeyed the old man as if he were her father, and she obeyed the old woman as if she were her mother. Yet at night she would go out of the *vezha* and lift her face to the Moon. She would stretch her arms toward the Moon and glow more brightly.

She learned to sew blankets and tent flaps of reindeer skins, and she decorated them with beads and silver.

When she wanted to play, she would call, "Niekiia—I'm not here!" and disappear. Only her laugh echoed nearby.

The old couple named her Niekiia, which means "I'm not here," because she repeated the word so often. Thus, Niekiia grew into a young woman. Her face was round and rosy, like cloudberries. Her hair was like silver threads. She stood slender and glowing all over.

Finally, a rumor reached the Sun that a maiden unlike all other earthly maidens was living on the island. The Sun sent his son, Peival'ke, to her. Peival'ke flew to the island and glanced into the old couple's *vezha*. When he caught sight of Niekiia, she immediately became dear to him.

"Try on my golden boots, my beauty," he ordered.

Niekiia blushed and began putting on the boots. Suddenly, she cried out in pain. "Oh, they burn! They hurt me!"

"Never mind," Peival'ke reassured her. "You'll get used to them."

He wanted to embrace Niekiia and carry her away with him, but when he tired, Niekiia cried, "Niekiia—I'm not here, I'm not here, not at all!" And, like a shadow, she melted away and disappeared.

The golden boots stood empty on the threshold.

Niekiia hid until night in the forest thickets. When the Moon rose in the sky, Niekiia followed her Mother's beam through the forest, across mountains, and across the tundra. Mother Moon led Niekiia to the sea and to a lonely house standing on a deserted shore.

Niekiia entered the house. No one was there. It was dirty and untidy. Immediately, Niekiia brought in a bucket of water and washed and cleaned everything.

After she had finished, she was tired and wanted to sleep. She turned herself into an old spindle, a wooden rod used in spinning thread. She stuck herself into the wall and fell asleep.

As twilight fell, Niekiia heard heavy footsteps. Warriors in silver armor, each stronger and more handsome than the last, entered the home. They were the Northern Light brothers, led by their oldest brother, Nainas.

"Our house is clean," cried Nainas. "A good housekeeper must have come to us. I don't know where she is hiding, but I sense her presence. I feel the gaze of her eyes."

The brothers sat down to supper. After they had finished, they started playing and staged a mock battle. In hand-to-hand combat, they slashed at one another with sabers, making white sparks and crimson stripes that danced in the sky. The brothers sang a song about the warriors of the sky, and one by one they flew away. Only Nainas remained home, like a pale shadow.

"Now please show yourself, whoever you are," he said. "If you are an old woman, you will be my mother. If you are my age, you will be my sister. If you are a young woman, you will be my bride."

"Here I am," Niekiia murmured. In the glow of early dawn, she stood before Nainas.

"Will you marry me, Niekiia?" he asked.

"Yes, I will, Nainas," Niekiia answered, barely audibly.

At that moment dawn blazed, and the edge of the Sun appeared.

"Wait for me, Niekiia," Nainas cried and in a flash he was gone, as if he had never been there.

Every evening Nainas and his brothers flew to their home, and every evening they played at their mock battle. At dawn they flew away again.

"Stay here, Nainas," Niekiia begged. "Please stay with me for just one day."

"I can't," Nainas answered. "The battle of the skies awaits me across the sea."

Niekiia began thinking of ways to detain Nainas. She made a curtain of reindeer skin and embroidered the silvery Milky Way and big stars on it. Then, she hung it from the ceiling.

Toward nighttime Nainas flew home with his troops. They played in the sky until they were weary and lay down to rest. Nainas slept soundly, but every now and then he opened his eyes. He saw a dark sky and the Milky Way above him, so he thought it was still night and too early to get up.

Niekiia awakened and went outside. She left the tent flap slightly open. Nainas opened his eyes and saw bright morning. Bear was pulling the Sun's sledge across the azure sky.

Nainas ran out of the house and called his brothers. But the Sun had already seen him and had sent down a shaft of fire that pinned Nainas to the ground.

Niekiia ran to her bridegroom and shielded him with her body. Nainas rose and became a pale shadow that melted into the sky. The Sun grabbed Niekiia by the braid. He burned her with his fiery gaze and called his son, Peival'ke.

"Kill me, if you like, but I will never marry Peival'ke!" wept Niekiia.

Furious, the Sun flung Niekiia into the arms of Mother Moon. Mother Moon caught her daughter and pressed her to her heart. She still holds her daughter to this very day. If you look carefully, you will see Niekiia's little face on the face of the Moon. Niekiia is watching, watching the pale stripe of color over the sea, watching the battles of the Northern Lights in the sky. She cannot tear her eyes away from her Nainas.

THE STAR MAN

(Greenland Inuit)

*A*n old man went out on the sea ice to hunt seal. He waited beside the breathing holes for the seal to appear.

Meanwhile, a crowd of children had gathered on the shore, quite near the old man. The children were playing in a ravine, running about and making a great deal of noise. Every time a seal came to the hole to breathe and the old man got ready to harpoon it, the noise frightened the seal away.

Finally, the old man could stand it no longer. He became angry with the children for spoiling his catch. "Close up over the children who are spoiling my hunting, Ravine," he cried.

Suddenly, both sides of the ravine closed over the children at play, entrapping them in a hill. A girl, who was carrying her little brother, had her fur parka torn. All of the screaming children were enclosed in the hill and could not climb out. The ravine had disappeared.

No one could get food to the children because only a tiny crack remained, through which the distraught parents peered at their dear ones and spoke to them. The grown-ups did manage to pour water down the crack, and the children licked it off the sides of the ravine as it trickled down. At last all of them died of hunger.

Now the people turned to the old man who had used magic to cause the ravine to close like a clam over the children and to shut them up in the hill. When the old man saw the people running toward him, he took fright.

Suddenly, he was lifted from the ground and became very bright. He rose higher and higher up into heaven. There, he became a great star.

Now we can see the star in the west toward dawn. The star stays low in the sky and never climbs very high. We call the star Venus, or Nâlaussartoq, which means "he who stands and listens." Perhaps it is so named in memory of the old man who stood on the ice listening for the breathing of the seal.

PART 3

TRICKSTERS AND FOOLS

KUIKYNNIAKU, THE RAVEN

(Koryak)

*W*ise old Kuikynniaku, the Raven, lived on the seashore. He was the ancestor from whom all ravens on earth originated. He was very learned and knew how to do many things. Objects obeyed his words. He was a shapeshifter and could turn into whomever he wanted to be. Besides having a reputation for being wise, he enjoyed a good joke. He understood that more might be learned from joking than from scolding and beating.

Now, listen to my story about Kuikynniaku, the Raven. One day Raven decided to amuse himself. He went to the seashore and gathered many old, empty seashells. He found a humpbacked salmon that had been flung onto the shore by a wave. He cut off the salmon's hump. Next, he gathered a bundle of sea cabbage.

Then, Raven left the seashore and went out upon the Arctic plain, which is called the tundra, with his collection. He set about building a reindeer skin tent, called a *yaranga*.

After Raven had constructed the *yaranga*, he began beating a shaman's drum. He blew on the hump of the humpbacked salmon and created an old man. It was a well-made old man, except that he was slightly humpbacked, like the salmon. "You will be called Papa Hump," Kuikynniaku, the Raven, told him.

Raven began beating the shaman's drum again and began chanting over the sea cabbage. He blew on it until it became an old woman. "And you will be called Mama Cabbage," Kuikynniaku said.

Raven began turning the empty seashells into reindeer until there were as many reindeer as there had been shells. The reindeer lay there, chewing and swinging their horns. However, they could not walk from one spot to another because they had no legs. "Now my camp is ready," declared Kuikynniaku, the Raven.

Raven spun on one leg, hit the shaman's drum, and blew on himself. Kuikynniaku, the Raven, became a young woman. She had ruddy cheeks, fat legs, and was in good health. She started a fire in front of the tent and sat down. She started kneading hides to soften them and make them into leather.

Meanwhile, Kuikynniaku's son, Èmemkut, went out into the tundra. Perhaps he had a reason for doing so, or perhaps he just felt like roaming around—we do not know. Perhaps Èmemkut himself did not know why he was wandering in the tundra.

He had not gone far when he came to his father's camp and was surprised. "Look at that," he said aloud. "A little camp has appeared in our tundra. Where could it come from? The people living in this camp probably crossed the mountain range from that direction over there. I'll go ask."

Disguised as a girl, Kuikynniaku, the Raven, saw his son and cried joyfully, "Hello, guest. Have you come to visit?"

"Yes, I've come to visit," Èmemkut answered. Meanwhile, Èmemkut kept looking at the girl.

Kuikynniaku shouted into the tent, "Hey, Papa Hump, come meet our guest. Hey, Mama Cabbage, entertain our guest."

"Well, come into our tent, dear guest," said Papa Hump.

Èmemkut went into the tent and turned his head around, looking the girl over. The old woman brought him refreshments. Èmemkut ate while looking around.

In a corner between two bed curtains, he noticed a shaman's drum. He jumped up and grabbed it. He turned the drum in his hands and wanted to strike it, but the girl cried, "Hey, guest, put the drum back where it belongs."

Èmemkut was glad that the girl had spoken, for now he could speak to her without offending her. He went over to the fire, where she was standing. "You have a nice drum," he said.

"Why wouldn't it be nice? I gave three deerskins for it."

"Did you get it far from here?" Èmemkut asked. He was eager to find out what tribe the woman was from.

"Yes, far away," the girl answered. "I got the drum beyond seven mountain ranges and beyond seven lakes." She began laughing to herself. The disguised Kuikynniaku thought it was funny that he had deceived his son.

The more the woman laughed, the more Èmemkut liked it. He began laughing with her. Then he remembered that it was impolite to visit for a long time. After all, it was the first time he had come. He said good-bye and set out for home.

While the girl, who was sitting by the campfire, could still see him, Èmemkut walked slowly. Once he was out of sight, he began running.

He ran home to his mother, Miti, and started telling her what had happened. "Some people crossed seven mountain ranges and seven lakes to set up camp nearby. They have a big herd of reindeer. They have already put up a tent. When I saw them, their daughter was sitting by the campfire kneading animal skins. She is pretty and merry and laughs all the time."

"Your father set out in that direction before you did. If you are speaking the truth, he should have come running with the news long ago. Something isn't right here."

"No, Mama, it's the truth! If you don't believe it, I'll tell you again. The girl has ruddy cheeks and fat legs. The deer must have gotten tired from the long journey. They are lying there without moving from the spot."

"The deer are just lying there? Just as I told you, something is not right."

"It's so, Mama, it's so! A beautiful shaman's drum is hanging in their tent. But the girl wouldn't let me beat it."

"She wouldn't let you beat it? Oh, I know these tricks. I'm going over there to see for myself."

"Go, Mama, go. Ask the girl's hand in marriage for me. I liked her very much."

"Quiet, simpleton!" Èmemkut's mother screamed.

Although Miti, Kuikynniaku's wife and Èmemkut's mother, was already an old woman, she rushed out into the tundra more agilely than a young woman.

Still disguised as a girl, Kuikynniaku, the Raven, saw her and said, "Greetings, dear guest. Have you come to visit?"

"Yes, I've come to visit," Miti answered while still running.

Again, Kuikynniaku called to the old man. "Come out, Papa Hump. Come, meet our guest."

Papa Hump came out, but Miti did not look at him. She went into the tent. There, Mama Cabbage brought her refreshments. Miti did not take the refreshments, but went straight to the shaman's drum. She tore it from the wall. The bells on the drum began jingling.

The girl by the campfire immediately cried out, "Don't touch the drum, guest. Put it back, or misfortune will come."

"I'll show you misfortune," said Miti.

She began beating the tambourine. She kept beating it until she grew tired. Then she put the drum down and looked around. Only the tundra surrounded her. It was as if the newcomers' camp had never been there. There were no tent, no reindeer, no Papa Hump, no Mama Cabbage. Only the hump from the humpbacked salmon was lying on the ground beside a bunch of dry seaweed and a pile of seashells. And it was not a red-cheeked girl sitting beside the campfire, but old Kuikynniaku, the Raven.

Miti rushed at her husband, scolding all the while. "Oh, you good-for-nothing! You would do better to go hunting than to amuse yourself with stupid ideas."

"What's it to you? Your business is in the home. Hunting is a man's occupation. Don't get involved."

"And why are you upsetting your son, old man? Just look at him. He's not himself."

Kuikynniaku, the Raven, began laughing. "So our simpleton believed everything."

"And you think that's funny?" Miti flew into a rage. She seized hold of her husband's hair. Kuikynniaku defended himself, laughing all the while. Finally, Miti grew tired.

"Why are you fighting with me?" her husband asked. "What will it accomplish? It was just a funny joke. You didn't believe it. You figured it out. It's time for our son to learn to figure things out, too. He's not little anymore. He shouldn't believe everything he sees. He must learn to think deeper and look closer."

Miti stopped being angry. "And what will we tell our son?" she asked.

"Tell him that the new neighbors went back across the seven mountain ranges and seven lakes."

Miti began laughing. They walked back to camp together.

RAVEN KILLS WHALE

(Dene and Alaskan Inupiat)

*R*aven was a glutton.[1] He was always hungry. One summer in Myth Time, Raven decided to go hunting.

"I'm going hunting for ducks," he announced. "Who wants to go with me?"

"I'll go with you," said Canada Jay, whom people called Camp Robber.

"You wouldn't make it, Camp Robber. You're too thin," Raven said. "I'd rather take Whale with me. He's solid enough."

In fact, Whale was overweight to such a degree that he could be considered obese. Whale agreed to accompany Raven on his hunting venture. Raven hopped into his canoe, and Whale lumbered into his own canoe. They set out paddling up the river.

After some time had passed, they beached their canoes. "There's a lake up ahead where there are plenty of young ducks that are molting now. They will be easy to catch because they won't be able to fly well without their feathers," Raven said. "You stay here and build a fire while I go to check on the duck situation there."

Raven went to the lake and walked around until he found a place with quicksand. He pulled a bunch of feathers out of his wings and painted them to look like duck feathers. Then he took the feathers to Whale.

"See all the feathers I found on the shore there. There are loads of ducks at that lake," he told Whale.

Raven and Whale cooked a meal over the fire that Whale had made. They ate the meal and pressed on. By the time they reached the lake, Whale was exhausted. Nevertheless, Raven insisted that they begin hunting right away.

"What? We won't be able to get any ducks in the dark. Let's wait until morning," Whale suggested.

"Why, night is absolutely the best time to hunt ducks. I'll show you how," Raven said.

Carrying his canoe over his head, Raven began walking toward the spot where he knew there was quicksand. "Follow me, Whale," he ordered.

Since Raven was light, he was able to prance over the quicksand without a problem.

Whale hesitated and then followed Raven. When Whale came to the quicksand, he began sinking because of his bulk. "Help," he called. "I'm sinking!"

"Of course, I'll help you," Raven replied. "Just let me set my canoe down in a safe spot first." Raven set his canoe on shore ever so slowly.

"Help, help!" Whale shrieked in desperation.

By the time Raven got back to Whale, the quicksand was up to Whale's waist. Instead of helping his friend, Raven began nipping at him.

"You've got too much fat. It's making you sink. I'm just snipping pieces off here and there to make you lighter," Raven said by way of explanation.

Finally, Raven ripped open Whale's belly and tore out his intestines. Raven dragged the intestines under some trees, where they became strong tree roots. In fact, the roots were so strong that from then on, the Koyukon people of Alaska used them as sinew with which to sew.

Gluttonous Raven returned to his friend and kept nipping at him until he had eaten up Whale completely. Only Whale's voice was left. Whale told Raven that he was mean-spirited. "I'm leaving this land, and I'm going to the ocean, where I'll never see you again," said Whale. From then on, Whale lived only in the ocean.

Raven prepared to leave and go home. He wondered what he was going to tell the people, who would surely miss Whale. Once again, Raven plucked some feathers from his body and painted them to look like duck feathers. Then, he hopped in his canoe and headed down the river. He sang a song for his dead friend, Whale. It was a mix between a funeral dirge and a love song.

When he reached camp, Raven acted very innocent. "Has my friend come home?" he asked, knowing full well the answer.

The people suspected that Raven had killed Whale because anyone who went hunting with Raven rarely returned. But what could they do about it? Camp Robber, in particular, was suspicious.

By way of explanation, Raven said, "Whale didn't want to hunt ducks at night, so I told him to sleep while I went hunting. I killed lots of ducks and brought them to Whale. I put them under his canoe as he slept. Then, I went to sleep. In the morning, my friend was gone and nothing was left of the ducks, except these feathers."

Camp Robber refused to believe Raven. "You killed Whale. I know you did," Camp Robber shrieked.

"If you don't believe me, I'm going to leave earth and stay up in the air, far away from you from now on," declared Raven.

The people noticed that Raven had hardly any feathers on his wings. "What happened to your feathers? How will you stay in the air without feathers on your wings?" they asked.

Raven explained that he had burned off his feathers while cooking a meal for Whale and himself.

There was a shaman in camp, and now the people consulted him. He gave the following advice. "Burn the feathers that Raven brought home. If they burn, they are duck feathers. If they don't burn, they belong to Raven and Raven has killed Whale."

None of the feathers burned. They just turned black. Now everyone knew for sure whether Raven had killed and eaten Whale. Everyone loved easygoing Whale, so they decided to avenge the death of their dear friend by killing Raven.

Raven decided that he had better get out of there fast. He snatched some of Camp Robber's feathers and put them on his own wings so that he would be able to fly. To this day Camp Robber does not have many feathers on his wings. Have you noticed?

Raven flew to the top of a tree just as the people started shooting arrows at him. He was too high for the arrows to reach him.

From his safe position, Raven made his confession. "You're right. I killed Whale," Raven mocked them, "and I ate him all up."

From that day on Raven has been living in the air and not on the ground.

THE LYNX WHO ATE HIMSELF

(Innu)

*T*here was a lynx who had a habit of marrying and eating Innu women. If he brought nothing home from the hunt, he would attack and eat his wife. One after another, his wives mysteriously disappeared.

Finally, rumor of Lynx's behavior reached the people, and no one would marry him, not even the ugliest, dirtiest woman. However, there was one very daring Innu woman who decided to teach Lynx a lesson.

"I'll marry Lynx," she declared, "and if he tries anything, I'll kill him before he kills me."

"It's worth a try, bold woman," said the people. Secretly, they thought that she was reckless to battle Lynx, who could be quite vicious.

The woman married Lynx, and everything went well until her husband became hungry. One day when he came home from the hunt empty-handed, Lynx said, "Go fetch some dry firewood and build a roaring fire."

His wife guessed right away what he was up to. She figured that he was going to throw her into the fire, roast her, and eat her up. She gathered the wood that Lynx had requested. Then she hid behind a tree and waited for her husband to return.

Lynx thought his wife was in the tent, so he rushed at it with his spear. He did nothing but ruin the tent because his wife was not there. He looked for her everywhere inside the tent. He called for her, but no one answered.

Finally, Lynx was so hungry and so desperate that he decided to eat himself. "Maybe I won't taste too bad," he thought.

He cut a chunk of meat off his leg, roasted it, and ate it. "Not bad," he declared. "Not bad at all."

Once his entire leg was gone, he tackled the other leg. Then, he cut bits off his entire body. All the while, he sang a little song. "I taste better than my wives," he crooned.

Finally, Lynx had eaten his entire body, except for his heart. "Now what?" he asked. "I'm still hungry. What will I do?"

Suddenly, he brightened. "I know what I'll do. If I roast my heart and eat it up quickly, at least I'll have a good meal before I die."

Lynx's wife watched from behind the tree as her husband grabbed his heart and threw it into the fire. Lynx fell down dead the moment his roasted heart touched his lips.

Lynx's wife laughed at his foolishness. "I didn't have to kill Lynx," she told the people. "He killed himself. I didn't have to do anything."

THE TEALS AND THE FOX

(Siberian Yupik)

*O*ne day a sly fox was walking along the seashore thinking, "There is no animal more clever than I am. No, siree, there is no animal more clever than I am."

A flock of wild ducks, called teals, was swimming on the sea. They caught sight of Fox and decided to play a trick on him.

The oldest teal said, "Let's make a boat with our wings, brothers. Let's get into two rows, side by side, so that our wings open inwards to form a boat. Then Fox will think that we are a boat sailing by."

They did just that. They got into two rows and spread out their wings. The middle wings formed a boat, and the outer wings looked like oars.

The teals swam on the ocean. The oldest teal called loudly, "One-two, one-two! Row harder!"

Fox's eyes were weak because of old age. He looked at the sea and saw a boat sailing by. He saw rowers sitting in the boat waving the oars in a friendly manner.

Fox stopped and called to them. "Hey, you, rowers, come moor your boat here on shore so that I can get in and take a little ride. Can't you see who is walking on the seashore? It's me, the Master of this place. Can't you see that I'm tired?"

The teals swam over to the shore. Fox plopped himself down right in the center of the boat. He sat with his chest proudly expanded. He spread out his tail and squinted with satisfaction. The boat sailed swiftly away from shore.

Suddenly, Fox heard the oldest teal say, "Well, brothers, we've had enough sailing. Now let's fly."

Fox had not managed to come to his senses before finding himself cast off into the water. The teals had already flown far away.

Fox swam to shore, thinking, "The teals played a trick on me and made a laughing stock of me to the entire world."

It was difficult for Fox to swim. His waterlogged tail was heavy and kept dragging him down to the bottom of the sea. "Tail of mine, my pride and glory, don't let me down. Help me swim to shore," said Fox.

Fox's tail stood out and began steering toward shore. Fox barely reached shore alive. He crawled onto a little hill and dried out in the sunshine. Meanwhile, the teals flew across the tundra and told everyone they met the story about Fox swimming in the sea.

Fox looked around. Animals, large and small, had gathered around him. They were staring at him and laughing. "Won't you tell us, oh respected Fox, how the teals bathed you in the freezing cold sea?"

Fox shook and pulled himself together. Then he grabbed his wet tail in his teeth so that it would be easier to run. Fox dashed off into the tundra in great shame. From that day on, Fox stopped walking along the seashore.

WOLVERINE AND THE BRANT

(Innu)

The most popular myth cycle among the Innu of Quebec and Labrador concerns Wolverine, or Kuekuatsheu. The myths describe several episodes of Kuekuatsheu's life. Wolverine is a sly trickster who is at once creator, destroyer, avenger, and a vain and foolish figure of fun. At times Wolverine acts like an irresponsible child; yet, he is nobody's fool.

One of Wolverine's misadventures happened when he decided to fly like a brant, a wild goose.[1]

One day Wolverine called the birds to an assembly, where he spoke to them like this. "Did you know that I am your brother? I will dress you in feathers, brothers, so that you can fly."

After Wolverine dressed the birds, he decided to make wings for himself. He put feathers along his arms to make wings and stuck some feathers in his back to make a tail. Then he flew up into the sky. "Whee-e-e!" exclaimed Wolverine. "See what I've been missing. Now I can fly anywhere I want."

A brant flew up to Wolverine and said, "We are going to fly far away. Would you like to come with us?"

"Oh, yes, indeed," said Wolverine. "I'll go with you."

"But you must be careful," warned the brant. "There are people where we are going. If they see us, they will call to us and make loud noises to cause us to get confused and fall down. Close your eyes when we fly past the people so that they can't bother you. If you open your eyes, you will fall from the sky."[2]

"Fine, brother, fine," Wolverine answered carelessly.

Wolverine was so delighted with his flight that he began to sing a song, at first softly, but later loudly. He sang, "My brothers and I are coming. Whee-e-e, we're flying!"

The people heard Wolverine's song. "Is that Wolverine?" they wondered. "He's always fooling around." Then the people shouted, clapped their hands, and made a great noise.

At first Wolverine kept his eyes closed while passing over the point of land where the people were shouting. The first turn he took went well, but during the second turn the brants made, Wolverine opened his eyes and looked below. "Shut up, silly people," he cried.

Down, down, down Wolverine fell, like a bunch of old rags. The people ran up to Wolverine, who lay on the ground.

"A brant has fallen," an old woman cried. "He will make a tasty dish for dinner." She grabbed Wolverine and began plucking off his feathers. Then, she disemboweled him.

A terrible odor came from Wolverine's bowels. "Ai, this brant isn't fit to eat," the old woman exclaimed. "Take the carcass, children, and throw it away. This brant is already rotten!"

"How could the brant be rotten?" asked another old woman. "It was just killed."

"Go see for yourself," the first old woman challenged her.

The second old woman went up to the carcass to take a sniff, but all that she found was Wolverine's dead body.

TWELVE CLEVER BROTHERS

(Vep)

*O*n the edge of a little village stood twelve little homes, six homes side by side on each side of the street. Twelve brothers lived in these cottages. Each brother had a wife and children, but the story is not about the wives, so we will not mention them again.

And so, there once lived twelve brothers. One winter they prepared to go to Sortaval[*] to make some purchases. One of them needed salt, another needed some calico cloth so that his wife could make a new dress, another needed some soap, yet another needed boots, and so on. Each brother harnessed his horse, took his seat in the sledge, and set out.

The brothers had to travel a great distance. Night fell before they reached their destination. They turned into a wayside inn beside the road to spend the night.

As they began unharnessing their horses, one brother said, "Don't forget to turn the shafts in the direction we have to travel."

"A good idea," said another brother.

"Right," said a third brother. "Then we won't have to guess which direction to take tomorrow."

"We'll just drive the horses on until we reach Sortaval," a fourth brother added.

The owner of the wayside inn overheard their conversation. Amazed at how simple-minded the brothers seemed to be, he burst out laughing. But he said nothing to them.

After the brothers put the horses in the stable, all twelve of them turned the shafts of their sledges in the direction of Sortaval. Then they went into the inn and went to bed.

The brothers had barely fallen asleep when the innkeeper came out, took the shafts, and turned them in the opposite direction. "I'm not doing this out of spite," he said to himself. "I'm just curious to find out if those brothers really know which way to go according to the direction the sledge shafts are facing."

The brothers slept soundly all night long. In the morning, they began harnessing the horses. As they were harnessing them, they praised one another. "If we hadn't turned the shafts in the right direction yesterday, we wouldn't know now which direction to take," said one brother.

---

[*] Sortaval is a town located in Sortaval Gorsovet of the Republic of Karelia. Its original name was Khelyulya.

"When you are traveling down an unknown road, the main thing is not to get lost," said the next brother.

"One head is all right, but with twelve heads we'll never get lost," said the twelfth brother.

The brothers traveled on. The innkeeper watched them set out, shrugged his shoulders, but said nothing. The brothers drove their horses on, rushing to reach Sortaval.

Suddenly, the brother in the lead said, "Look, brothers. This place seems familiar. It's exactly like the one we rode past yesterday. The birch tree is growing beside a boulder, and there is a ditch beside it, just like yesterday."

"The spot really is similar," said the second brother.

"There are lots of places in this world that look alike," said the third brother.

"What's amazing about it?" asked the fourth. "In our country every tree is a birch, every boulder is a stone, and you come upon ditches everywhere!"

The twelfth brother said, "You'd do better not to be gaping all around."

An hour passed in silence, then a second and a third hour. No one said a word. The brothers just urged on their horses.

Suddenly, the fifth brother said, "It seems to me that we passed through this village yesterday."

The brothers turned their heads and looked.

"It's not the same village," said the sixth brother.

"It's not," declared the seventh brother.

"The other village was on the left," said the sixth brother.

"Yes, it was on the left," agreed the seventh brother, "and this village is on the right."

"Indeed, it's on the right," said the sixth brother.

"Why discuss it?" asked the twelfth brother. "Get a move on, or else we'll have to spend another night on the road."

Once again they rode on, and once again they were silent. Another village loomed up ahead of them.

The eighth brother said, "If I didn't know for sure that we were going to Sortaval, I would think that the village up ahead was our village."

"That little knoll is the same," said the ninth brother.

"And there are six cottages in a row on either side of the street, just as it is in our village," said the tenth brother.

"Well, I said that there are lots of places in this world that look alike," the third brother reminded them.

"You did say that," agreed the eleventh brother. "But a place like ours, a village like ours, cottages like ours, you won't find anywhere on earth."

The twelfth brother raised his voice. "Stop wagging your tongues!" he said. "Whether it's our village or not our village, we must ride on."

No sooner had the words escaped his lips than a brown dog ran up to the sledge wagging its tail.

"I don't know whose village it is," said the twelfth brother, "but the dog is mine."

"Well, if the dog is yours, then it's our village," said the first brother. And he turned into his yard.

Thus, the twelve brothers never got to Sortaval.

"Rather than ride around senselessly, it's better to stay home," said the twelfth brother. And every one of his eleven brothers agreed with him.

A TALE ABOUT A SILLY OLD MAN

(Even)

*T*here once lived a little boy who had no mother or father. He lived with his two sisters.

One day the boy was swinging and singing, "Who will push my swing? If only I had a father, he would push my swing. If only I had a mother, she would give my swing a push."

An old man was walking past. He heard the boy's song and said, "I'll give your swing a push, son."

After the old man had pushed the swing for a while, the boy said, "Now I'd like to invite you to our lodge. My sisters are cooking some tasty meat today."

The old man sat down in the lodge and ate the meat the boy's sisters had prepared until he had his fill. Then, he fell asleep.

The boy's sisters decided to play a trick on the old man. They glued deer fur onto the old man's eyelashes as he lay sleeping. They painted the fur red.

The old man awoke without suspecting anything and plodded home. That evening as he and his old wife were drinking tea, the old man looked at the smoke hole and said, "Wife, take a look. I think our lodge has caught fire."

The old woman ran outside in a panic and began throwing snow at the lodge. Eventually, she understood that there was no fire at all.

She returned to the lodge and asked, "Old man, why are you lying to me? Nothing is burning."

"No, it's burning, I tell you. Take a good look up there."

"What's wrong with you, old man? Look at me!"

The old man looked at his wife. She noticed the red fur glued to his eyelashes. "Why have you glued fur to your eyelashes?" she asked.

"I don't know anything about it. I haven't glued on anything," the old man replied.

"Then, who else glued the fur on?" the old woman continued to question him. "Where were you today?"

"Today I went for a walk. Then, I ate some tasty meat and rested at the lodge of some young women. They must have done it. I'm going to visit them again and scold them for gluing reindeer fur onto my eyelashes."

The old man plodded back to the young women. As he approached their lodge, he saw that just like yesterday the little boy was swinging on a swing near the lodge and was singing.

"Let me give you a push," said the old man.

"No, you'd better go see my sisters. They'll give you something to eat," the boy replied.

The old man went into the lodge. Once again the young women gave the old man a tasty meal. After the old man had eaten, he fell asleep. Using a piece of coal and red dye, the young women took the opportunity to cover the sleeping old man's face with tattoos.

The old man awoke and without suspecting anything set out for home. On the way home, the old man decided to drink some water from a river. He approached the river and bent over to get a drink.

To his surprise, he saw a stranger's face in the water. The stranger was looking at him. The old man thought that a woman was in the water, a very beautiful woman with an artistically decorated face.

"Why are you living in the water, woman?" asked the old man.

There was no reply. "What a haughty woman," the old man thought. "She doesn't even want to talk to me."

Then, the old man addressed the woman. "Haughty woman, come on out of the water!"

Again there was silence. "Apparently, she doesn't want to come to me because I already have a wife," thought the old man. He was very taken and enamored of the woman in the river.

"Woman, I'll kill my wife and come to you," the old man promised. "I'll bring all of our possessions with me."

The old man went home. He killed his poor, old wife. Then, he gathered all their things and dragged them to the river.

Once again he bent over the water, and again he saw a beautiful woman. "Haughty woman, I killed my old wife and brought you all our things," said the old man. "What will you do with my possessions? Do you need them?"

It seemed to the old man that the woman in the water was nodding her head "yes."

"I'll throw the things into the water, and you grab them," the old man said,

The old man threw a blanket into the water. It did not sink, but rather it sailed down the river with the current.

"The woman must be wealthy," the old man thought. "She has no need of my blanket."

Part 3: Tricksters and Fools

Then, the old man threw the scraper for dressing reindeer hides into the water. The scraper immediately sank to the bottom of the river.

"My, but she is a wealthy woman. She didn't even take my scraper! How will she dress the reindeer hides without a scraper?"

The old man threw the rest of his property into the river. Then, he said "Dear woman, now I will come to you!"

The silly, lovesick old man jumped into the water headfirst to join his beloved and, of course, he drowned.

SOMEONE ELSE'S URASA

(Yukaghir)

The Yukaghirs are divided into Forest Yukaghir, who live in the Sakha Republic (Yakutia), and Tundra Yukaghir, who live in the Magadan area. The name Yukaghir is said to mean "icy people" or "frozen people." The Yukaghirs' traditional dwelling is called an urasa. *An* urasa *is a collapsible dwelling. It is covered with animal skins, and sometimes with birch bark, that have been sewn together.*

*O*ne evening three brothers were sitting in their *urasa*. The oldest was named Loshiia, the middle brother's name was Lopchuo, and the youngest was named Akchin-Hondo. Bored, they sat with nothing to do.

"Let's sing songs and exercise our voices," the oldest brother, Loshiia, proposed. "I'll begin first." He began singing, "Loshiia-ia! Shiia! Loshiia!" And he sang on in that vein.

"I have a good voice," he said, praising himself. "Now you sing," he instructed his middle brother.

The middle brother began singing, "Lopchuo-o! Chuo! Lopchuo!" And he sang on like that.

"I sing well, too," Lopchuo said. "Now let's see how well our youngest brother sings."

The youngest boy sang, "Akchin-Hondo! Hondo-Hondo! Akchin!"

When the youngest boy had finished singing, his brothers said, "Something just isn't right when he sings. Let's try singing together."

They began singing. Each brother sang his own song so that the song did not harmonize. The oldest brother became angry and blamed the youngest brother. The youngest brother became angry and blamed the middle brother. And the middle brother became angry and blamed the oldest brother.

"Why are you singing your own names? Sing mine. Then the song will harmonize," said the middle brother.

"The song won't work well with your name. We must sing mine," screamed the oldest.

"And I don't even want to know your names!" the youngest brother said, continuing the quarrel. "I know only my own name." And he struck up his song. "Akchin-Akchin-Akchin-Hondo! Hondo-Hondo-do-do-Akchin!"

The middle brother and the oldest brother rushed at him. They began hitting him, but he would not relent. They overturned the kettle on the fire. Its contents poured out over the hearth, extinguishing the fire. While they were rolling about on the floor, they broke all of their arrows.

"It's not good to fight in the *urasa*. Let's go outside," said the oldest young man.

Obediently, the brothers went outside. But they began fighting on the grass immediately. The oldest young man knocked his youngest brother onto the ground.

The youngest young man lay face up on his back. He noticed the starry sky above and cried out, "Stop, brothers, trouble's coming!"

"What trouble? Where's trouble?" the middle and oldest young men asked.

The youngest brother jumped up and pointed to the stars in the sky. "Look, strangers have cut down a dry willow tree and are using its branches as torches. An army is using the torches to light up the road. They are moving in on us!"

The brothers took fright. "We must run away. There are many of them and few of us!"

They ran to the river and jumped into their canoe. They grabbed the oars and began rowing the same way they had sung songs in the *urasa*. One rowed backward. Another rowed forward. Yet another lowered and raised the oars, going neither backward, nor forward.

The canoe circled around on the same spot. Water splashed against the sides so that it seemed to the brothers that the canoe was traveling fast.

The oldest brother glanced up and said, "They're catching up!"

They rowed on. Then, the middle brother glanced up and cried out, "It seems that we're beginning to outdistance them."

They kept swinging the oars. The youngest brother craned his neck and declared, "We've lost them."

It was dawning. The stars, which the brothers understood to be the burning willow branches in the hands of a hostile army, were growing dim in the gray sky, so their enemies were no longer visible.

"I know why we were able to outdistance them," said the oldest young man. "While we were rowing, they were robbing our *urasa*."

"Of course, they robbed us!" said the middle brother.

"They've carried away the kettle and have taken the animal skins off our *urasa*. What should we do?" the youngest brother asked.

Suddenly, the brothers saw an *urasa* on the bank of the river. It was a splendid, big *urasa*.

"This is probably the dwelling of those hostile warriors," said the oldest brother.

"And whose else would it be?" the middle brother added. "Of course, it's theirs."

"Since they robbed our place, let's destroy their *urasa*!" the youngest brother cried, and he hopped out of the canoe.

The other two young men jumped out after him. Letting out a whoop, they rushed toward their enemy's dwelling. They broke the poles and tore down the animal skins. They grabbed the kettle and put it into the canoe. In short, they destroyed it completely.

They began digging on the spot where someone else's *urasa* had stood. The youngest brother found a bow. He raised it and shouted, "This is my bow. I made it myself!"

"It can't be. What drivel are you talking?" asked the oldest brother, ignoring his words.

Then, he saw his own bow. "Listen," he said, pushing the middle brother. "It appears that Akchin-Hondo isn't completely dumb. I found my bow, too."

Lopchuo, the middle brother, held another bow in his hands. He looked it over and shook his head. "It turns out that the bows are ours. Maybe it's our *urasa*."

The brothers sorted through the animal skins that they had thrown into a heap. They recognized all of them. "This is the deer I shot!" said one of the brothers.

"And this is my deer."

"And this is the bear skin that Father gave us!"

The brothers looked at one another. Then, they asked," How did this happen? We rowed all night long and came back to our own *urasa*."

Finally, the brothers decided that a shaman had heard their song and was jealous of their singing. In his jealousy, the shaman had placed a fog over their eyes and had sent down calamities.

So they decided, and so they think to this very day. Not one of them came to the conclusion that the "shaman" had a name. But we, dear readers, know the shaman's name, don't we?

RAVEN AND WOLF

(Chukchi)

*T*hey say that one day Raven was sledding on his tail feathers down a cliff that hung over the sea. As he was sliding down, he cried out in pleasure, "Whee-e, how nice! The sky is flashing by, and I'm zipping along!"

When Raven reached the end of the cliff, he jumped and flew up into the air. Then, he slid down the cliff all over again.

Suddenly, Wolf came into sight. After watching Raven for a while, Wolf said, "Brother, let me take a turn."

Raven tried to dissuade him. "No, you shouldn't try it. You don't know how to fly. You'll fall into the water below."

"I won't fall into the water. My legs are long. Please, brother, let me slide down the cliff just once," begged Wolf.

"Well, all right," Raven finally agreed. "Only you're going to fall into the water. Just you wait and see."

Wolf slid down the cliff. As he was sliding, he cried out in pleasure, "Whee-e, how nice! The sky is flashing by, and I'm zipping along!"

Thus, he slid to the edge of the cliff where he had planned to dig his heels into the snow. However, he could not manage it. He was going so fast that he missed his chance and plunged into the water.

"Brother, please pull me out," cried Wolf.

"No, I won't pull you out," Raven said. "Didn't I tell you that you'd fall into the water? Now, crawl out on your own."

"Please, please, brother. Pull me out, and I'll drive a herd of mice your way for your dinner."

This time, too, Raven said, "No, I won't pull you out."

Wolf begged again, "Please, dear little brother, pull me out. I'll give you a herd of ground squirrels for dinner."

Raven persisted in his refusal to help Wolf. "I won't pull you out," he repeated.

Wolf did not give up. Again, he begged, "Brother, dear little brother, please pull me out. If you want, I'll give you some porridge stuck to a spoon."

This temptation made Raven tremble with joy. Raven never could resist the offer of food. "Well, why didn't you say so before? You've spent needless time freezing in the cold water."

Raven pulled Wolf out of the icy water. He wiped the water from Wolf's fur.

Instead of thanking Raven, Wolf said, "I did a good job of fooling you."

Raven became angry. "Oh, you! I'll never believe you again."

Wolf was silent for a moment. Then, he said, "Now I'm going in that direction, where it is getting dark. Where are you flying off to?"

Raven did not deign even to look at Wolf. "Right now I'm flying in the direction opposite from you, where it's getting light."

Wolf and Raven parted and went in different directions. Since that day, they have no longer been friends.

PART 4

LEGENDS AND *POURQUOI* TALES

THE LITTLE WARRIOR MOUSE

(Siberian Yupik)

*M*ouse was sitting beneath a big burdock plant when Man passed by. Man and Mouse did not see one another because Man was too big and Mouse was too small. But Mouse heard the song that Man was singing.

"Songs are sung about Man and stories are told about him, but no one says anything about us mice. I wonder why that is," mused Mouse. "People become warriors. They have great battles, races, and bow and arrow contests. They are hunters and heroes. What can I do to make people sing songs and tell stories about me?"

"I know. I'll gnaw through this tree and carry it up that high hill."

Mouse began gnawing at the tree. He gnawed for a long time. He gnawed a strip around the tree. Then Mouse grabbed the trunk and rocked it from side to side.

"O-o-oh," Mouse grunted. But the tree did not budge, so Mouse started gnawing again.

"O-o-oh," Mouse cried. The tree began to crack, and it fell over.

At first Mouse was frightened. Then he saw that it was not a tree that had fallen over, but a blade of grass.

Mouse felt wretched and frustrated. It's good that people didn't see what happened, or they would have laughed at Mouse.

"But what can I do to become famous?" asked Mouse.

Mouse walked across the tundra deep in thought. He descended a mountain and saw several big lakes. The lakes extended one after another in a chain.

"If I swim across such a lake and dry out my *kukhlianka** and *torbasy*** on the other shore, people passing by will notice me. 'What a swimmer! That's a real swimmer,' they'll say."

Mouse swam across the lake. It was difficult. Several times he dove down, swallowed a mouthful of water, and almost drowned. Still, he swam to the other shore.

---

* Reindeer-skin shirt.
** Reindeer-skin boots.

Mouse dried his *kukhlianka* and *torbasy*. He was happy.

At that moment, a hunter approached the lake. The hunter stepped over the lake and did not even notice the brave swimmer. Several more big lakes formed behind the hunter. Wherever the hunter stepped, he crushed the earth and formed a big hole that filled with water. The second chain of lakes that the hunter made stretched into the tundra.

Mouse felt miserable. He sat for a while by the lake. Then he put on his *kukhlianka* and pulled on his *torbasy* and walked on. He continued walking until he stumbled on a hill. Although it looked like a hill to Mouse, it was actually a small stone.

Mouse stopped in front of the hill and thought, "The hill is too high to climb, and it's far too big to go around it." Then Mouse lifted the hill onto his back.

Mouse walked along the seashore for a long time carrying the hill on his back. He put it down on the highest bank of the Bering Strait. "Now I am a real warrior!" Mouse declared loudly, sitting down beside the hill.

Mouse rested on the high precipice overlooking the sea, and then he decided to go back to camp to drink tea. Mouse began descending the steep precipice. At that moment, the wind began blowing. The little stone that Mouse had carried up the precipice began rolling down again.

People heard Mouse talking and saw the stone rolling down the precipice. People composed a story about Mouse. They named the high place on the shore of the Bering Strait in honor of Mouse. In the Yupik language, they called it Avsynikhom—"The Mountain Transported Here by Mouse."

THE ORIGIN OF THE PTARMIGAN

(Inuit)

The ptarmigan (aqiggiq) is important to the diet and culture of the Inuit. Ptarmigan stay around for the winter when other birds have flown south. Their plumage turns white in winter so that they are difficult to see in the snow. They provide nourishment for the Inuit, even when larger animals, such as caribou and sea mammals, are scarce. The Inuit named children born in summer "ducks" and children born in winter "ptarmigans." Whenever ball games or song battles were held, the "ducks" and "ptarmigans" formed opposing teams. Moreover, it was forbidden to burn ptarmigan feathers for fear that the act would affect the weather and cause a thunderstorm.[1] Following is a legend about how the ptarmigan came to be.

*M*any years ago, when the land was young, there lived an old woman who liked to play tricks on people. It was a time when people, birds, and animals were shapeshifters. People could become birds and animals, and birds and animals could become people. At any rate, the old woman was in the habit of joking and playing tricks on people, both to their consternation and to their amused delight.

One day the old woman decided to play a practical joke on some children who were playing games intently and who were not observing what was going on around them. The old woman crept quietly up behind the children and clapped her hands loudly.

Frightened out of their skins, the children jumped into the air. When they did so, they turned into ptarmigan and flew away.

The children were very young, so they did not know how to turn back into children. They remained ptarmigan forever. And that is how the birds called ptarmigan came to be.

The willow ptarmigan, or willow grouse, breeds in the tundra and forests of Canada, Scandinavia, Alaska, and Siberia. It is Alaska's state bird and the topic of "The Origin of the Ptarmigan." Photograph by Paul Northcott.

INUKSHUK

(Arctic)

Travelers in the Arctic may come across piles of stone that are called inukshuk *(also rendered as* inuksuk *and* inutsuk*) in the singular and* inukshuiit *(also* inuksuit*) in the plural.[1] They are very noticeable because there are no tall trees to hide them on the tundra. They stand out on the barren rock and snow, towering over the landscape like sentinels. Inuk means person, and inukshuk means something that acts for a person.[2]*

Inukshuiit *play an important role in the life of the Inuit, Yupik, and Inupiat of Green-land, Canada, Siberia, and Alaska. An* inukshuk *is a stone marker that indicates that some-one has been there before. It may point out the location of a food cache. Or it may indicate where good hunting and fishing grounds are located. Several may be used to create a caribou run that leads the caribou to hunters. It may mark trails or routes used by the caribou. Or it may serve as a guide to travelers on the sea. The territory of Nunavut, which was carved out of Canada's central and eastern section of the former Northwest Territory; Nunavik in northern Quebec; and autonomous Nunatsiavut of Newfoundland and Labra-dor adopted the* inukshuk *as a symbol for placement on their flag. It was also a symbol for the 2010 Winter Olympics in Vancouver, Canada.*

Inuit Peter Irniq makes a distinction between the inukshuiit *that are piles of stones and the more elaborate* inunnguat *(*inunnguaq *in the singular) that are what he refers to as "pretend people," or imitations of people with arms, legs, and head.[3] He cautions that these monuments are of later development and differ from* inukshuiit *in origin and purpose. Nevertheless,* inunnguat *are frequently grouped with* inukshuiit. *In Labrador, there is a legend about how the first* inukshuk *was constructed[4]:*

A young Inuk girl named Niqaak fell in love with a hunter from the south named Iqaluk. After Niqaak's reluctant father agreed to their marriage, Iqaluk returned to his tribe to make preparations for the wedding. Niqaak feared Iqaluk would not return, so Iqaluk constructed a pile of rocks as tall as himself and called it an *inukshuk*.[5] Iqaluk told Niqaak that his spirit lay within the rocks and that she was to guard the *inukshuk* until he returned.

The young girl stopped grieving because she knew Iqaluk would return to reclaim his spirit. Indeed, he returned in summer, and they married. After the wedding, Niqaak followed Iqaluk to his land. They built *inukshuiit* at intervals on the way to Niqaak's adopted land so that her family could follow and visit them.

Their story became legend and the building of inukshuiit became a tradition. In this legend the role of the inukshuk both as marker to act as guide for Niqaak's family's visitation and as an imitation person that contains Iqaluk's spirit is mentioned, pointing out the inukshuk's dual function.

Inuksuiit at Igloolik, Nunavut. *Inuksuiit* are used by the Inuit for navigation and to mark good hunting and fishing places. Photograph courtesy of Kira Van Deusen.

TOADMAN TAKES A WIFE

(Innu)

The Innu live in Labrador and northern Quebec. They call their homeland Nitassinan. They believe that every animal kingdom has a master. The most powerful master of them all is Caribou Spirit, who rules over the other animal masters. The story that follows is about Toadman, or Anikunapeu, Spirit of Frogs and Toads.

A shaman can communicate directly with the animal spirits during the shaking tent ceremony. A conical tent is constructed for the shaman, who enters it. The tent begins shaking upon his entry, and the voices of the shaman and the animal spirits are heard. The shaman is helped by the Mishtapeu, legendary giants who come to the shaman's aid in times of need. The shaking tent ceremony was practiced until 1957 in Davis Inlet (called Natuashish today) and up to 1973 in Sheshatshiu.[1]

Toadman lives in Nitassinan in a mountain named Petshikapushkau near Michikamau (Meshikamau) Lake. One day two girls went to Nitinuk Island on Michikamau Lake to pick berries.[2] They were looking for berries in a swampy area when one of the girls walked on quicksand and began sinking down into the mud.

When the other girl saw her friend sinking, she screamed, "Help! Help!" She ran home to tell the others to get help.

People came rushing to pull the girl out of the mud. They pulled and pulled, but the girl slowly sank, despite their efforts, until only her head was visible. She was being pulled down into the mud by Toadman (Anikunapeu), who had grabbed her feet.[3] The more she screamed, the faster she sank until only one of her hands was visible.

Suddenly, the people saw Toadman's hand rise from the swamp. They caught hold of Toadman's hand and cut it off with an ax so that he could no longer pull the girl down into the mud. Toadman's hand grew right back again. Then they cut off Toadman's hand at the wrist, but again it grew back into place. In desperation, the people kept cutting, but Toadman's hand kept reappearing.[4]

Finally, no trace of the girl could be found. She had disappeared in the mud, pulled to the bottom by Toadman.

That evening, the people decided to make a shaking tent and ask the spirits to tell them what had happened to the girl. They made a shaking tent of caribou skin, and the shaman brought Toadman into the tent.

The girl's father entered the tent and asked, "What have you done with my daughter? Where is she now?"

"I took your daughter," replied Toadman. "She is happy with me and will live forever as long as she stays with me in my mountain home beside Michikamau Lake."

"And I will always stay here, too, to be near my daughter," the father replied.

This is a true story of long ago. To this day Toadman watches over Michikamau Lake and the surrounding area, including the Smallwood Reservoir.[5]

THE STOLEN SONG

(Siberian Yupik)

*S*pring came. Two snow buntings flew from warm countries to the craggy cliffs of the Bering Strait. There, they built a nest on a high cliff by the sea's edge.

Mother Snow Bunting laid an egg and set about keeping it warm. She dared not fly away from her nest for fear that a cold wind might blow on the egg. Hungry and sleepy, she covered the egg in the rain with her body.

Finally, a little son hatched and popped out of the egg. He was a fine, handsome chick. In fact, a more handsome chick could not be found on the entire coast.

The chick had only one bad trait—he was very loud, so much so that his parents could neither drink nor eat nor sleep. Whenever his father flew off to hunt for food, his mother sang a lullaby to the little chick.

One day Mother Snow Bunting was sitting on the edge of the nest singing her son a song.

> *Whose little feet are these?*
> *Whose little wings are these?*
> *Whose dear little head,*
> *And whose dear little eyes?*
> *Whose? Whose? Whose?*

Raven was flying by and heard the song. Raven stopped and perched close by, listening all the while to the song. Raven listened and listened, but still he could not get his fill. He liked the song more than anyone could possibly describe.

"Give me your song," he requested of Snow Bunting. "Oh, please give me your song!"

"What on earth are you thinking?" asked Mother Snow Bunting. "I can't give the song away. It is our only song. We have no others."

"I beg you to give me the song," Raven said persuasively. "I can't live now without that song."

"And my son can't sleep without the song. Don't ask. I won't give it to you."

After hearing those words, Raven became angry. "If Snow Bunting won't give me the song willingly, I'll take it by force," he muttered.

Raven flew up to Mother Snow Bunting. He snatched the song from her throat and flew away. Snow Bunting's son began shouting and crying. Mother Snow Bunting wept.

Soon Father Snow Bunting returned from his hunt. He heard his son crying and saw his wife shedding tears. "What's wrong with you?" he asked. "What misfortune has occurred?"

"A terrible misfortune has occurred," Mother Snow Bunting answered. "Raven flew down and carried off our song. Now our son won't fall asleep, no matter what. He'll just keep crying. How will we survive?"

Father Snow Bunting grew angry. His eyes sparkled, and he stamped his foot. "Give me my hunting gloves, my battle bow, and my arrows that never miss their mark. I'll find the thief and tear the song from his throat!"

Father Snow Bunting flew on and on. He saw many birds, but not one raven. He saw a ptarmigan running among the rocks and a plover whistling merrily. Finally, he spied a flock of ravens on the cliffs. He alighted a short distance away. He laid his arrow on the bow, drew the bowstring, and waited. He planned to shoot whoever began singing his song.

The ravens went about their business. The old ravens warmed themselves in the sun and gossiped. The young ravens played games. No one sang a song, not Snow Bunting's song, or any other song. Once or twice the ravens began croaking, but how could that be called a song?

Father Snow Bunting flew on. He saw Raven sitting on a tree branch, and Father Snow Bunting began circling above him. Raven lifted his beak, closed his eyes, and rocked from side to side as a song poured forth from his beak.

Whose little feet are these?

Whose little wings are these?

Whose dear little head,

And whose dear little eyes?

Whose? Whose? Whose?

After singing the song, Raven began again.

Whose little feet are these?

Whose little wings are these?

"That's the villain!" exclaimed Father Snow Bunting. "There he is, the thief who stole the best song in the world."

Father Snow Bunting alighted on a branch of the same tree. He drew his bow and shot an arrow into Raven. The arrow slid along Raven's wing feathers and fell to earth. Raven did not even notice anything. He did not even open his eyes. He continued singing, the song pouring forth from his throat.

Then, Father Snow Bunting grabbed all the arrows in his quiver. He placed them between his fingers and began shooting them at the thief, four arrows at a time.

Raven kept singing.

Oh, whose little feet are these?

Oh, whose little wings are these?

Oh, something hit me in the side.

Oh, whose dear little head. . . .

Oh, something jabbed me!

Oh, whose dear little eyes. . . .

Oh, oh, I can't go on! Caw! Caw!

And Raven released the song from his beak. Father Snow Bunting grabbed the song and flew quickly to his nest. As he ascended, he heard his son crying and his wife weeping.

"Don't cry. Don't weep," said Father Snow Bunting. "I've taken our song back from evil Raven. Here it is!"

Mother Snow Bunting rejoiced and began singing the song. Her little son grew quiet and fell asleep.

Since that time, whenever snow buntings catch sight of Raven flying overhead, they grow silent. They are afraid even to open their beaks. In that manner, they have preserved their song. Once again snow buntings sing to their crying children. Raven, on the other hand, was left with an ugly "caw."

RAVEN AND OWL

(Inuit and Upper Yukon Dene)

*I*t is hard to believe, but once upon a time both Owl and Raven were as pure white as the driven snow. But Raven was a whimsical creature and was always scheming.

One day Raven caught sight of Owl. "Aren't you sick of being white?" he blurted out without giving his question a second thought. "Wouldn't you rather try wearing a different color?"

"I suppose so," Owl replied hesitantly. "Let's try wearing a different color. How can we change?"

"I'll make up some paint by mixing this black soot with the oil in the lamp," proposed Raven. "Then, you paint me first, and later I'll paint you."

Owl knew of Raven's reputation as a trickster. "Oh, no," Owl said. "Since it was your idea, you have to paint me first."

"Oh, all right," Raven replied.

Raven poured some hot oil from the lamp. The oil was already black with soot, but Raven added even more soot to it until it was a jet-black color. Then, he pulled a tail feather out to use as a brush. "Ouch!" he yelled.

Raven set to work painting beautiful black spots all over Owl. He painted big spots, medium-sized spots, and small spots until Owl's new dress was beautifully speckled.

Owl looked at Raven's work admiringly. "I really am quite beautiful in my new clothes, Raven. You did a wonderful job. Now let me paint you."

In her gratitude for Raven's hard work, Owl made a pair of whalebone boots for Raven. Then Owl painted carefully and meticulously with the feather paint brush. She measured every stroke of the feather brush.

Unable to stand still, Raven kept hopping about as Owl worked. "Ouch, ouch, ouch!" Raven squawked.

Nevertheless, in the end Raven was handsome and elegant. He was a speckled work of art. Owl stepped back to look at her work. She was stunned by the brilliance of her

---

masterpiece. She realized that now Raven was better looking than she was and that she had outstripped Raven in her artistic ability. The green worm of envy gnawed at Owl's heart.

Suddenly, Owl grabbed the pot of sooty oil and dumped it on top of Raven's head. It ran down his feathers until it covered his entire body. Not a patch of white was left. "That's what you get for hopping about so," said Owl, attempting to justify her behavior.

"Caw, caw," croaked the enraged Raven. "What have you done to me, nasty bird? Now I have lost all of my white color and am blacker than midnight."

Owl knew that nothing good would come of Raven's rage. She flew away rapidly. Raven set out in pursuit.

To this day Raven remains black. Have you ever seen a raven that was not black as the blackest of nights?

THE ORIGIN OF RAVEN

(Inuit)

*O*nce Raven was a man whose people were getting ready to move to another place. As they were in the process of gathering their household goods, Raven kept reminding them not to forget the deerskin bed blanket, which is called the *kak* in the Inuit language.

"Don't forget the *kak*. Don't forget the *kak*," he kept repeating.

Raven repeated the word so often that everyone grew sick of hearing it. "Get the *kak* yourself," the annoyed villagers told Raven.

Raven rushed to and fro in a veritable panic in his zeal to get the blanket. He hurried so much that he transformed from a man into a bird—a raven.

Still, Raven kept repeating "*kak, kak*" until *kak* became the sound of his song. To this very day when Raven flies over camps that are moving to another location, he cries "caw, caw, caw!" It sounds very much like "*Kak, kak, kak*! Don't forget the blanket."

THE CUCKOO

(Nenets and Ket)

There once lived a poor woman who had four children. The children did not obey their mother. They ran about and played in the snow from dawn to dusk. If they got their clothes wet, their mother dried them. If they dragged the snow on their boots into their reindeer tent home, which was called a *chum,*[*] their mother cleaned the snow off the boots.

Their mother caught fish for them in the river nearby. Life was hard for her, and the children did not help out.

Finally, their mother grew ill from such a difficult life. She lay in the *chum* and called for the children. "Children, my throat is dry. Please bring me some water," she requested.

The mother asked for water more than once or twice. She asked many times. But the children did not fetch the water she had requested. They made excuses. The oldest child said, "My boots aren't dry, so I can't go out."

Another said, "I lost my hat." And so it went. The children ignored her and ran off to play. Soon they forgot all about their mother.

Finally, the oldest child grew hungry and wanted to eat. He glanced into the *chum*. His mother stood in the middle of the *chum* putting on her reindeer fur jacket. Suddenly, the fur jacket was covered with feathers.

The mother picked up the board on which she scraped animal skin, and the board became a bird's tail. Her iron thimble became a beak. Her arms became wings. The mother turned into a bird and flew out of the *chum*.

"Brothers, look, look! Our mother has turned into a bird and is flying away," cried the oldest son.

Then, the children ran after their mother. "Mama, we have brought you some water!" they cried.

"Cuckoo, cuckoo, cuckoo! It's too late. I won't be coming back."

---

[*] Pronounced "choom."

The children ran after their mother with a dipper of water. They ran for many days and nights. They ran on stones, through swamps, and over tussocks of grass. Their feet got scraped and were bleeding. Wherever they ran, they left a bloody trail.

The mother, who had become a cuckoo, abandoned her children forever. Since that time, the cuckoo has not built a nest. She does not raise her own children. Instead, she places them in the nests of other birds to be cared for. And since that time a red moss has spread across the tundra where the children left their bloody footsteps.

THE GIANT CANNIBAL DOG

(Greenland Inuit)

*O*n the coast of Greenland, there once lived an old couple with two sons and a daughter. The sons were hunters famous for their skill and strength. They used to bring seals home that were attached one after the other to a long towline.

One day their sons did not return from the hunt, and the old people became very worried. Shortly thereafter, a neighbor came with sad news. "I have seen your sons," he said. "They are hanging upside down from a cliff. The inlanders did that to them."[1]

The people of the village rushed to the spot where the young men were hanging. They tried their best to reach them, to cut them down, but it was impossible. The young men hung there, exposed to the elements until they died.

The old couple mourned their loss. One of their neighbors had a dog that had given birth to several puppies. In an attempt to raise the spirits of the old people, the neighbor gave them one of the puppies. The old couple sent their daughter to the neighbor's to fetch the dog.

The old woman adopted the puppy and treated it like her own flesh and blood. She always had it beside her, and she nursed it with her own milk. The dog became like a son to her.

The dog grew up with great strength and magic powers. He grew to be gigantic and was able to haul whale and narwhal home to his parents from the sea on towlines that were attached to holes that the old man had cut in the dog's jaws. By pulling on the lines, the dog could change the direction he was pulling the whales.

When the old folks wanted to go on a journey, they mounted the dog's back. The dog took them wherever they wanted to go. The old man gave his adopted dog-son an amulet made of hard wood. It protected the giant dog against death.

One day the dog attacked a man and ate him up. The old couple could no longer stay where they were living because their neighbors had grown frightened of the dog and were afraid that it might eat them, too. The old couple moved to a new place where the dog's behavior was unknown to the local people.

One day a stranger approached in a kayak. The old man hurried to secure his dog before it could eat the stranger. He took the dog up into the mountains and gave him a bone to gnaw to keep him busy.

A friendship developed between the old man and the stranger, but one day the dog got a whiff of the stranger while he was visiting. The dog became agitated and barked viciously. The old man managed to hide the man and his kayak so that the cannibal dog could not eat the man.

In time the giant dog became more and more vicious. Although the old man had saved one stranger's life, he was not always so successful. People heard stories about the dog's bad behavior. One day another stranger arrived in a sledge pulled by three dogs as big as bears. The stranger intended to kill the cannibal dog.

The cannibal dog sensed the stranger's intent. As the old man went out to meet the stranger, the dog skulked behind him, pretending to be afraid. When the stranger's dogs attacked him, however, he crushed the skulls of all three in his teeth, as if they were mere splinters of wood.

Soon the cannibal dog took to wandering off into the hills. Sometimes he returned with the leg of an inlander. The old man knew the legs belonged to the inlanders because the boots on the legs were hairy in the inlander style and not covered with sealskin in the coastal style. The dog thought he was doing a good deed because he knew that inlanders had killed the old man's sons several years ago. He brought the legs to his parents, proudly showing them that he could avenge his brothers' deaths.

The inlanders became terrified of the cannibal dog. They had a habit of searching for women who had lost their way in the fog. The inlanders kidnapped these women and took them home to be their wives.[2] Now they stopped kidnapping coastal people, as they used to do so frequently.

Finally, the dog's foster mother began to fear him. "How can I get rid of the dog?" she wondered.

She devised a plan. In the spring after the old couple had loaded the boat and were ready to leave for their spring and summer camp, the old woman asked the dog to go back to the house to get something she had forgotten. As soon as the dog's back was turned, the old couple pushed off from land and began their journey.

When the giant cannibal dog saw that he had been left behind, he chased after the old couple, following along the shore and barking. The dog followed them until they were barely visible on the horizon. He remained on that spot for a long time, whining and howling.

People say that this story explains why dogs follow departing boats along the coast, barking and whining. Just like the giant, cannibal dog, they howl at people in the boat until they become a tiny speck in the distance.

DOG IN SEARCH OF A FRIEND

(Evenk and Mordvinian)

*L*ong, long ago, Dog lived in the forest, alone and lonely. She was bored and wanted to find a friend—not just any friend, but a worthy one who feared no one.

Dog met a rabbit and said to him, "Rabbit, let's be friends and live together."

"Let's," Rabbit agreed.

That evening they found a place to spend the night and went to sleep. During the night, Mouse ran past them. Dog heard the rustling noise that Mouse made. She jumped up and began barking loudly.

Rabbit awoke in fright, his ears trembling with fear. "Why are you barking?" he asked Dog. "If Wolf hears you, he'll come here and eat us up."

"What kind of friend is this?" thought Dog. "He's a coward. He's afraid of Wolf. But Wolf probably isn't afraid of anyone."

In the morning Dog said good-bye to Rabbit and went in search of Wolf. Dog came upon him in a remote ravine and proposed, "Wolf, let's be friends."

"All right," Wolf agreed. "It will be more enjoyable to live with someone."

That night they went to sleep. Frog hopped past them. Dog heard the sound of Frog's hopping. Dog jumped up and began barking loudly.

Wolf awoke in terror and began scolding Dog. "What are you carrying on for? Bear will hear and come here and tear us apart!"

"So, Wolf is afraid, too," thought Dog. "It would be better to be friends with Bear, who doesn't fear Wolf."

Dog went up to Bear. "Bear, let's be friends and live together," Dog proposed.

"All right," Bear said. "Come into my den, Dog."

That night Dog heard Snake slithering past the den. She jumped up and began barking.

Bear got scared and began scolding Dog. "Stop it! Man will come and take the fur off our backs."

"So, it turns out that Bear is a coward, too," Dog thought.

Dog ran away from Bear and went in search of Man. Soon Dog came upon Man, who was hunting in the forest. "Man, let's be friends and live together," Dog said.

"Let's," said Man. Man led dog to his home. Man fed Dog and built her a warm kennel near his home. When night came, Man lay down to sleep.

At midnight Dog began barking at a noise. Man awoke, but he was not afraid. "Sing if you want, Dog, but don't keep me from sleeping!"

Dog understood that Man was afraid of no one. They began living together. They live in friendship to this day. And out of gratitude for Man's kindness, Dog guards Man's house and possessions.

WHY RABBIT HAS LONG EARS

(Mansi)

*W*hen animals first appeared in the forest, Elk* was thought to be the oldest and wisest of them all. One day Elk was talking to his wife when Rabbit came running. Rabbit heard their voices and stopped. "I'll just listen to what they are saying," he said. He sneaked up closer, hid behind a tree stump, and listened.

"I have some antlers here," said Elk, "which I must give to the animals. But there are many animals and few antlers. To whom shall I give them?"

Rabbit listened and thought, "I would like to have those antlers. I am no less deserving than the other animals."

"To whom shall I give the antlers?" Elk repeated.

Rabbit was on the point of opening his mouth to shout, "Give me the antlers!" when Elk's wife suggested, "Give the antlers to Reindeer. He is your relative, so you should give them to him."

"All right," said Elk. "Here are some antlers for Reindeer. Now who else should get a pair of antlers?"

Elk's wife was just about to answer when Rabbit, unable to bear it any longer, leaned out from behind the tree stump and shouted, "Give them to me, Elk!"

"What sort of idea is that, brother?" asked Elk. "Why do you need such big antlers? What would you do with them?"

"What would I do with them?" Rabbit repeated Elk's question. "Why, I need antlers to scare my enemies so that they will fear me."

"Well, then, all right, take them," said Elk, and he gave Rabbit the antlers.

Rabbit was overjoyed. He put the antlers on and began jumping and dancing around. Suddenly, a big cone fell from the cedar tree right onto his head.

Rabbit jumped up in fright and began running. He made a dash but came to a crashing stop. He had not gotten very far. His antlers had become entangled in some bushes. Unable to get free, he began squealing fearfully and trembling all over.

---

* European elk, which is akin to the North American moose.

Elk and his wife laughed. ""No, brother," said wise Elk, "antlers are not for the likes of you. The longest antlers in the world won't help a coward. Give them back to me and take these long ears instead, so that everyone will know that you are an eavesdropper who likes to listen to what other people are saying."

That is how snoopy Rabbit lost his antlers. The ears that Elk gave him grew and grew. Every time Rabbit listened to words that were not meant for him, his ears became a little longer.

HOW MOSQUITOES CAME TO BE

(Tlingit)

*M*any years ago in Myth Time, there lived a cannibal giant who killed people in order to eat their meat and drink their blood. The giant considered the human heart to be the tastiest of morsels.

The frightened people assembled to discuss how they might rid themselves of this monster. "If we don't get rid of the giant, no one will be left alive," they reasoned.

"I have a plan," one man said. He went to the path where the giant usually walked. Then he lay down on the path, and he pretended to be dead.

Soon the ground began to shake, and the man heard the heavy footsteps of the giant. The giant came up to the man lying in his path and said, "You've saved me a great deal of trouble, human. I didn't even have to catch you. You died here on my path undoubtedly of fright."

The giant prodded the body and felt it. "Wonderful!" he exclaimed. "He's still warm. Fresh meat will make a fine meal, and as for his heart—what a delicacy it will be!"

The cannibal giant threw the man over his shoulder. The man pretended he was dead and let his head droop over the giant's back. When the giant reached home, he dropped the man down in the middle of his dwelling near the fireplace. Noticing that there was no wood, with which to start a fire so that he could cook the human, the giant left to fetch some.

As soon as the giant was gone, the man bounded up and grabbed the giant's enormous knife that he used to skin human hides. The giant's son, who was bending low to enter the home, interrupted the man.

The little boy was the size of an adult, so the man who had been pretending to be dead held the enormous knife to the boy's throat. "Tell me where your father's heart is, or I'll slit your throat!" he threatened.

The young giant was so frightened and surprised that he answered without thinking, "Dad's heart is in his left heel."

After the giant's son had uttered these words, the giant's left foot suddenly appeared in the entryway. The man who had been pretending to be dead thrust the knife into the giant's left heel. The monster let out a shriek and fell down dead.

As he was breathing his last breath, the giant uttered these words. "You may have killed me and I may be dead, but nevertheless I will continue eating you and all humans on earth forever! It's a promise and a curse."

"We'll see about that!" said the man. "I'll make sure that you won't be able to eat anyone again."

The man cut the giant's body into tiny pieces and threw them, one by one, into the fire. After they had burned, he scooped up the ashes and threw them into the air. The wind blew them in all directions.

As the man watched, each particle of ash turned into a mosquito. The cloud of ashes changed into a swarm of mosquitoes.

The giant's laughter rang out. "I'll eat you humans as long as you exist, until time ends. Ha, ha, ha!"

Even as the cannibal giant was speaking, the man felt a pinch. A mosquito had bitten him and was sucking his blood. Then many more mosquitoes bit him, and he began scratching. Since that day, people have been pestered by mosquitoes.

TWO BROTHERS AND A GIANT

(Kaska)

Two brothers lived together. The older brother stayed home and kept house while the younger brother went out every day to hunt. Although this arrangement worked well, the older brother, who was the housekeeper, came to dislike his younger brother. He began neglecting to give him anything to eat when he came home with game to be prepared for dinner. The younger brother suffered because it was winter and he needed to eat a great deal to keep warm.

One day the younger brother killed a porcupine. He was so hungry that he made a fire and cooked the porcupine suspended on a hook over the fire on the very spot where he had killed it.

When the porcupine was partially cooked, a giant came along. The boy caught sight of the giant approaching and ran up a tree. The giant lifted the porcupine in his enormous hands and smelled it. He threw the porcupine away in disgust. Then, the giant spied the boy's snowshoes and ate out the sinew strings. Finally, the giant began chopping down the tree, where the boy was hiding.

"Brother, come help me!" the younger brother called.

The older brother came running. The giant noticed the older boy approaching and was happy because he regarded the young man as a potential meal.

"I'll give you a hand," the older brother said to the giant, and he took up an axe.

"My brother is a very bad and mean boy. I'll chop down the tree so that we can get him and eat him."

The older brother swung the axe with great force. The giant was standing a little too close to the axe, so he received a blow on the forehead from the back of the axe.

"Stand farther away," said the older brother to the giant. "You're too close. I might hit you accidentally."

The older brother began swinging the axe again, chopping forcefully and wildly. When the opportunity presented itself, he gave the axe a great swing—and cut off the giant's head. In the end, you see, family ties were stronger than any temporary animosity.

The younger brother climbed down from the tree and together the two brothers opened the giant's head. When they did so, the giant's brains turned into mosquitoes and flew away.

This is the reason that giants are so foolish and that mosquitoes exist today. It is all thanks to the two brothers who opened the giant's head, thereby releasing mosquitoes into the world.

WHY RAVEN'S BEAK IS CROOKED

(Yukon River Dene)

*O*ne day Raven changed himself into a little old man who was lame and who had a long, white beard. Raven is a great glutton, so he was thinking all the while of food and was hungry as usual. Raven walked through the forest until he came to a village beside the ocean. People were fishing there. Raven decided to join them.

Raven caught and ate enough fish to feed an entire village, but still he was hungry. He caught sight of some fishermen baiting their hooks and throwing them into the ocean. Raven decided that the bait would make a tasty bite. Ravenous Raven dove into the water and gobbled up the bait on the end of the fishermen's hooks, one by one. When each fisherman felt a tug on the line, he pulled it in, only to find nothing on the end—no fish and no bait.

The most expert of the fishermen gave a quick jerk when he felt a tug at the line. He had hooked something that weighed a great deal. It was Raven's jaw. As the fisherman reeled the line in, Raven pulled in the opposite direction. In desperation, Raven grasped at the rocks at the bottom of the ocean and begged them to help him. The rocks did not reply to his pleas. Ultimately, Raven's struggles were in vain.

In terrible pain, Raven finally cried out, "Ouch, ouch, ouch! Break off, jaw." His jaw obliged him by falling off.

The fisherman reeled in his line and saw something ugly at the end. It was Raven's jaw attached to a white beard. The fisherman shuddered. The other fishermen gathered around to have a look at the puzzling jaw. They took to their heels, frightened by the thought that the jaw was an evil spirit.

The bedraggled old man, Raven in disguise, crawled out of the water. He covered his face with a blanket and followed the fishermen, who ran to the village chief. They showed the chief the jaw. The chief looked in puzzlement at the jaw, which he handed from one person to another. No one knew what to make of it.

Finally, Raven mumbled through his blanket, "Let me have a look."

When the fishermen handed him the jaw, Raven quickly stuck the jaw under his blanket and replaced it. He worked so quickly that no one noticed what he had done.

The old man, Raven in disguise, turned back into a bird and flew through the smoke hole of the chief's home with his jaw, which had now become a beak, firmly attached. Now the fishermen knew that it was gluttonous Raven who had stolen their bait.

Later, Raven realized that his beak was no longer straight. It was crooked, with a curve in it that served for the rest of time as a reminder to Raven of the day when in the form of an old man, he lost his beak.

THE FIRST TEARS

(Alaskan Inupiat)

*L*ong ago an Inuk was hunting seal at the edge of the sea. He saw a large group of seals crowded together along the seashore. Overjoyed with his find, the hunter crept closer to the seals. "One of these seals will feed my hungry wife and son for many days," he mused.

It seemed that the seals had not noticed the hunter's presence. But suddenly, they began running toward the water. In a flash, they were gone. They slipped into the water and swam far away before the hunter even had managed to take out his knife. "My family's meal is gone," thought the desperate hunter.

One seal moved more slowly and kept to the back of the group. It may have been old and unable to move as fast as the others.

"Aha!" thought the Inuk. "This seal will provide our store of meat for the winter. My wife and son will be so very proud of me."

The hunter crept very cautiously toward the seal that lagged behind the others. He thought that the seal did not notice him, but he was wrong. Suddenly, the lagging seal leapt into the water and made a big splash.

Slowly, the Inuk stood up. A strange emotion flooded his entire being. He thought of his hungry wife and son, and he was sad. Water began flowing from his eyes. He touched the drops of water and tasted them. They were salty, like seawater. Moreover, strange gasping sounds were coming from his chest and mouth.

His son heard the strange noise and came running. "Father, what is wrong? What has happened to you?" he asked.

When the Inuk did not answer, the boy called his mother to come. The boy and his mother ran to the water's edge and saw water pouring from both of the Inuk's eyes. They were frightened.

The Inuk told them how he had been hunting seals and how they had escaped. Now they would have no celebration feast and no store of meat for the winter.

As they listened to his story, tears began flowing from the eyes of the Inuk's wife and son. They, too, wept because their livelihood had been lost. They wept the first tears, and this is how people learned to cry.

There were other, happier days ahead for them. Later, the Inuk and his son caught a seal together and used its hide to make snares to catch more seals.

GUILLEMOTS

(Eastern Inuit)

Guillemots are northern shorebirds. They have webbed feet and like to dive into the water. There are legends about these birds. The legend that follows explains how guillemots originated.

*O*nce some children were playing on top of a high cliff that hung over the sea. The children were in high spirits, jumping, shouting, and having a good time. The older children watched the younger ones carefully to make certain that they did not lose their footing and fall from the cliff onto the seashore below.

The sea below was covered with ice. The ice had not yet opened near the shore so that seals could hop onto the ice and approach the shore.

Suddenly a wide crack in the ice opened along the shoreline and the water became filled with seals. The children did not notice the seals. They continued to play, cheering one another on in their games and shouting at the top of their lungs.

A group of hunters noticed the seals and hurried to the shore to put their kayaks into the water so that they might pursue and kill the seals. When the children observed the commotion, they shouted all the louder, urging the hunters on. The cries of the children frightened the seals, and they dove out of sight.

One of the hunters was very angry with the children for chasing away the seals. "I wish the cliff would topple over onto those noisy children and bury them for scaring away the seals," he said.

No sooner were the words out of his mouth than the cliff fell and began burying alive the noisy children. As chunks of huge rocks were falling onto the poor children at the bottom of the cliff, they were changed into guillemots, sea pigeons with red feet. To this day guillemots live among the rocks and debris at the foot of cliffs beside the edge of the sea.

Perhaps guillemots never forgot that once they had been human because another story is about a talking guillemot. Here it is.

There was a man from the south who heard about a guillemot that could talk. Someone told him that the talking bird lived somewhere in the north, so he set out for the north in his *umiak*, a boat made of skins stretched on a wooden or bone frame. A crew of women rowed the *umiak*, as was the custom.

Finally, he and the women came to a village and stopped. "I am looking for a guillemot that can talk," he explained to the villagers.

"You will find it three days journey away from here," the villagers replied.

The man stayed in the village only one night and continued on his way the next morning. Eventually, the man from the south came to another village. There, he asked again where he might find a talking guillemot.

"Tomorrow I will take you there," one of the villagers offered, "because I know the way and because I have no wife to keep me here."

Next morning the two men set out together in kayaks, leaving behind the women and the *umiak*. They rowed on until a cliff came into view. They got out of their kayaks and stood at the foot of the cliff looking up. It was a high cliff.

"I wonder where the talking guillemot is," said the man from the south.

"The nest of the talking guillemot is here," said the man who had served as a guide, pointing to a nest.

The man from the south was careful not to frighten the bird when it came out of its nest. After the guillemot emerged from the nest, it went to the edge of the cliff and stared down at the men. It stretched its body and strutted about. Then, it settled down and said quite clearly, "I think this might be the southern man who has come here from afar to hear a guillemot speak."

The bird had hardly spoken when the man from the south fell forward onto his face. The guide lifted him up, but he was dead. The man from the south had died of fright when he heard the guillemot speak.

The guide covered up the body and left it at the foot of the cliff below the guillemot's nest. He went home and told the villagers and the women who had come with the man from the south in the *umiak*. The crew of women stayed in the village during that winter.

When summer came, the women got ready to go back home to the south. They had no man to go with them, so the guide, who had no wife, agreed to accompany them.

On the journey, the wifeless guide caught fish for the women. After he had caught a pot full of fish, he would row in with his catch. In that manner, the wifeless guide led them to the south to their own country.

The women had grown so fond of the guide that they did not want him to return home to the north. Finally, the guide chose a wife from among the women, married her, and stayed with the southerners.

People say that the skeleton of the guide is still lying there in the south to this very day.

BEAVER AND PORCUPINE

(Dene, Tlingit, and Tahltan)

*P*orcupine and Beaver were once good friends. They traveled everywhere together. Porcupine used to visit Beaver frequently, but Beaver dreaded the thought of Porcupine's visits because he left his quills everywhere. Beaver was a very good housekeeper and despised messes.

One day Porcupine asked to visit Beaver, and Beaver decided to play a nasty trick on him. "Very well," Beaver said. "Sit on my back, Porcupine, and I'll take you to my house."

Instead of going to his house, Beaver took Porcupine to an old, rotten tree stump in the middle of the lake. "Get off my back," said Beaver. "This is my house."

Beaver dropped Porcupine abruptly and left him there. Meanwhile, Beaver swam ashore. Beaver knew how to swim, but Porcupine did not.

Porcupine clung to the stump and gazed around sadly. After his initial fear, Porcupine began singing a song. "May the lake freeze, may the lake freeze so that I can cross on the ice and go to Wolverine Man's place."

Soon the surface of the lake froze, and Porcupine walked home. However, Porcupine did not forget Beaver's nasty trick, even though he played with Beaver daily as he had always done.

Some time later, Porcupine said, "You must come to my house now, Beaver. It's my turn to carry you on my back."

Beaver climbed onto Porcupine's back. Porcupine knew how to climb trees, but Beaver did not. So, Porcupine took Beaver to the top of a very high tree—and he left Beaver there.

Beaver stayed at the top of the tree for a long time. He did not know how to get down. He shuddered when he looked at the ground. Eventually, his paws began to ache.

When no one came to rescue him, Beaver understood that he was going to have to get down the tree by himself. Finally, Beaver screwed up his courage and slid down the tree quickly.

He scratched the tree bark with his paws on his way down so that the tree had scratches on it from top to bottom. From that day on, because of Beaver's bumpy trip down the tree, tree bark has had a scratched, or broken, appearance.

THE WOODPECKER'S REWARD

(Evenk)

Wolverine and her old husband were looking for a new place to live. They had heard that there was more food on the other side of the river, so they decided to ferry their *chum*,* a skin-covered tent, and all their worldly goods across the river, where they planned to settle.

Wolverine's husband went into the forest to strip some birch bark off the trees to make a boat. While he was gone, Wolverine put their possessions into bags and sat on the riverbank waiting for her husband to return.

Suddenly, she caught sight of a little boat sailing down the river. In it was Fox. Curious Fox sailed toward Wolverine and offered to ferry the bags full of Wolverine's possessions across in the little boat.

Wolverine was delighted. She grabbed her bags and dragged them into the boat. The boat was filled to the brim. Finally, Wolverine started to sit down on top of her bags.

"Wait a minute," said Fox. "Don't sit there. It's dangerous. You could drown. First, I'll take your things across. Then, I'll come back and get you." Wolverine agreed, albeit uneasily.

Fox pushed off from shore with her oar and sailed downstream. Further and further Fox sailed until Wolverine understood that clever Fox had no intention of coming back to get her and that she had been tricked. She sat on a stone by the water's edge and burst into tears.

Woodpecker was flying by. He heard Wolverine crying. "What's wrong?" he asked. After he learned about Wolverine's trouble, Woodpecker flew straight through the forest after Fox.

By flying to the tip of a big cape, he got ahead of Fox. He sat on a twig on a bush and waited for the sly creature to sail by.

Fox's boat appeared in the distance. When the boat came even with the bush on which Woodpecker was sitting, Woodpecker pretended to be sick. "Dear little Fox, please take me with you in the boat," he begged.

---

* Pronounced "choom."

Thinking that a fat woodpecker would make a tasty dinner, Fox agreed to take him into the boat. Woodpecker hid behind Wolverine's bags and disappeared from sight.

They sailed on. Fox sat at the stern. Meanwhile, unnoticed, Woodpecker buried his beak into the boat and pecked at it. The thick birch bark tore open and water began to collect in the boat.

"What's this? The boat must have sprung a leak," said Fox, frightened.

"That's right, it's leaking," answered Woodpecker. "A seam must have come apart somewhere on the birch bark."

They rowed ashore. Fox jumped out and said to Woodpecker, "Take the luggage out of the boat. Then, pull the boat onto shore. Meanwhile, I'll go into the forest to look for some spruce pitch to plug the hole. We'll stop the leak with the pitch and sail on."

As soon as Fox had disappeared into the forest, Woodpecker heaped some twigs together and poked them into the hole. Then he sat in the boat and sailed back to Wolverine.

Later, Fox ran out of the forest bringing the spruce pitch. The boat had already sailed far up the river. "Woodpecker, you robber, come back this very minute!" she shouted.

"No, Fox, I won't go back," answered Woodpecker.

Woodpecker sailed with the bags to the place where Wolverine's *chum* had stood. There sat Wolverine and her husband, weeping over their loss. When they saw Woodpecker, the old wolverines rejoiced. "Well, said the husband, "what should we give good Woodpecker as a reward?"

Lady Wolverine decided to sew a suede jacket for Woodpecker. She decorated it with colored clay and made a bright red cap for his head. Woodpecker tried on his new outfit and looked very handsome. Since that time, Woodpecker has gone about in the colorful clothes that Wolverine made for him.

Wolverine's husband was a good blacksmith, so he forged a strong steel beak and sharp claws for Woodpecker. Now, with the sharp claws, Woodpecker is able to climb the highest tree, and with the steel beak, he is able to chisel through the toughest bark to reach the insects on which he dines.

THE ORIGIN OF FOG

(Greenland and Canadian Inuit)

Long before the Inuit came to the Arctic, the Tuniit, who belonged to the Dorset culture, lived there. The Inuit are descendents of the later Thule people, who came to western Alaska around AD 1000 and migrated eastward across the Arctic. We know very little about Inuit encounters with the Dorset Tuniit, but in legend the Tuniit are described as strong giants, who are the shy enemy of the Inuit. They were easily frightened off and disliked conflict. Eventually, the Tuniit disappeared entirely, perhaps because of their inferior technology or perhaps because of exposure to western diseases.[1] An Inuit legend about how fog originated describes what happened when an Inuk hunter met a giant Tuniq.[2]

This story took place many long years ago when the Tuniit and Inuit lived on the same land. They shared the land, but they disliked and avoided one another.

One day an Inuk hunter, who was a well-known shaman, went fishing. He sat beside the water all day long, but he caught nothing. Then he began roaming the land, looking for game, because his family was hungry.

Finally, he caught sight of a man who was approaching from far away. He was just a speck in the distance. Gradually, the man came closer, and the hunter saw that it was a giant Tuniq. The hunter knew that his life was in danger. To save himself, he fell to the ground and pretended to be dead.

When the giant reached the Inuk, he lifted him up and listened to hear whether he was breathing. The hunter held his breath.

"No question about it," said the Tuniq. "He's dead. I'll take him home. He'll make a tasty morsel for dinner."

The Tuniq grabbed the hunter and carried him under his arm. The hunter did not move. He held his hands out and grabbed at the trees and bushes, thus slowing the giant and making himself seem as heavy as possible.

"This fellow certainly feels heavy for such a puny, little Inuk," declared the giant.

Forced to use all his strength, the Tuniq soon grew tired. Finally, the giant arrived home exhausted and threw the hunter down onto the ground.

He greeted his family. "I've brought home a corpse for us to eat," he announced to his wife. "Go gather some wood so that we can cook him for dinner. I'm tired, and I'm going to take a little nap." The giant lay down to sleep.

Suddenly, the voices of his children awakened him. "Father, Father, the corpse just opened its eyes. It's not dead at all."

"Don't be silly, children. It's just your imagination making you think he's alive," said the Tuniq. And he went back to sleep.

As the giant lay snoring, the hunter took his axe and hacked the giant to pieces. Then he started running home.

However, the Tuniq's wife, who was outside gathering wood for the fire, noticed the hunter. At first she thought he was her husband. "Where are you going?" she asked. "I've got enough wood here to build a fire. Now I'm going to cook the hunter. Soon dinner will be served, so don't rush off."

The hunter did not answer. He just ran all the faster.

The Tuniq's wife got suspicious. She ran after him, crying "Stop!"

As she came closer and was on the verge of overtaking him, the hunter decided to use his magic shamanic powers. He was running on flat ground, so he created high mountains by giving the command, "Rise up, mountains!" Suddenly, many mountains appeared behind him. The Tuniq's wife had to climb the mountains to reach him, and she lagged behind.

But not for long! Soon she was gaining on the hunter again.

The hunter saw a little stream and hopped over it.

When he reached the other side, the hunter said, "Overflow your banks, little brook."

The brook became a river, and the Tuniq's wife could not get across. "How did you manage to cross the river?" she screamed.

"I drank the water until a dry spot appeared," said the hunter. "You can get across the river, too, if you drink up the water."

The Tuniq's wife began drinking. At first she drank great gulps of water until she was full. She grew bigger and bigger with each gulp. Then she took little sips until a dry spot appeared that she could walk across. By now she was full of water and enormous in size. The giantess began waddling across the river coming ever closer to the Inuk hunter.

In desperation, the hunter screamed, "Oh, look! What's that ugly thing hanging down between your legs?"

The Tuniq's wife bent down to see what the hunter was talking about. When she did, it put too much pressure on her belly. Her big belly exploded, spraying fine drops of warm water everywhere.

The tiny drops of water became fog, the first fog people had ever seen. Droplets of water floated in a cloud over the river and nestled at the foot of the mountains. And that is how fog came to be.

The hunter-shaman waited until the wind had blown the fog away and returned home to his family.

PART 5

STORIES ABOUT ANIMALS AND MARRIAGES WITH ANIMALS

WHO SHALL I BE?

(Siberian Yupik)

A bear cub by the name of Kainekhak became very stubborn and refused to obey his parents. "I don't want to be a bear anymore," he said. "I want to be someone else."

After uttering these words, he ran away from home. He wandered on and finally came to the treeless plain known as the tundra. The sun was shining, and there were many beautiful flowers covering the earth. A ground squirrel was sitting beside her burrow with her front paws hanging down, leaning for support on her tail and whistling as if she were singing a song.

"I want to stand rooted to the ground, too, so that I can whistle like the ground squirrel," said the cub.

Kainekhak got up onto a little knoll. He let his front paws hang down and leaned on his tail, just as the ground squirrel had done. Then he began whistling. Instead of a whistle, a tremendous roar came out of his mouth. The ground squirrel got scared and ran away.

The little bear cub was annoyed. He wandered on further and came to a herd of grazing deer. He went up to one of them and asked, "Who are you? I've never seen an animal wearing such a head of antlers before."

"I am a deer."

"I want to be a deer, too."

"All right. It will be more enjoyable to have a friend," said the deer. "Let's run and see who is faster."

While the bear cub was huffing and puffing and hobbling along on his crooked paws, the deer disappeared without a trace.

"It's not so interesting being a deer," Kainekhak mumbled, and he walked on.

He came to a lake. Not far from the lake, he caught sight of a duck. "It would be better if I became a duck," decided Kainekhak. "The duck doesn't walk as fast as the deer, and she knows how to fly."

The bear cub stood on his back paws and waved his front paws as if they were wings. He jumped into the air with all his might—and dropped with a thud onto the ground.

"Let me teach you the right way to fly," the duck proposed. "Go over to the cliff by the shore of the lake, and it will be easier to begin."

The duck went up to the very edge of the cliff, spread her wings, and glided over the water.

Kainekhak followed her. He went to the steepest part of the cliff and leapt into the air. He glided down-down-down—and plopped into the water. He fell head first into the lake and began flailing about with his paws. He swallowed water and snorted it out. The bear cub barely made it back to dry land, where he stood shaking the water off for a long time. The water was ice cold and his teeth were chattering, so the little bear cub found no pleasure in his swim.

He dragged himself away and walked on. Suddenly, he met up with his father and mother and brother. He had never been so happy to see them as he was at that moment.

The little family walked on together in the direction of a berry patch. They were chatting and laughing.

"It's better to be a good bear than to disgrace oneself in front of other animals," Kainekhak decided. From then on, he had no desire to be anyone other than what he was—a bear.

THE WOMAN WHO ADOPTED A POLAR BEAR

(Greenland Inuit)

*T*here once was an old woman living in the Arctic. She lived all alone beside the sea in a sod hut with stone walls and seal-gut windows on one side. When the people living in the village above went hunting, they always brought back meat and blubber for her, too, because it was their custom to share with the elderly, the helpless, and those who had no one to hunt for them the food that had been caught.

One day they came home with a polar bear. The hunters cut off a piece from the bear's ribs for the old woman, and the old woman took the meat home.

Soon afterward, the wife of the man who had killed the bear came to the window of the old woman's dwelling. "Dear little old woman, would you like to have a bear cub?" she asked. "The bear that my husband killed had a cub. Now the little polar bear has no mother and is all alone."

The old woman went to fetch the polar bear cub. He was frozen stiff. The woman took him to her home and set him up on the drying rack to thaw out. After some time had passed, the old woman noticed that the cub moved ever so slightly. She took him down to warm him.

She cooked some blubber because she had heard somewhere that bears like to eat blubber. At first, she fed the cub just a few drops of melted blubber at a time. Later on, she added the bits of skin and meat that had fallen to the bottom of the melted blubber as sediment. At night the polar bear cub slept beside her, and she began to regard him as her son.

The little polar bear grew quickly. The old woman talked to him all the time. It was thus that he acquired the mind of a human being and came to understand human speech. When the bear wanted food, he would sniff to let his adopted mother know that he was hungry.

The old woman never went without food. The people in the village brought food for her, as did her polar bear cub.

Sometimes the village children came to play with the polar bear. At such moments, the old woman always would say, "Remember to sheathe your claws when you play with the children, little bear, so that you don't hurt them."

The children would come to the window in the morning and call to the bear. "Little bear, come out and play with us."

The cub was clumsy, so he broke the children's toys and hunting harpoons, but he never forgot to sheathe his claws if he pushed one of the children. Nevertheless, at last the bear grew so strong that playtime almost always ended with the bear's causing the children to cry. That is why the grown-ups began playing with the bear, in this manner helping the old woman and giving the bear the exercise he needed to grow strong. Finally, not even the village men dared play with the bear because he had grown too strong even for them.

"Let's take the bear with us when we go hunting," one man suggested. "The bear might be able to help us find seals. He might be able to find their breathing holes better than we can."

One morning at dawn, the men came to the old woman's window and cried, "Come hunting with us, bear. Come and earn your share of our catch."

Before he left, the polar bear sniffed at the old woman. Then he went with the men.

"You must keep downwind from the seals, little bear, or they will smell you and run away," one of the men explained.

One day the hunters returned home and stopped at the old woman's house. "Hunters from the north almost killed the little bear today. We barely managed to save his life. Give us some mark by which the bear might be known, old woman, such as a large collar of braided sinew that the bear might wear around his neck."

The bear's adopted mother braided a sinew collar for the bear, large and thick and broad as a harpoon line. Thereafter, the bear never failed to catch seal. He was stronger than the strongest hunter but no bigger than an ordinary bear. Even in the stormiest and snowiest weather, the bear went hunting. Everyone knew the bear, even people in other villages. They sometimes mistook him for a wild bear, but they always let him go when they saw his special collar.

Only a man living beyond Angmagssalik[*] to the north claimed that he would kill the bear if he caught sight of him.

The man's friends scolded him and tried to convince him otherwise. "You mustn't do that," they said. "How would the bear's adopted mother manage without his help? If you see a bear with a collar, leave it alone."

The bear's adopted mother instructed the bear, too, to avoid violence. "Treat all people as if they were your family," she said. "Never hurt them unless they attack you first."

The little polar bear did as he adopted mother said. The old woman kept the bear with her. In summer the bear fished and hunted in the sea, and in winter he hunted on the ice. The other hunters got to know the bear, who gave them shares of his catch.

One day the bear was away hunting during a storm. He returned in the evening. First he sniffed at his adopted mother and then leapt onto the bench where he slept.

[*] Angmagssalik is the largest town on Greenland's East Coast.

The old woman went outside and found the body of a dead man lying there, which the bear had hauled home. She hurried to the nearest home and shouted at the window, "Are all of you at home?"

"Why?"

"The little bear has brought home a dead man and I don't know who he is."

In the morning light, they recognized the man from the north, the one who had threatened to kill the bear earlier. They saw that the dead man had been running fast because he had thrown off his furs and was dressed only in his under breeches. Later, they learned that the dead man's friends had urged the bear to fight back because the man would not leave the little bear alone, but kept pestering and taunting him.

The bear's adopted mother could not forget the horrible incident. It bothered her for a long time. Finally, she said to the bear, "You had better not stay with me anymore. I'm afraid that you'll be killed if you do, and that would be very sad. You had better leave me."

The old woman wept as she spoke. The little polar bear wept, too, lowering his snout right down to the floor. Such was his grief when he was told to leave the only person he had known as a mother.

After the old woman had made the difficult decision to send the bear away, she went out every morning at dawn and looked to see what the weather was like. If there was even one little cloud as big as one's fist in the sky, she said, "It's not a good day to leave, little bear. The weather is bad."

One morning when she went out, the sky was clear. There was not a single cloud, and the sun was shining brightly. "Little bear, today you had better leave. Go find your own kin out there on the ice," the old woman said, and then she sighed.

The bear's adopted mother wept inconsolably. Before the bear set out, she dipped her hands in oil and smeared soot onto them. Then, she stroked the bear's side before he left. The bear did not notice what his foster mother had done. He sniffed at her and went away. All that day the old woman wept. The people living in the village mourned the loss of the bear, too.

People say that far to the north when many bears have gathered and are walking about, sometimes they catch a glimpse of a polar bear as big as an iceberg with a black spot on his side. They like to think that it is the old woman's bear.

The story ends here.

THE OWL AND THE SIKSIK

(Canadian Inuit and Alaskan Inupiat)

The Inuit call the Arctic marmot, or ground squirrel, siksik *because "sik-sik" is the clicking sound that the ground squirrel makes. The animal looks very much like its relative, the prairie dog. They are herbivores that collect seeds in autumn and live on their seed cache when they awake from hibernation in their underground tunnels. The* siksik *has been around for a very long time. Yukon miners have found ancient nests that date back more than 90,000 years.[1]*

*O*ne day an owl was out hunting *siksik*s. He spied one near a hole that was the entrance to its burrow. As the owl walked over to the *siksik* to grab it, the little creature darted into the burrow.

The owl approached the burrow and began coaxing the animal to come out. "It's warm outdoors. It's a beautiful day. Come out and play," the owl said.

"You'll just block the entrance to my home," the *siksik* complained.

Still, the owl persisted. "Oh, please do come out and play, *siksik*."

Finally, the *siksik* gave in and ventured out.

The owl immediately stood in front of the entrance to the animal's hole so that he could not go back inside. The *siksik* understood that the owl did not have good intentions. Indeed, the owl planned to catch the *siksik* and eat it for dinner.

The clever little creature decided to distract the owl. "It's a beautiful day, just as you said. I am so happy that I'm going to do a little dance. Will you sing for me while I dance?"

The owl began singing, "Who-who-who-o-o-o! I've blocked the *siksik*'s burrow, *sik-sik, siksik*."

As the owl sang his sinister song, the *siksik* darted toward the safety of the burrow with a sharp clicking sound—*sik-sik, sik-sik*. Just as the little creature neared the entrance, the owl stood directly in front of it and stopped the *siksik* from going inside.

"How do you suppose you'll get into your burrow now, *siksik*?" asked the owl.

"Oh, I wasn't going to try to get into my house," said the *siksik*. "I was just running over to get this blade of grass."

Then, the *siksik* said, "What a pretty song. Sing louder, cousin. Spread your legs wide and sing for me while I dance."

The owl spread its legs, and the *siksik* danced around the owl faster and faster until the owl complained, "You're making me dizzy."

"Then, close your eyes, owl. And spread your legs wider so that you won't lose your balance."

The owl spread his legs apart even wider and closed his eyes. He sang, "Who-who-who-o-o! I've blocked the *siksik*'s burrow, *siksik*, *siksik*, who-who-who-o-o!"

As the owl was singing, the animal made a dash for the hole with a sharp squeak—*sik-sik*, *sik-sik*. This time the *siksik* was able to squeeze through the owl's legs and get safely into the burrow.

THE BOLD LITTLE MOUSE

(Nenets)

*S*pring had come. The sun was warming the earth and breaking up the ice on the river. Ice floes were making a ringing sound as they piled on top of each other and drifted down the river.

Mouse, hearing the noise, jumped onto a knoll and shouted, "Ice, oh, Ice, float a little further from shore. My nest is beyond the cape. Watch that you don't destroy it!"

A big chunk of ice answered Mouse. "When Ice is floating, no one can bring it to a stop."

Mouse got angry. Her fur bristled. "You needn't be so proud, Ice," she said. "Right now you are sitting in the shallow part of the river with Sun warming you. When Sun has melted you, nothing will be left of you."

The block of ice became silent. Having overheard the conversation, Sun said, "Hey, there, Mouse, you are very insolent and presumptuous. Is it any of your business that I melt Ice? Why have you forced your neighbor, who is older than you and therefore deserving of respect, to be silent?"

Little Mouse lifted her head boldly and shouted, "And you needn't be proud either, Sun. I see Storm Cloud coming. When Storm Cloud covers you up, what use will you be then?"

Sun fell silent. Then Storm Cloud said, "Why are you so quarrelsome, Mouse? Is it any business of yours that I sometimes cover Sun? Why have you made your neighbor, who is older than you and therefore deserving of respect, silent?"

Mouse screamed at the Storm Cloud. "You don't have any reason to put on airs either, Storm Cloud. When Wind blows, it will drive you wherever it wants. It will rip you to pieces."

Storm Cloud became silent. Then Wind began blowing. "You have a bold tongue, Little Mouse," said Wind. "If I chase Storm Cloud around the sky, what is it to you? Why have you made your neighbor, who is older than you and therefore deserving of respect, silent?"

There was no calming Little Mouse. "I don't even want to listen to you, Wind. You've got nothing to brag about. You can't fly far. And when you bump into the Ural Mountains, · that's the end of your strength."

Wind, knowing that it was impossible to fly over the Ural Mountains, became silent. The stones of the Ural Mountains heard the words of angry little Mouse and began to rumble. "You are less than a grain of sand, Mouse, and yet you quarrel with your elders. What business is it of yours if I block Wind's way?"

Mouse turned toward the Ural Mountains. "Maybe I *am* small, and maybe you *are* big. So what? Anyone who wants to can trample all over you. At this very moment Wolverine is climbing over your stones, and you can't even drive her away."

The Ural Mountains fell silent, and Wolverine spoke. "Don't interfere in something that is none of your business, Mouse. Don't make me angry, or I'll gobble you up, together with your claws and tail."

"Go ahead and get angry to your heart's content, Wolverine. What will you have to say when you fall into a wooden trap?"

Wolverine fell silent. Little Mouse waited to hear what the wooden trap would say to her. But the trap did not say anything. It was made of wood and did not know how to talk.

Mouse decided that she had out-argued everyone. She stuck her nose high in the air, waved her tail, and walked toward her nest.

When she got there, her nest was gone. While she had been quarreling, Ice had rounded the cape, and pushed against the shore. Ice carried her home away.

Mouse considered what had happened and said, "I guess I didn't win the argument after all. I only wasted time needlessly."

After making that observation, she set to work building a new nest, wiser than she had been before.[1]

THE EAGLE AND WHALE HUSBANDS

(Inuit)

*T*wo little girls were playing with bones they had found on the beach. One girl had found an eagle's bone. "This bone will become my husband," she declared.

Her sister had found a whale's bone. Not to be outdone, she said, "And this bone will become my husband."

Suddenly, the eagle's bone disappeared and an eagle came soaring through the air toward them. He swooped down, grabbed the girl who had been playing with the eagle's bone, and spirited her off to his nest on top of a high cliff. "Now you are my wife," said the eagle.

"But I am too young," the girl said. The eagle just ignored her words.

At the same time, the whale's bone disappeared, but an enormous whale came into view, spouting water. The whale snatched up the sister who had been playing with the whale's bone. "You will be my wife," the whale declared. He dragged the girl down to the bottom of the sea.

The girl said that she was too young to marry, just as her sister had done. The whale did not listen.

Every day the eagle went hunting for food. The girl with the eagle husband was very unhappy because the eagle brought only birds back to his nest. The diet was monotonous.

The young bride devised a plan. She began gathering sinew from the wings of the birds that the eagle brought home and knotting it together to make a rope. She encouraged her husband to bring many more birds home, and the sinew rope grew longer and longer. Finally, the day came when the sinew rope reached the bottom of the cliff.

One day when the eagle had gone hunting, the little girl saw a lone kayaker sailing along the shore. She shouted, "Please send a boat to rescue me. An eagle is holding me prisoner."

Soon a boat appeared. The little girl slid down the cliff on her sinew rope. She boarded the boat and reached home, where her dear parents and two brothers were eagerly awaiting her return.

When the eagle returned to his nest and found his wife missing, he raced after her. In an instant, he was at the beach, where originally he had found her. It was not long before he spied the girl's home. He beat his wings and swooped down to scoop up his wife, but a hail of arrows greeted him. His wife's brothers were shooting at him.

Finally, one of the brothers cried, "If you want to show that you have married into our family, spread your wings wide."

When the eagle did so, the brothers shot many arrows into his vulnerable body. The eagle fell to the ground dead. In time the eagle became a bone once again.

The other sister, who had been kidnapped by the whale, lived in the whale's enormous home at the bottom of the sea. The whale built the house of his bones and fed his wife his flesh. The whale was jealous. Whenever his wife had to go outside to the toilet, he tied her to the bottom of the sea by a rope and would not let her out of his sight for fear that she would run away.

The girl found the whale's attentions oppressive and longed for the freedom of home and her dear sister and brothers. She sat tied up and bored all day long while her husband went hunting. When he returned, her only amusement was picking whale lice from his body.

Meanwhile, her brothers began building a swift-sailing boat called an *umiak,* with which to rescue their sister. They convinced a guillemot, a shore bird, to race with them. The guillemot flew past them easily.

"This won't do," they declared. Then, they took the *umiak* apart and built a new, swifter boat. Once again they raced with the guillemot. This time they outdistanced it. The brothers set out to fetch their sister.

Their sister heard their approach and said to the whale, "I must go outside."

"Go," her husband said, "but I will hold the end of the rope so that you can't go far."

The girl was barely out the door when she felt her husband tugging at the rope. "I'm still in the passageway," she shouted.

Once outside, she loosened the rope and twisted it around a stone. Then she ran to her brothers' *umiak* and hopped in. The *umiak* dashed away.

The pesky whale learned of her escape in no time at all. Once again, he pulled on the rope to get hold of her and discovered a stone at the other end. He chased the boat and came upon it so quickly that it seemed as if the *umiak* was standing still.

As the whale drew near the boat, the girls' brothers screamed, "Throw your outer jacket into the water."

Their sister threw her jacket into the water, and the whale snapped at it. When he realized that it was only his wife's jacket, he set out in hot pursuit again.

When he got too close, the girl threw her inner jacket at him. The sea foamed and the whale stopped, but not for long.

"Drop your trousers into the water," screamed the girl's brothers.

She did so. The whale whipped the seawater into foam as he dove for the trousers.

Soon the whale was upon them for the fourth time. The brothers cried, "Throw out your mitten!"

The girl threw out her mitten, and the sea foamed again. Before the whale could overtake them, they had reached the shore.

The whale tried to follow, but he was cast onto the shore as a white, sun-bleached whale's bone.

Both sisters returned to their home and lived there happily for many years. They never mentioned husbands again until they were of marriageable age.

A Chukchi family seventy years ago in Chukotka, the Russian Far East. Courtesy of Zina Sergeevna Nikitina.

A Chukchi woman of seventy years ago in Chukotka, the Russian Far East. Courtesy of Zina Sergeevna Nikitina.

Performance of Karelian folk dancers and singers. Photograph by Bonnie C. Marshall.

Performance of traditional Nenets songs and dances. Photograph by Bonnie C. Marshall.

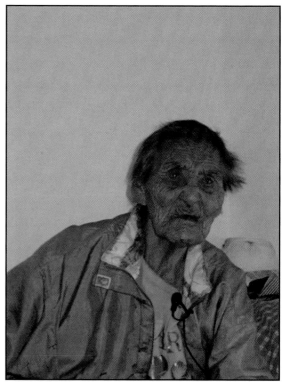

Inuit elder Niviuvak Marqniq telling the story of Kiviuq in 2004. She was one of the last elders to have facial tattoos. Photo courtesy of Kira Van Deusen.

Inuit throat singers Trisha Marie Ogina and Jerilyn Kaniak, Cambridge Bay Nunavut, 2004. Photo courtesy of Kira Van Deusen.

Forty Mile River, Alaska. Photograph by Joyce Hill.

Russian-style onion dome in Skagway, Alaska, testifies to Russia's presence in Alaska prior to the 1867 purchase of Alaska from Russia by the United States. Photograph by Joyce Hill.

Northern polar lights or *Aurora borealis*. Auroras are light displays, energized by solar winds. They are a common sight in the Arctic Circle. Photograph by Paul Northcott.

Sunset viewed through caribou antlers at Lobstick Lake in Labrador. Photograph by Paul Northcott.

A cabin with a sod roof. Photograph by Joyce Hill.

Smelt and sea trout are common foods of the Arctic and Subarctic peoples. These were caught at Mulligan Bay, which is located on the northern shore of Lake Melville, Labrador. Photograph by Paul Northcott.

This polar bear resides at the Moose Creek Lodge Museum, located between Minto and Dawson City, Yukon Territory, Canada. Photograph by Eva Irene Muir.

Caribou from the George River herd. In autumn they migrate south to Labrador and Quebec. The George River is in Nunavik, Canada. Its mouth is at Ungava Bay. Photograph by Paul Northcott.

Osprey nest. The osprey is a raptor that nests near water and eats fish. This nest was found on Forebay, which is part of the reservoir that supplies water to the Churchill Falls Power Plant in Labrador. Photograph by Paul Northcott.

Fishing seagull. The seagull is the heroine of "The Man Who Married a Seagull." The white Arctic gull, or Ross's Gull, breeds in the Arctic of North America and Siberia. Photograph by Paul Northcott.

Siberian birch bark box. Birch bark is waterproof and is thought to have antibacterial properties. Boxes were used to store liquids and food. Photograph by Bonnie C. Marshall.

Wolf spirit mask for skill at hunting. Cottonwood bark mask by Adam John, Athabaskan of Alaska. Photograph by Bonnie C. Marshall.

Doll handmade by the Sakha, who were once called Yakuts. The Sakha Republic (Yakutia), located in the far north of eastern Siberia, is almost half the size of the United States. Photograph by Bonnie C. Marshall.

Totem pole. Photograph by Joyce Hill.

Miniature Siberian boots hang from a decoration made of reindeer skin. Reindeer provide the basic food and clothing of Siberia's reindeer herders. Photograph by Bonnie C. Marshall.

THE MAN WHO MARRIED A SEAGULL

(Inuit)

A childless old bachelor used to pretend that the skulls of seals were his children. He played a game with the skulls, placing them on the beach before going out seal hunting in his kayak.

Once out on the sea, he would turn to the seal skulls and before parting he would say, "Now be good, children, and go straight to the house."

When he returned, of course the skulls were in the very place he had left them. They had not budged an inch. "Are you deaf and dumb, children?" he would ask. "Didn't I tell you to stay away from the water before I set out this morning?"

Then he would grab a skull and throw it into the sea. "See, your little brother has fallen into the water!" he would point out to the other skulls in admonishment.

On one occasion, feeling sad and lonely, he ran inland far from the sea and came upon many naked women bathing in a lake. They had placed their clothes on the shore of the lake.

As the old bachelor watched them, an idea came to him. "I think I know how to get myself a wife and have children of my own," he thought.

The old bachelor crept noiselessly up to the place where the women had placed their clothes. He grabbed the garment belonging to the most beautiful woman of all and stepped forward, holding it.

The women noticed him and rushed to the spot where their clothing lay. After hurriedly throwing on their clothes, they turned into seagulls and flew away. Only the beautiful woman who had been robbed of her clothing remained.

The old bachelor walked up to her. "Would you like to be my wife?" he asked.

"I will be your wife if you give back my clothes," the woman agreed.

The old bachelor gave the beautiful woman her clothing, but he held onto her just in case she should be tempted to fly away with the others. He took her home and married her.

The next morning, for the first time in a long while, he did not venture out in his kayak because he was afraid that his beautiful wife would take flight while he was gone. Eventually, he gave up kayaking altogether.

Finally, one day his wife said, "You may leave me now without fear. I won't fly away because I have come to love you truly. You may depend on me."

The man, no longer an old bachelor now, began going seal hunting again. He and his sea bird wife lived together happily.

The day came when his wife gave birth to a son. When the son grew into a young man, another son was born to them. Thereafter, they had no more children.

When the boys grew up, their mother sometimes took them for a walk. On their journey, she would tell the boys to gather bird wings and feathers that they found near the sea. "Pick up all the feathers that you find, sons, and put them into your sealskin sacks. Always remember that your relatives are birds."

One day she fastened a pair of wings she had fashioned from the collected feathers onto the oldest boy, who immediately became a seagull and flew away. She did the same to his younger brother, who flew after him. Then, she put on a pair of wings and followed her sons in the shape of a seagull. "We are going home to our people," she cried.

The old husband came home and found that his wife and sons had left him. He grew very sad. Nevertheless, he continued to go out in his kayak, although he no longer chased seals.

One day he disembarked close to a sand hill. He left his kayak on the beach and crossed the hill. Traveling on, he walked a considerable distance into the countryside.

Eventually, the old husband came to a man sitting beside a lake with his back turned toward him. The man was working away at a piece of timber with his axe. As the old husband approached the man, he noticed that the man's legs were visibly trembling and that the chips of wood were falling into the lake and turning into salmon.

"What direction are you approaching from?" asked the trembling man.

"I'm approaching from your side," replied the old husband.

"Fine. If you had been approaching me from behind, I would have killed you on the spot," said Salmon Man. He did not want the husband to see that he was hollow inside from his backside to his mouth.

"Have you seen my wife and two sons?" the old husband asked.

Salmon Man remained silent.

"Tell me where they are, and I will give you my new kayak."

"I have no need of your kayak. And I haven't seen the three people you mentioned."

"I see that you are working with wood. I'll give you my new axe. Just let me know whether you have seen my wife and sons."

"Well, my axe is getting rather worn. All right, I'll help you. Another man has asked your wife to marry him, and you may be too late to stop the marriage. Go down to the river and sit on the tail of the giant salmon that is waiting there for you. But mind that you don't open your eyes, even when you hear children's voices."

The old husband did as Salmon Man instructed. After reaching the river, he sat on the salmon's tail and was whisked along the water. The old man shut his eyes tightly. When he heard waters rushing, the old husband opened his eyes a slit and peeped. He noticed that a rapid current was carrying him up the river. He shut his eyes again and heard nothing at all.

Suddenly, he heard the voices of children crying. Still, he did as instructed and did not open his eyes. The salmon flipped its tail and flung the old husband ashore.

The old man heard children crying, "Mother, Father is coming!"

"We left your father, and he has no way to reach us. He can't possibly find us."

The boys persisted. "But it's true, Mother. Father is coming!"

The old husband stood and walked toward a big house with fine, sealskin windows. He peered through a window and noticed that many women were in the house.

His seagull wife was sitting close to the back wall. A man with a pug nose was sitting opposite her, repeating, "Will you marry me?"

The seagull wife replied, "No, I won't marry you. I already have a husband."

Everyone left the house so that only the seagull wife and pug-nosed man remained. Finally, the pug-nosed man left, too. The old husband entered the house and tried to take his wife back, but she rushed out, following the pug-nosed man.

As the old husband pursued his wife, she turned into a seagull and joined the rest of the women, who had become gulls as well. The pug-nosed man turned into a wild duck that rushed after the gull women.

The rejected husband turned around and looked at the place where the fine house had been. The house was no longer there. It had turned into a little hill of turf and moss that had formed on top of a mound of bird guano.[*]

* Manure.

THE FOX WIFE

(Inuit)

There once was a hunter who lived alone. One day when he returned home from hunting, he found that everything in his home had been put in order, just as if he had a dutiful wife. The house had been cleaned, his meal was cooking on the stove, and his old pair of skin boots, or *kamik*s, had been scraped and were drying beside the fire.

No one was inside the house, so he looked outside. Not a soul was there. Puzzled, the hunter ate the meal prepared for him and lay down to sleep.

The next day, he went hunting as usual and returned to find that once again someone had done the housework. And once again there were no tracks, no sign of anyone's presence.

This happened for several days. Finally, curiosity got the best of the hunter. He devised a plan to find out who had been caring for him and his home.

The next day, he left his home as if he were going on a hunt. But instead, he hid behind a pile of rocks and watched the entrance of his house.

After a while, he saw a fox enter his home. "That fox must be after my food," he said.

Then he slipped quietly into his house. Once inside, he could not believe his eyes. He saw a beautiful woman dressed in fine skin clothing with a lovely red topknot on her head. A fox skin was hanging on the wall.

"Are you the one who has been cleaning my house and cooking my food?" he asked.

"Yes, I have been cleaning your house and cooking your food because I am your wife. Isn't that what a wife is supposed to do? Are you happy with my work?"

"Very happy, indeed," the hunter replied. "Will you stay with me from now on without leaving when I come home?"

"I will stay on one condition," Fox Woman replied. "You must promise never to complain about me."

The hunter agreed to her condition without giving it too much thought. Thereafter, they lived together happily as man and wife.

One day the hunter smelled a musky odor in the house. "What is that bad smell?" he asked the fox wife, turning up his nose.

"The smell is coming from me," Fox Woman admitted. "You have broken your promise never to complain about me. If my smell is objectionable to you, I must leave."

Fox Woman threw off her fine, fur dress and put on her fox skin, which had been hanging on the wall. She slipped quietly out of the house in the form of a fox.

Fox Woman never visited the hunter again. She had gone forever. From that day on, the hunter had to live alone and do all of the work himself.

THE CRANE'S FEATHER

(Sakha/Yakut)

*S*tories are told about a brave hunter named Yudzhian. Stories are told about his little brother Khodzhugur, too, stories about their life together and about what happened to them.

The two brothers had no mother or father. The older boy, Yudzhian, was both mother and father to his brother. He could be found hunting in the forest as soon as the rim of the sun peeked over the horizon while his little brother was still sleeping. When the sun rose higher in the sky, Khodzhugur, the younger boy, would get up, sweep the yard, and feed the horses and cows. Toward evening he would make a fire on the hearth and Yudzhian would return from the hunt.

Yudzhian always brought home a great deal of wild game. He drove fur-bearing animals out of their burrows before the light of day. At the dawn's light, he chased after three-year-old elk. At twilight, he wrestled with bears. Whenever he caught sight of a pack of wolves, he felled them without making an error. The brothers always had enough soft fur skins, fat, and meat in their nomad's conical tent, called a *urasa*.

One day Yudzhian had gone off to hunt as usual. Little Khodzhugur remained at home. When Khodzhugur came out of the *urasa* to sweep and clean the yard, he heard a cry overhead. He looked up and saw seven white cranes circling overhead. Their wings were flecked with a rosy color when the sun shone on them, and their wings reflected a blue color in the shadow. Khodzhugur waved to the cranes, and they flew lower.

"Who is home?" they asked.

"I am home alone," Khodzhugur answered. "My older brother has gone hunting."

"Shall we play with the little boy, sisters?" a crane asked. "It would be fun for him, and it wouldn't be boring for us."

The cranes descended to the middle of the big yard. They circled around the yard on their long legs. Then, they threw off their skins and white feathers and became beautiful girls. They organized interesting games. They played hide-and-seek, danced, and set up races with Khodzhugur. They went into the *urasa* and put everything topsy-turvy. They played and laughed all day long.

At sunset they hurried to gather their skins and white feathers. They threw them on and turned into cranes again. Flapping their wings, they flew away.

Yudzhian, the older brother, returned home with his catch. He looked around. The yard was not swept, the cows in the shed were mooing, and the unwatered horses were whinnying in their stalls. The wood had not been chopped, the water had not been fetched, and the fire had not been made in the *urasa*.

"Why haven't you done your work?" Yudzhian asked Khodzhugur.

"I'm sorry, brother," Khodzhugur answered. "I slept all day long. I thought it was sunrise, and it was sunset."

The older brother laughed. He did not get angry. They did the work together quickly. They fed the cows, watered the horses, and prepared food for themselves. After eating, they lay down to sleep.

The next morning, as soon as his brother was out of the yard, Khodzhugur jumped up. He did not luxuriate on the soft skins or lie about on the downy coverlets. He ran out of the *urasa*, looked up, and saw the cranes already circling in the sky above the yard.

"He's gone! My brother's gone!" Khodzhugur called to them. "Come down quickly!"

The cranes alighted and became girls. They organized the same games as they had the day before. Again, Khodzhugur failed to notice the day passing. When they left, the cranes said, "Don't say anything about us to your brother. If you say a single word, we won't fly to you anymore."

The cranes flew away, melting into the blue sky, like snowflakes. Khodzhugur set to work, but it was too late. His brother was already returning home, leading a deer with big antlers by the snout.

Yudzhian looked around and saw that nothing had been tidied up; nothing had been cleaned. He got angry. "Are you going to say that you slept through the day again today?"

"Yes," Khodzhugur answered.

Yudzhian shook Khodzhugur not out of spite, but to teach him a lesson. "Something isn't right," Yudzhian thought. "There must be a reason for my brother's behavior. He never was lazy before. He did what had to be done and willingly."

The next morning Yudzhian rose early, as usual. He grabbed his bow and arrows and went out of the *urasa*, but he did not leave for the forest. He fell to the ground and jumped from the ground like a flea. He hid in a trench in the garden. He hid, and he waited.

Khodzhugur did not sleep or luxuriate, oh, no. He ran out of the *urasa*, stood in the middle of the yard by the tethering post, and raised his head. The "flea" stuck its head out of the trench and looked up, too, Cranes were circling overhead.

They spoke in human voices with a crane's cry. "Hey, little Khodzhugur, has your brother gone?"

"He's gone. He's gone!" Khodzhugur cried, waving his arms joyfully. "Come down, come down quickly!"

The cranes did not alight. "Why is there a shadow on your yard? Why is your home and fire shrouded in a dark fog?"

"It just seems so to you," Khodzhugur answered. "The sun hasn't risen very high yet. You can see the sun over there, but it hasn't come here yet."

"Then your brother isn't at home?" the cranes asked again.

"No, no! He has already reached the forest and is tracking an animal."

The seven cranes alighted in the middle of the big yard. They threw their skins and feathers onto the tethering post and turned into girls.

Yudzhian became lost in admiration of them. All of the girls were beautiful, but one of them—the one whose skin was hanging on the edge of the tethering post—was more beautiful than the others. The crane girls played and ran about, but she ran faster than the others. They danced, but she raised her feet more easily, as if she were not touching the ground. Little Khodzhugur kept closer to her and kept striving to play with her.

The day was declining. "Soon your brother will return. It's time to leave," the girls told Khodzhugur.

While sitting in his trench, Yudzhian thought, "My little brother told the truth. I didn't notice how the day passed either. It is as if I had a lovely dream."

The girls went up to the tethering post and extended their hands toward the crane skins. Like a flea, Yudzhian jumped to the post ahead of them. He turned near the tethering post and grabbed the skin hanging on its edge.

Six white cranes rose into the sky. One girl writhed on the ground and begged the hunter to give back her skin.

Yudzhian would not give back her skin. "I have been looking at you all day long," he said. "I have been admiring you. Now, look at me. If you don't like me, take your skin and fly wherever you want. If you like me, stay and be my wife."

Through her tears, the girl looked at the hunter. Then, she dried her eyes and smiled at him. "I'll stay," she said softly.

"What should we do with your skin?" Yudzhian asked. "Should we hang it on a pole in the *urasa* or throw it into the fire?"

The girl's face turned as pale as newly fallen snow. "Don't throw it into the fire. If you do, misfortune will come of it. And don't hang it in the *urasa*. I'll be tempted to fly into the sky some spring day, and then I'll forget everything and will have no mercy on you or on myself. I'll fly away! Bury it somewhere where no hands can touch it and no eyes can see it."

Yudzhian hid the skin and the white feathers in a trunk forged with iron. He locked the trunk with three locks. He hung the keys on a peg by the door.

Yudzhian and his beautiful wife lived well. When they awoke in the morning, they greeted one another. His wife would get her husband ready to go hunting, weeping all the while as if he were leaving forever. In the evening, Yudzhian would hurry home as if he had not seen his wife for a year.

The *urasa* was always tidy. The inviting fire was always burning; it never went out. The cattle were fed, and the yard was swept.

The only bad thing was that the boy Khodzhugur had gotten quite out of hand. Formerly, the household work had been his responsibility. Now the young bride did everything. Khodzhugur ran about all day long, dreaming up various amusements. Thus, autumn passed, as did winter.

One day Yudzhian's beautiful wife went to fetch water. She went up to the river and forgot why she had come. The bright sky caused the water to turn sky blue. Singing birds had begun weaving their nests. Everything was in bloom. She stood there for a long time. Finally, she remembered what she had come for. She scooped up some water and carried it home.

For a long time, the boy Khodzhugur had dreamed of becoming a hunter and helping his brother. Yudzhian kept dissuading him, saying that he was still too young, that he did not know how to use a bow and arrow. While his sister-in-law was fetching water, Khodzhugur remembered his brother's old bow and arrows were somewhere, but he did not know exactly where they were. If only he could find them, he could learn on the sly how to shoot. Then, Yudzhian would be amazed.

Khodzhugur rummaged through the *urasa*, looking into every corner, but there was no bow anywhere. "Could it be hidden in the trunk?" he asked.

He took three keys from the peg and opened the three locks on the trunk. He lifted the heavy lid. Although he found no bow and arrows, he saw a crane's skin with white feathers. He took it out and began inspecting it. What beautiful feathers!

His sister-in-law came in. She stopped short and stared. "Give me the skin," she ordered. Her voice seemed to be unlike her normal voice. It seemed that the voice of a crane was resounding far, far away in the sky.

Khodzhugur hid the skin behind his back. "I won't give it to you," he said. "Yudzhian had a reason for locking it in the trunk. I took it out by accident. Now I'm putting it back."

"Let me just hold it," the beautiful girl said. "I'll give you my golden pendants if you let me hold it."

"I'm not a girl! Why would I want your golden pendants?"

"I'll give you my belt, the one embroidered in silver."

"A man has no need of a woman's belt."

"I'll give you my knife in exchange for the skin. The knife with the handle with designs on it and with the decorated sheath."

Khodzhugur's eyes began to glow. "Your special hunting knife?" asked the boy. "Give it to me!" He grabbed the knife and threw the crane's skin to his sister-in-law.

The Crane's Feather

She threw the skin over her shoulders and turned into a white crane. She went out into the yard, stepping carefully on her long legs. She was afraid to flap her wings. She was afraid she would be torn from the earth and carried away into the sky. Yudzhian would miss her, and she would wither away of melancholy without him.

She wanted to throw off the skin, but she heard a crane's call. Six cranes were circling above the *urasa,* calling her to join them. She jumped, stretching her wings wide with a mournful cry.

Khodzhugur ran out in fright when he heard the cry. He rushed toward her. He wanted to grab her by the wing but did not succeed in doing so. The crane flew away. Only a feather was left in Khodzhugur's hand.

Seven cranes made a parting circle over the *urasa.* They circled higher, higher, and higher until they were hidden behind the clouds.

Khodzhugur followed them with his eyes. He waved and said, "But you asked only to hold the skin. I'll never believe a woman again!"

He sat in the middle of the yard. He put the feather down beside him and began playing with the knife. That is how his brother found him when he returned from the hunt.

"Where did you get that knife?" Yudzhian asked.

"Your wife gave it to me."

"And where did that feather come from?"

Khodzhugur was silent. His brother grabbed him by the shoulders and shook him. He understood that something bad had happened.

Khodzhugur started crying. "I found the skin accidentally. Your wife asked me to let her just hold the skin. But she put on the skin and flew away. The other cranes called her to go with them."

Yudzhian never had spanked his brother out of spite, but now Khodzhugur learned for the first time in his life how frightening an angry person can be. Yudzhian hit him with a whip and called him a dog.

After alleviating his anger, Yudzhian calmed down. He pushed Khodzhugur away and rushed to the stable. He led his horse out of the stall and mounted it. The golden brown piebald horse with the blonde mane and tail bounded beneath him. Yudzhian scooped the white feather up from the ground and left the yard without looking back at his brother.

Holding the rein in one hand and the crane's feather in the other, Yudzhian galloped away on his piebald horse. The feather turned, pointing out the direction in which to ride.

Yudzhian rode on for a long time. He crossed rivers on his horse, rode around lakes, forced his way through thick forests, and galloped up and down ravines. He spent nights under the open sky, sheltering himself from the wind behind his horse's broad back. He lost count of the days and nights.

Finally, he reached the foot of a high mountain. The feather stood straight, pointing up with its sharp end. Yudzhian left the horse pasturing in a green meadow, and he began climbing. The mountain slopes were steep. The first day Yudzhian mastered only a quarter of the height. The second day, he was only halfway to the top. Then, his strength increased. He saw a white *urasa* at the top. The cliffs became steeper, the crevices wider, and the stones sharper. He kept crawling and clambering until he reached the summit.

He went into the white *urasa*. It was neat and beautiful. A merry fire was blazing on the hearth. A golden cradle was standing in the middle of the room, and Chychakh Bird was rocking the cradle.

Having noticed that a man had come in, the bird was alarmed and began crying, "Cheep, cheep, cheep." Then, it spoke in a human voice. "Aren't you called Yudzhian? Are you looking for your wife?"

"My name is Yudzhian, and I am looking for my wife," Yudzhian answered, but he could not take his eyes off the cradle.

"Well," said Chychakh Bird, "look at your son."

Yudzhian bent over the cradle. A handsome child was lying there. He noticed Yudzhian and stretched his chubby little arms toward him.

"Cheep-cheep," said the bird. "The part seeks the whole. Blood is thicker than water. Amuse your son, Yudzhian. I have grown tired of rocking the cradle."

Yudzhian turned into a white ermine and ran up and down in the cradle, jumping and turning somersaults. The little boy laughed.

Then, light footsteps were heard. The door squeaked, and the bird said, "If you don't want your wife to see you, hide quickly!"

Yudzhian, disguised as an ermine, hid behind some animal skins. Having lost his amusement, the child cried loudly. A white crane ran into the *urasa*. She quickly threw off her skin, rushed to the child, and took him up in her arms. Feeling his mother's warmth, the child quieted down.

The ermine came out from under the sealskins and became Yudzhian again. He grabbed the crane's skin and threw it into the fire.

His beautiful wife let out a cry and looked around. "Oh, why did you do that?" she whispered, reproaching her husband. And she fell down dead.

Yudzhian picked her up in his arms and clasped her to his chest. He warmed her with his breath, hoping to return her to life. But his wife was not moving. She was locked in a deathly dream. Yudzhian placed her body on the sealskins. He hung his head.

"My unlucky day has come. A time of sorrow has come. She told me everything beforehand. She predicted it. 'If you throw the skin into the fire, misfortune will come of it.' But I gave will to my ardent heart and quick hand, and so misfortune has struck. I, myself, am guilty, and I will answer for it. I'll battle weakness with strength and simplicity with cunning. I'll atone for my impulsiveness with patience."

Yudzhian ran out of the *urasa*. He saw a light cloud that lingered near the mountain. He took a run and leapt onto it. The cloud sailed away, rocking and swaying. The sun had already set. The sky was turning dark. The cloud sailed along a great starry path. It sailed to a constellation and stopped.

Yudzhian stepped from the cloud onto the ground. He looked around. It was the same kind of place on the constellation as it was on earth below. There was earth, a home, and a fire. A girl was sitting on an eight-legged copper pedestal. She was letting down her eight *sazhen** silken scarlet hair, winding it on a silver staff and combing it with a golden comb.

"Daughter of the Constellation Yurgial',"** Yudzhian said to her. "Oh, Fearsome Shaman Yurgiuk, I have come to make you my wife. Will you marry me?"

The Daughter of the Constellation Yurgial' looked at him. The man who had come courting her was stately and handsome. "Yes, I'll marry you," she answered softly.

"Then, gather your attire and prepare for a journey. I'll wait for you at the top of the high mountain."

Fearsome Shaman Yurgiuk began bustling about. She gathered her apparel, her head-dresses, and called to the cattle that were part of her dowry.

Yudzhian traveled on. He came to the Moon's *urasa*. There, a girl was sitting on an eight-legged copper pedestal. Having let down her eight *sazhen** silken silvery hair, she was combing it with a golden comb while winding it on a silver staff.

"Daughter of the Moon, Shaman of the Moonlight," Yudzhian said to her, "I have come to marry you. Will you be my wife?"

Daughter of the Moon looked at him. Boldness was depicted on Yudzhian's face. The eyes of her suitor sparkled with intelligence.

"I'll marry you," she said. "Just give me time to gather my dowry."

"I don't have time," said Yudzhian. "Do everything as quickly as possible. Then come to the top of the high mountain. I will await you there."

Daughter of the Moon, Shaman of the Moonlight, began bustling about gathering her attire and headdresses. She called to the cattle that were part of her dowry.

Yudzhian traveled on. While he was walking, night ended. The Sun's *urasa* was shining in the distance. Yudzhian went toward it.

Beside the shining *urasa,* a girl was sitting on an eight-legged copper pedestal. She was combing her eight *sazhen** silken sunny hair with a golden comb while winding it on a silver staff.

"Shaman Kiuyogial', Daughter of the Sun," said Yudzhian, "I have come to marry you if you wish and if you will have me."

Shaman Kiuyogial' looked at her father, the Sun, without blinking. But while looking at Yudzhian, she squinted. Her love for the suitor, who had come to ask her hand in marriage, had blinded her.

---

* A *sazhen* is equal almost to fifty-six feet.
** Yurgial' is the Pleiades. —Kira Van Deusen

"I'll marry you. Why not?" she said to Yudzhian.

Yudzhian ordered her to gather her things and go to the top of the high mountain. Shaman Kiuyogial' prepared her dowry, and Yudzian hurried on.

He ran to the edge of the earth and jumped onto the same cloud that had brought him there. Then, he set out on his return route. The cloud sailed to the high mountain and came down at the summit.

In the *urasa* Chychakh Bird was rocking Yudzhian's child, and his dead wife was lying on the sealskins. Yudzhian dressed her in his clothes and tucked her hair into his cap. Then he carried her out of the *urasa* and placed her in front of the entrance. He hid behind the *urasa*.

He just managed to do everything before his brides arrived on three horses from three different directions. Each had a rich dowry. In their saddle straps were dresses and precious furs. Each had eighty herds of horses and ninety herds of cattle. The herds covered the slopes of the mountain.

The brides got off their horses. They noticed one another. "Friends, sisters," they said, "as it turns out, all three of us are wives of the same man. It appears that it won't be boring living here. But where is our husband? Let's go into the *urasa*. Maybe he's asleep."

They walked with light, heavenly steps toward the *urasa*. Suddenly, all three of them stopped. One said, "Oh, sisters, a dead man is lying there."

Another said, "Isn't that our husband?"

Yet another looked and said, "It's he! It's he! He's wearing the same clothes he wore while courting us."

Shaman Kiuyogial', Daughter of the Sun, asked, "Oh Fearsome Shaman, Daughter of Yurgial', do you know how to bring back the dead?"

"To say that I know how to bring back the dead would be a lie, and to say that I don't know how to bring back the dead would be a lie," Fearsome Shaman answered. "I can bring the dead to life so that they are lying there unconscious."

"Well, that's not a great deal, and it's not enough," said Daughter of the Sun. Then she asked Daughter of the Moon, "And do you have any great skill, Shaman of the Moonlight?"

"I know how to put a dead person into a deep sleep," she answered.

"And I can bring a dead person back to consciousness," said Shaman Kiuyogial', Daughter of the Sun. "I can awaken him from a deathly dream."

"Well, what about it, sisters?" asked the three. "Let's get to work. Let's revive our husband."

First, Fearsome Shaman, Daughter of the Constellation Yurgial', jumped over the dead body. The dead person's breast began barely rising up and down. A scarcely noticeable exhalation came from the mouth.

Next, Shaman of the Moonlight jumped over the body. Color returned to the pale face, and the eyelashes quivered.

Then, Shaman Kiuyogial', Daughter of the Sun, came forward. She jumped over the body, and the dead person rose from the earth. The hat fell from the dead person's head, and her long hair cascaded down her shoulders.

"Oh, sisters, it's plain that we didn't revive the man we intended to revive. It's not our husband but an unknown woman."

While hiding behind the *urasa*, Yudzhian had heard and seen everything. He ran up and embraced his dear wife tightly. She hid her face on his broad chest, blushing from happiness.

The shamans watched and exchanged glances. Suddenly, a child began crying in the *urasa*. When the beautiful woman heard the cry, she tore herself away from her husband and rushed into the *urasa*. Yudzhian ran after her.

"What shall we do, sisters?" asked Daughter of the Sun. "Our intended has a wife and child. We heavenly shamans can't play the role of younger wives. Let's return home."

Daughter of the Sun jumped onto her horse. The horse galloped straight into the sky. The other two shamans followed her.

When halfway home, Fearsome Shaman, Daughter of Yurgial', suddenly cried out, "Oh, sisters, what have we done? We've forgotten our dowries and left them down there."

Shaman Kiuyogial', Daughter of the Sun, laughed proudly. "My father's wealth is greater than the pitiful cattle that I left down there. Father will give me as many as I want."

"And my father won't utter a word of reproach," said Shaman of the Moonlight, Daughter of the Moon, not to be outdone.

Shaman Yurgiuk, Daughter of the Constellation Yurgial', blushed. "Let my dowry go to waste. My father isn't as rich as yours, but he doesn't deny me anything."

They never returned for their dowries. Yudzhian was left with all of their wealth, with all three dowries. He prepared to journey back to his native land. He gave a hero's whistle, and his piebald horse came galloping out of the green valley.

The family traveled home—Yudzhian on his piebald horse with his wife seated in front of him and the cradle with his son lying in it bound tightly at his left knee. Chychakh Bird, faithful nanny that she was, sat on the cradle singing songs to the little boy.

Three times eighty herds of horses galloped ahead of them. Three times ninety herds of cattle ambled behind the horses.

Thus they traveled, and thus they arrived. A handsome young man with wide shoulders came out to meet them.

"Are you Khodzhugur, my brother?" asked Yudzhian.

"Don't tell me that I've grown so much that you don't recognize me?" Khodzhugur laughed. "I see that you have brought back your wife, my dear sister-in-law. Forgive me for causing so much trouble."

From then on, they lived together, and they lived well. That's the story that is told. It is said to have happened that way.

Part 5: Stories About Animals and Marriages with Animals

MACHENKAT

(Khant)

Once upon a time there lived a brother and sister who had no memory of their parents, so long ago had they died. The siblings lived together in the coniferous forest called the taiga. Machenkat, the sister, prepared the meals, and the brother traded in animal skins. One day when hunting time came, the brother set out for the taiga.

"Machenkat," he said, "if guests come, meet them with courtesy. If a chipmunk visits, feed it. If a magpie comes flying, feed it."

The brother left, and Machenkat began sewing a fur coat. She worked for a long time, but neither a chipmunk nor a magpie came. Instead, it was a bear that came to see her.

The bear entered the house and bowed. Machenkat was frightened. She jumped over to the stove, grabbed some ashes from inside, and threw them into the bear's eyes.

The bear covered its eyes with a paw in an attempt to protect them. After giving a roar, the bear ran down the path Machenkat's brother had taken earlier.

Time passed, and the snow began melting. Machenkat waited for her brother to come home. She waited one day, then another, but no one appeared. She skied to the edge of a dried up swamp and noticed a blizzard blowing in the distance. It seemed as if her brother were coming to meet her. She looked again, and the blizzard had disappeared. Her brother was nowhere to be seen.

"My brother must be angry with me," she thought. She continued to wait. Then she turned around and skied home.

Evening passed, night passed, but her brother did not come home. Even by morning, he had not appeared. Machenkat began living alone, without her brother.

Soon the snow had almost disappeared. Again, Machenkat put on her skis and set out to meet her brother. She went to the swamp, and it seemed to her again that her brother was coming to meet her in a blizzard. "Brother must be angry," she thought. "I'll go to meet him if he won't come to me."

She went to the spot where the blizzard had whirled, but her brother was not there. It was as if he had disappeared without a trace. Finally, she came upon his ski tracks. She saw bear tracks nearby.

The sister followed the bear tracks. She came to the edge of the taiga. Her brother's *narta,* or sleigh, was standing there. But her brother was nowhere to be seen.

"Apparently, Brother was coming home, and the bear met him," the girl thought. "Where should I search for my brother?"

That evening she made a knapsack. She did not sleep a wink all night long. In the morning, as soon as it was light, she dressed in a fur coat lined with otter skins and went outdoors.

She took her skis and pushed them up the river. The skis stopped sliding along and made a turn, as if they had a mind of their own and wanted to block her path. "That's not the way I should go," she said. "The skis don't want to go in the right direction."

She directed the skis toward the estuary of the river. The skis kept sliding along of their own accord. "This is the way I should go!" she said. Machenkat got on the skis and set out in the direction the skis had taken of their own accord.

It is not known whether she skied for a long or short time. When evening approached, it was time to gather wood and make a fire. She would have to spend the night.

Machenkat fetched some rotten tree stumps. She would have to break up a birch stump for kindling. As she was breaking open the stump, a frog jumped out.

"What a disaster," the frog cried. "You have smashed my home. Do you want me to freeze to death?"

"I smashed your home, but I'll set it right. After all, I didn't know that you were living there," Machenkat said.

"Let's spend the night together," the frog said. "We'll be sisters. I'll make a fire and set the kettle boiling. Then I'll fix supper." The frog set to work. She sprinkled pieces of rotten wood into the kettle.

"We don't have to eat rotten wood," Machenkat said. "We'll boil some meat. I have a supply with me."

The frog was delighted. "Then let's eat meat!"

They cooked supper and ate. Then they lay down to sleep.

In the morning, the frog made the following proposal. "Let's swap clothes and skis."

Machenkat agreed without hesitation. She put on the frog's rough-hewn skis and wore the frog's fur coat, which was full of holes. The frog put on Machenkat's swift-running skis and her otter-lined fur coat.

Machenkat tried to ski up a mountain, but the rough-hewn skis began going backward. She had never skied on such rustic skis, and she fell down. She caught up to the frog only with difficulty.

For her part, the frog was delighted. "Oh, boy, what wonderful skis you have! They ski up and down the mountain by themselves."

"Oh, what bad skis you have," said Machenkat. "I can't get up the mountain with them."

So they changed clothes and skis again. The frog put on her tattered fur coat, full of holes, and Machenkat put on her otter-lined coat.

"Girl, you begrudge a friend nothing. The time will come when I will repay you for your generosity," said the frog.

They prepared dinner and ate. Then they continued on their way.

Whether they traveled for a long or short time is not known, but suddenly they heard the sound of chopping, as if the forest were being chopped down. They went closer and saw that some people were building a big city.

"Now our bridegrooms will come to meet us," said the frog. "My bridegroom will have golden stockings, and yours will have stockings laced with thongs."

"What are you saying, little sister?" Machenkat asked the frog. "We have come to an unfamiliar city. What bridegrooms could be waiting for us here?"

At that moment, two young men were walking down a mountain and approaching the river's shore to meet them. One was named Kana, and the other was named Kol'ket.

Kana was a capable person. He knew everything and could do everything. Machenkat looked at Kana. He had golden stockings. Kana went up to the frog and bowed down to her. He placed his hand on her shoulder, and she turned into a beautiful maiden.

Kol'ket went up to Machenkat and bowed low. His blue eyes smiled, and his curls flowed in ringlets. Kol'ket took Machenkat by the hand. "I have waited a long time for you," he said.

Machenkat pulled her hand away. "How dare you? Never in my life has someone led me by the hand. I came here on my own, and I'll walk up the mountain on my own."

Nevertheless, Kol'ket helped Machenkat ascend the mountain. A great crowd of people came to meet them.

In the morning the city dwellers began arranging a marriage ceremony for the two couples. They placed tables all around. Everyone gathered for the celebration. There was a great feast. After the wedding ceremony, the two couples began living in happiness.

Perhaps Machenkat and Kol'ket lived in happiness for a long or short time, no one knows. Then one day the snow began melting. The ice broke into large chunks that were carried down the river.

"I must go back to my native land and look for my brother," Machenkat said to Kol'ket.

Kol'ket agreed to accompany her. Then Kana and his frog wife decided to join them. Kol'ket and Machenkat and Kana and his frog wife prepared for the journey. They made a covered boat. Then they sailed up the river to Machenkat's home.

After they had gone a little, or perhaps a great, distance, they noticed fresh wood chips floating down the river. "Who chopped this wood?" they wondered.

They went a little further and noticed two little bear cubs sitting atop a cedar tree. The cubs were dividing cedar cones into two piles. They were having a discussion. "I'll give my cedar cones to Auntie," said the big cub.

"And I'll give mine to Uncle," said the little cub.

Then, they slid down the cedar tree to the ground. They ran to the river's edge and struck the ground—and turned into children.

"Uncle, Auntie!" they cried when they spied the travelers. "Take us in the boat."

"It seems we've found your brother's children, Machenkat," said Kana.

They put the children into the boat and sailed on.

"Auntie, Mother got really angry when she heard you were coming," said the older cub. "Father isn't angry. He'll come out to greet you, but Mother has turned into a bear. Don't be afraid. Just approach her in a normal manner."

They came to the home of Machenkat's brother on the riverbank. Machenkat's brother met them at the entrance to his home. He was happy to see his sister and asked the couple to come in.

Soon a bear came into the house. Machenkat took a big piece of silk cloth out of her pocket and bowed low to the bear. "Forgive me," she said, and she covered the bear with the piece of silk.

The bear went outside. She shook her hide off and became a woman. After shedding the bearskin, she entered the house. There are no words to describe her beauty. It was as if silver were flowing from her brows and hair.

Machenkat and the bear woman made peace. They kissed and embraced.

Machenkat noticed that her brother's wife had a burn on her cheek. Machenkat guessed what had happened. She said, "I wouldn't have thrown ashes at you if I had known who you were. Brother told me to feed a chipmunk if it came and to feed a magpie if it came flying, but you were neither a chipmunk nor a magpie."

"There is a law in the taiga that whoever comes to visit should always be met graciously," said Machenkat's brother. "Friendship sustains the world."

Later, the feasting began. There were meat pies, venison, and elk fat. Friends and family feasted for a long time in celebration of their love and friendship.

PART 6

SPIRITS, SHAMANS, AND SHAPESHIFTERS

TSHAKAPESH, THE MOON SPIRIT

(Innu)

One day a man and a woman went to the forest to search for wood with which to make snowshoes. They left their little girl behind at home.

Angry that the noise of their axe chopping trees had awakened him, Mammoth rushed up to see what the man and woman were doing.[1] Mammoth gobbled up the man first. Then, Mammoth attacked the woman, who was pregnant with a son. Mammoth tore her to pieces. He ripped out her womb and threw it onto a pile of snow.

When her parents failed to return, the little girl went searching for them. She saw that her mother and father had been killed and that some distance away her mother's womb was lying in the snow. As she approached the womb, a baby boy crawled out of it. By some miracle, he was alive!

"Are you my brother?" she asked, because she knew that her mother had been almost ready to give birth.

"Yes, I am your brother, Tshakapesh, the Moon Spirit, who has been flung so unexpectedly and abruptly into the world," replied the boy.

The little girl took her brother home and kept him in a huge bucket, lined with animal furs to keep him warm. In no time at all, Tshakapesh had grown into a strong young man. Whereas his sister grew by days, Tshakapesh grew by hours.

One day Tshakapesh asked, "Where are our mother and father, Sister?"

Tshakapesh's sister told him the terrible story about their parents' deaths.

"I'm going to kill Mammoth for what he did," Tshakapesh said.

"You are too young, brother," his sister said.

"We'll see about that," replied Tshakapesh.

Tshakapesh decided to make himself a bow. He cut down an enormous birch tree, a tree that is supple, as everyone knows, and he made an enormous bow. He used some smaller trees as arrows.

When his sister saw how serious Tshakapesh was about taking revenge for his parents' deaths, she said, "Don't go near Mammoth, Brother. He is very dangerous."

But Tshakapesh did not listen to her. He went to the place where his parents had been killed and called for Mammoth.

Mammoth heard his call and went to Black Bear. "Go kill Tshakapesh for me," Mammoth ordered.

Black Bear approached Tshakapesh. "Are you Mammoth?" asked Tshakapesh.

"No," said Black Bear.

"Then, go away. I want Mammoth," said Tshakapesh, and he began calling again.

This time Mammoth sent Polar Bear to kill Tshakapesh.

"Are you Mammoth?" asked Tshakapesh.

"No," replied Polar Bear.

"Then, get lost. I want Mammoth," said Tshakapesh, who was now more than a little annoyed. Once again, he began calling Mammoth.

This time Mammoth sent Grizzly Bear to kill Tshakapesh.

Although Grizzly Bear looked frightening, Tshakapesh asked, "Are you Mammoth?"

"No," admitted Grizzly Bear, "I'm not."

"Then, go home. I want Mammoth, not you," Tshakapesh cried in frustration.

Grizzly Bear told Mammoth what had happened.

"Is Tshakapesh big?" asked Mammoth.

"Not very. You could crush him with your foot," said Grizzly Bear.

"Then I'll go to see him myself," Mammoth decided.

The earth shook as Mammoth lumbered toward Tshakapesh, but Tshakapesh, the Moon Spirit, seemed undaunted by Mammoth's size and bulk.

Mammoth ran to attack Tshakapesh when he caught sight of him, and the ground trembled even more. Mammoth grabbed Tshakapesh and flung him to the ground. He did so several times until he finally threw Tshakapesh to the spot where his birch tree bow lay.

Tshakapesh grasped his bow and arrows and spoke to Mammoth. As he spoke, he grew taller and stronger.

"How strong are you?" asked Tshakapesh.

"I'm as strong as that tree over there," Mammoth replied, pointing to the tallest tree around.

Tshakapesh, the Moon Spirit, shot an arrow into the tree, and it tumbled to the ground.

"I'm as strong as that boulder over there," Mammoth said, pointing in the other direction.

Tshakapesh shot an arrow into the boulder, and it crumbled to pieces. Chips of rock flew in all directions.

When Mammoth saw what Tshakapesh had done, he began running away, but Tshakapesh shot an arrow that killed Mammoth instantly.

Tshakapesh, the Moon Spirit, cut Mammoth up into pieces that grew wings and turned into birds that flew away. Only Mammoth's ears did not fly away. They were so soft and downy that Tshakapesh decided to make them into mattresses.

Inside Mammoth's stomach, Tshakapesh found his mother and father. He blew on their hair and saw that it was still alive. He knew that he could breathe on them and bring them back to life, but he decided not to. "If there are too many people on earth, it will be hard for the earth to hold all of us," he reasoned.

That was the end of Mammoth. Come to think of it, when did anyone last see a mammoth?

WHIRLWIND'S SISTER

(Ket)

*T*wo sisters lived in a small camp. Their *chum*,* a tent covered with reindeer hides, was located on the edge of the camp site. The sisters were always together. They slept side by side in their animal-skin blankets and chopped wood for the campfire together.

Whether they lived together for a long time or a short time no one knows, but one day the older sister said to her younger sister Aisa, "I'm going to the forest now. The berries have probably already ripened. If so, I'm going to pick a few. You lie down and sleep. Cover up tightly beneath the blanket. If you hear a rustling sound, don't make even a tiny noise."

Aisa obeyed her sister and lay down, wrapping herself up in the blanket. After she had been lying there for a time, she heard a rustling sound outside. Aisa continued to lie there quietly.

Someone opened the door and came in. The person sat down by the hearth.

Aisa was gripped by curiosity. She raised the edge of the blanket slowly and stole a peek. She glanced out from under the blanket and—oh, horror of horrors! An elderly woman who resembled nothing human was sitting there.

An idea suddenly flashed through Aisa's mind. "That's Whirlwind's Sister!" Aisa gave a shudder and slowly wrapped herself tighter in the blanket. "Now she'll eat me up," Aisa thought.

Whirlwind's Sister sensed that the young woman was not sleeping. "Get up," she said. "I won't eat you up."

Aisa shrank into a little ball. Whirlwind's Sister bent over her. She pulled back the edge of the blanket and looked at Aisa. "You are very beautiful," she said. "I won't eat you up because you will be my brother's wife."

"No, no, I don't want to be your brother's wife," said Aisa, "because both of you are cannibals."

* Pronounced "choom."

Aisa covered herself quickly with the blanket. Without giving it much thought, Whirlwind's Sister rushed at her and began tickling her. Aisa fainted.

After the passage of some time, Aisa came to. She glanced around. She saw that she was in a new, strange place. The *chum* was enormous with a long hearth. A man named Whirlwind sat in front of the hearth. He was handsome. The woman who had tickled Aisa sat behind him. Meat was roasting over the fire. Fat was dripping off the spit. Whirlwind was chewing raw meat, and blood was dripping from his mouth. Aisa's body shrank with fear.

"You will be my wife," said Whirlwind.

"I'll never be your wife! You and your sister are cannibals!" Aisa cried.

"I'll bring all kinds of earthly birds for you to eat," said Whirlwind. "You won't have to eat humans like my sister and I do."

After a little, or perhaps a great deal, of time had passed, Whirlwind fell to the ground. As he struck the ground, his arms became wings. Now in the form of a bird, he flew through the smoke hole and flew up beyond the clouds. All that was left behind was a snakeskin that reminded Aisa of a glittering beast. The snakeskin lay on the spot where he had been sitting.

"Now we will go to bed," Whirlwind's Sister told Aisa.

That night while Aisa was sleeping, she had a dream. In the dream her older sister said, "Don't marry Whirlwind, or you'll give birth to cannibals. There are enough cannibals on earth as it is. Here's what you must do, sister. Take Whirlwind's skin from Whirlwind's Sister and burn it up. When Whirlwind descends to earth, he'll die of a heart attack."

Aisa awoke. She looked and saw a snakeskin lying there. Whirlwind's Sister sensed that the young woman had bad intentions. She grabbed her brother's skin and thrust it into her bosom.

"What shall I do with her?" Aisa pondered. After some time had passed, Aisa came up with an idea. "She tickled me, and so…."

Aisa rushed over to Whirlwind's Sister. She grabbed her from behind, gripped her feet, and began tickling them.

Aisa kept tickling Whirlwind's Sister until she fainted. Aisa threw her onto her back and looked at her. She was still. Apparently, Whirlwind's sister had died of laughter.

Breathless, Aisa removed the snakeskin from the bosom of Whirlwind's Sister. She took a moment to recover her breath. Then, she made a big bonfire. She threw the snakeskin into the fire and placed some logs on top of it.

All the while Whirlwind had been flying overhead high above the clouds. He had been searching for the meat of various earthly birds in a land beyond the sky. He felt that something bad was happening on earth, so he headed back.

As Whirlwind came closer to earth, people looked up at the sky. "Oh, my, storm clouds are touching down," they cried.

In bird form, Whirlwind's wings roared and thundered, like the sound of ice cracking. Soon feathers began falling from his wings. Craters formed on the mountains where his feathers fell. Lakes, too, formed wherever his feathers fell.

As soon as he landed on earth, his heart burst, and he died. People were happy that both cannibals had died.

"Now I'll go back to my own land," said Aisa.

When she got home, she told her sister, "I burned the cannibal's skin."

Aisa married a man from among her own people. She gave birth to children and told them the story that I am telling you. And you, children of the future, tell this story to your children. May this tale pass from generation to generation. May it be recorded and told to Russians and to other peoples of the world.

FART MAN

(Innu)

Fart Man (Matshishkapeu) is both an amusing and a powerful spirit. He speaks to the Innu through flatulence. Fart Man can sing, speak, imitate other sounds, express an opinion, or give advice.[1] It is said that he can even predict the future. The Innu listen for his counsel, which he gives in a humorous way. When someone lets gas, the sounds are interpreted by the older people in the community. In this manner, flatulence becomes a form of divination.

Although Caribou Spirit (Kanipinikassikueu) rules over all of the other animal spirits, Fart Man is rumored to be even more powerful than Caribou Spirit. The story that follows tells of an occasion when Fart Man got the better of Caribou Spirit.

*O*n one occasion Fart Man (Matshishkapeu) got the better of Caribou Spirit (Kanipinikassikueu) and showed him that he was more powerful. It happened like this.

That year Caribou Spirit was stingy and refused to give caribou to the Innu. People were starving everywhere. Things got so bad that the people called upon the shaman for help.

The shaman set up the shaking tent and entered it to speak to Caribou Spirit. "Please help us, Caribou Spirit," he begged. "Our people are dying of hunger. Give us some caribou meat. Send the caribou our way so that we can slay them and eat again."

"No, I won't," roared Caribou Spirit.

Then the shaman called upon another spirit, Fart Man (Matshishkapeu) and explained the situation to him. "I will help you," Fart Man declared.

Fart Man went to Caribou Spirit and said, "I am asking you to give some caribou to the Innu people."

"Well, I won't," declared Caribou Spirit.

"If you do not do as I ask, I will cause you pain," warned Fart Man.

"Do as you please. I'm not afraid of you," said Caribou Spirit.

Fart Man

Fart Man said not a word. Instead, he caused Caribou Spirit to be constipated. As time went on, Caribou Spirit felt worse and worse until he was in danger of dying. No matter how hard he tried, he could not relieve himself. His belly grew large.

Finally, Caribou Spirit screamed, "Enough! I give up! I agree to give caribou to the Innu people!"

Then, Fart Man released his power over Caribou Spirit, who ran to the bush to relieve himself. That is how Fart Man provided caribou for the Innu. And that is why some people say that Fart Man (Matshishkapeu) is more powerful than Caribou Spirit (Kanipinikassikueu).

THE FOREST SPIRIT

(Khant)

*L*ong ago a man and his wife were living near a river. They had a daughter who liked to play outside for days at a time. She built toy houses and played with her dolls there.

One day she ran home and said, "Mama, give me my very best outfit. Forest Spirit Vonlok has come to make me his bride and become your son-in-law. He doesn't like it when people look at him, so put a kerchief over your face so that you can't see him."

"Don't be silly, daughter," her mother said.

However, the girl got dressed in her finery and went out. That evening, when her father returned from fishing, there was no daughter there to greet him. The couple searched for her everywhere, but they did not find her.

Time passed, and the couple grew old because of their grief. Then one day, a woman came to them. She set her child down on the floor. The little boy ran around the floor, laughing and playing.

The woman sat down and said, "Mama, Forest Spirit Vonlok, my husband, and your son-in-law, has come to visit. He doesn't like it when people look at him, so put a kerchief over your face so that you can't see him."

The mother looked at the young woman and thought, "Is she really my daughter?"

The daughter and her son lived for a long time with her parents. Time flew quickly. It does, of course, when you are living with someone you love.

One day the daughter said, "It's time for us to go home now. We've stayed long enough."

All that time Forest Spirit Vonlok, the old couple's son-in-law, had been living under the same roof, but no one had seen him.

The old couple accompanied their daughter and grandson out to the porch. The young woman and her son walked a few steps into the distance and then disappeared.

Only the old couple remained to live out their old age alone.

The Forest Spirit

161

THE GIRL AND THE MOON SPIRIT

(Chukchi)

*T*here was a Chukchi man who had an only daughter. The girl was her father's best helper. Every summer she guarded the reindeer herd out on the treeless plain tundra, not far from her camp. In winter she took the herd even further away into the depths of the tundra. From time to time she rode back to camp on her reindeer to get food.

One night her reindeer raised his head, looked up at the sky, and said, "Look! Look! Here comes the Moon Spirit."

The girl looked up at the sky and saw that indeed the Moon Spirit was descending in his sledge, which was drawn by two reindeer.

"Where is he going? And why?" asked the girl.

"He wants to kidnap you and take you away." The reindeer answered.

The girl became alarmed. "What can I do? He's going to carry me away to the sky!"

The reindeer brushed some snow away with his hoof and made a hole. "Quick! Get into the hole," said the reindeer.

The girl crouched down in the hole. The reindeer covered her with snow so that nothing was visible, except a big snowdrift.

The Moon Spirit descended from the sky. He told his reindeer to halt and got out of the sledge. He walked around, looking everywhere, searching for the girl. He could not find her. He approached the snowdrift and looked at the top, but he did not guess that someone was hiding inside the drift.

"How extraordinary!" the Moon Spirit said. "What happened to the girl? I can't find her. I'll leave now, but I'll come back again. Then, I'll find her without fail, and I'll take her away to my home."

He got into his sledge, and his reindeer dashed off into the sky.

As soon as the Moon Spirit was gone, the reindeer raked aside the snow with his hoof.

The girl came out of the snowdrift and said, "Let's get to camp quickly. If the Moon Spirit sees me, he'll descend again. Then, there'll be no place to hide."

Part 6: Spirits, Shamans, and Shapeshifters

She got into her sledge, and her reindeer rushed on at top speed. Snow swirled and whirled as they came galloping into camp. The girl ran into her family's *yaranga,* a round tent covered with reindeer hide that served as their home. Her father was not there. Who would help her now?

The girl's reindeer hurried her. "You must hide, or else the Moon Spirit will come after us!"

"Where can I hide?"

"I'll turn you into something, perhaps into a block of stone."

"He'll know it's me."

"Well, then, I'll turn you into a hammer."

"He'll know it's me."

"Then, I'll turn you into a tent pole that supports the *yaranga.*"

"He'll know it's me."

"Then, I'll turn you into a hair on the flap that covers the entrance to the *yaranga.*"

"He'll know it's me. He'll know!"

"What else can I do? I'll turn you into an oil lamp."

"Fine, fine!"

"Sit down."

The girl crouched down. The reindeer struck the earth with his hoof, and she turned into an oil lamp. The lamp burned brightly and illuminated the *yaranga.*

No sooner had the girl become an oil lamp than the Moon Spirit dashed into camp. He had already searched for her among the herd.

He tethered his reindeer and entered the *yaranga,* which he searched from top to bottom. He searched and searched and peeped into every corner, but he could not find the girl. He looked among the tent poles, and he inspected all the utensils. He looked at every hair on the hides that covered the *yaranga.* He inspected every twig from under the bed and gazed at every bit of earth on the floor of the girl's home. He could not find the girl anywhere.

He failed to notice the oil lamp because it was bright, just like the Moon.

"Strange," said the Moon Spirit. "Where on earth is she? I see that I'll just have to come back."

The Moon Spirit went out of the *yaranga* and untethered his reindeer. He got into his sledge. He was preparing to leave when the girl poked her head out of the *yaranga.* She thrust her body to the waist out of the tent flap.

Suddenly, she burst out laughing and cried out, "Here I am! Here I am!"

The Moon Spirit abandoned his reindeer and rushed back to the *yaranga*. The girl turned into an oil lamp again.

The Moon Spirit searched for her. He searched among the twigs and leaves. He searched among the strands of wool and bits of earth on the floor, but the girl was nowhere to be found.

"Oh, how extraordinary! Where is she? Where has she disappeared? It's plain to see that I'll have to return again."

He left the *yaranga* and began harnessing his reindeer when once again the girl thrust her body to the waist out of the tent flap.

She laughed and cried, "Here I am! Here I am!"

The Moon Spirit rushed to the *yaranga*. He began searching again. He searched for a long time and rummaged through everything. He overturned everything several times, but still he could not find her.

The Moon Spirit grew weary of the search. He grew thinner and weaker. In short, the Moon Spirit began to wane. His feet barely carried him anymore, and he could barely raise his thin arms.

From then on, the girl stopped being afraid of him. She took on her form as a girl and acted boldly as she had earlier. She jumped out of the *yaranga* and rushed at the Moon Spirit. She threw him onto his back and tied his hands and legs together.

"Oho! You'll kill me," said the Moon Spirit. "Well, go ahead and kill me. I deserve it. I wanted to kidnap you and take you away from Earth. I have only one request. Before I die, wrap me in a blanket of reindeer hide and warm me because I am freezing."

The girl was amazed. "How can you be freezing? You wander about eternally at will. You don't have a *yaranga*. You're homeless. Stay outside now, too. You don't need a reindeer hide."

"If I am eternally homeless, then let me go outside. I will be an amusement for your people," begged the Moon Spirit. "Let me go and I will turn night into day. Let me go, and I will measure the months of the year for your people. First, I will be the Moon of the Old Stag, then the Moon of the Newborn Calves. Then, I'll be the Water Moon, the Leafy Moon, the Warm Moon, the Horn Shedding Moon, the Reindeer Love Moon, the Moon of the First Winter, and the Moon of Shortening Days."

"If I let you go, will you come after me again when you become strong and your arms and legs get their strength back?"

"Oh, no, I won't. I'll forget all about it. You are very clever. But, no, I'll never come down from the sky again. Let me go, so that I can light up the sky."

The girl released the Moon Spirit, who returned to the sky and stayed there. To this day he shines on high for the Chukchi and the rest of the world to see.

FIRE SPIRIT

(Selkup)

*T*his story is said to have happened long, long ago among the Selkup people, who live in Siberia by the River Taz. It happened in a camp where seven families lived, where there stood seven conical tent-like dwellings called *chums*.*

One day all of the Selkup men went off to hunt. Only the women and children remained in camp.

For two whole days everything went well, but here's what happened on the evening of the third day. In one of the *chums,* a woman was cooking some food. She had thrown a greater quantity of wood than usual into the fire and had hung a kettle filled with venison over it. She and her small child were sitting near the hearth. The child was sitting on her lap and laughing. The woman was smiling.

Suddenly, a log cracked and sparks flew out of the hearth. One spark fell onto the child's hand and burned him. The little boy burst into tears.

"What on earth are you doing?" the woman scolded the fire. "I feed you logs and take care of you, yet you hurt my child!"

When the child heard his mother shouting, he began crying louder. The woman walked about with him, rocking him in her arms. In dismay over his outburst, the woman spanked the little boy. The child became even more upset. The woman should have blamed herself for the child's tears, but instead she blamed the fire.

"See what you've done?" she shouted. "If you do anything like that again, I won't add any more wood to you. I'm going to hack you to pieces and pour water onto you."

The fire crackled and sparks flew again. Then, the woman put the child down in the cradle and grabbed an axe. True to her word, she struck the fire with the axe. She took some water in a jug and splashed it onto the hearth. The fire began sputtering and went out.

"That will teach you not to hurt my son," the woman said. "Not a single flame, not a single spark will be left of you!"

The fire stopped burning. It grew cold and dark in the *chum*. The child began crying pitifully. He was freezing.

---

* Pronounced "chooms."

Suddenly, the woman came to her senses. She bent over the fire and raked together the ashes. It was just as she had said it would be—not one spark remained.

Her son kept crying. "I'll run next door," the mother said. "I'll borrow some of their fire to light a fire on my hearth."

She ran to the neighbor's. As soon as she entered the neighbor's *chum,* the flame on their hearth began sputtering and growing lower. Then the last blue flame went up in a stream of smoke and died.

The woman ran to another neighbor. She had scarcely opened the door-flap of the neighbor's *chum* when their fire went out. She did not even enter, but closed the door-flap immediately.

Thus, she went around the entire camp, and the fire went out everywhere she went. Yet a fire was still burning in the last *chum.*

An old woman lived there and had been living there for a century. She knew a great deal and had seen a great deal. Afraid to enter, the young woman stood in front of the old woman's *chum.* But what else could she do? Her little son might freeze to death. She went in.

The old woman's fire blazed, smoked, and then died out. The child's mother began crying.

The old woman raked up the ashes and searched for a live coal or spark in the ashes. There was no coal, no spark. The hearth was cold and dark.

"I've never seen the like of it," the old woman said. "I take care of my fire and feed it all the logs it wants. When I lie down to sleep, I cover the coals with ashes. Why has the fire gone out? Have you perhaps done something wrong, my cold little frog?" the old woman asked the young mother. "Have you perhaps insulted the fire on your hearth?"

The woman hung her head and was silent.

"I thought so," said the old woman. "What's to be done now? Well, let's go to your *chum,* and we'll see."

They went out together. They walked through the camp. It was quiet and dark everywhere, as if people had abandoned their homes, as if the camp had been deserted.

In the young woman's *chum,* the child had cried himself out, so that he could no longer cry. The old woman took some sulfur buds and set about making a fire with them. She labored long, but the fire would not start.

The old woman lowered her tired hands and said to the young mother, "The fire on the hearth is sacred. It gives us life. It gives us light and warmth and feeds us. The fire's going out is the same as the sun's disappearing. Without fire, we'll freeze—we'll be done for. Without fire, a cruel death awaits us."

The old woman got down on her hands and knees. It was then that she saw the Fire Spirit. The Fire Spirit was sitting in a corner of the hearth. Her clothing was gray, the color of ash. Her skin was luminescent, like a coal covered with ashes.

The Fire Spirit was rocking back and forth. "Why are you even trying to start the fire?" she asked the old woman. "You won't be able to light it. That woman has offended me greatly. She chopped up my face with an axe. She poured water on my eyes and screamed evil words at me."

"Don't be angry, Fire Spirit," the old woman begged. "Take pity on us. This foolish woman is to blame, not the rest of us."

The Fire Spirit began shaking her head. Her hair shimmered like blue smoke.

"Tell us what to do," said the old woman, so that fire will once again burn on our hearths. Everything you command will be done."

"There are no words, no powers either in me or in you to make the fire blaze like it did before. Now it can be rekindled only from a human heart."

The young woman sat weeping and holding her child close to her breast.

"See what you have done?" asked the old woman. "All seven families must perish because of you, foolish woman. Hunters as brave as angry bears and as strong as elks will die because of you. Hardworking women will grow weak beside their cold hearths. Little children and old women and old men will die because there is no life without fire."

The young woman dried her eyes. She stood up and gave the child to the old woman. "Take care of him for me," she said.

Then she threw herself onto the stone hearth. The Fire Spirit touched the woman's breast with her finger. A flame leapt from the woman's heart. Once again the fire began humming and raging on the hearth. The Fire Spirit could be seen grabbing the woman with her flaming hands and bearing her along through the smoke hole with the sparks.

"From this *chum* a legend will spread about how fire was kindled from a living heart," said the old woman. "The Selkup people will remember what happened in our camp forever, and they will take good care of the fires on their hearths from now on."

FLYING TO THE MOON

(Greenland and Canadian Inuit)

At the time when great shamans lived, there was a very great shaman called Kukiaq.[1]
He lived in the Netsilik land around Kinngait.*

O ne day he was standing by a breathing hole waiting for a seal to stick its snout through the hole to catch a breath of air. It was a fine, crisp winter's night with no wind and a full moon. As Kukiaq stood looking at the moon, it suddenly seemed that it was coming nearer. It was a full moon. Kukiaq continued to stare, and the moon came nearer and nearer, as if it were falling from the sky. Finally, it hung over the snow above the ice. Kukiaq saw approaching a phantom team of four dogs, a sledge made of whalebone jaws, and the Moon Spirit sitting in the sledge. A fifth dog trotted along unharnessed beside the sledge.

As the dogs came up to Kukiaq, the Moon Spirit had trouble making them obey, so eager were they to see Kukiaq. At last, the Moon Spirit got the dogs under control and waved his arms to indicate that Kukiaq should go with him. Kukiaq ran over to the big, angry-looking Moon Spirit, who stood with his back to him.

"Get into the sledge, and close your eyes," the Moon Spirit said.

Kukiaq did as he was told, and the sledge began to move. Kukiaq felt the wind whirling around him and heard a swishing sound. The sledge was speeding along. Because he wanted to see where they were going, Kukiaq peeped through his eyelids, but he did not open his eyes wide. He looked down into an enormous black hole, lost his sense of balance, and almost fell off the sledge.

Afterward, Kukiaq was so afraid that he closed his eyes tightly and did not open them again. They drove on, and Kukiaq could tell from the noise of the sledge runners that they were on glare ice that had no snow cover.

Soon the sledge stopped, and Kukiaq opened his eyes. He saw a large village with many houses and many happy people playing and jumping about. Two of his friends who had recently died came running up to him and slapped him on the back so hard that it hurt. He was in the Land of the Dead, which is located in the sky.

---

* Inuktitut name for Cape Dorset, a village on the southwest coast of Baffin Island in Nunavut, Canada.

The Moon Spirit invited Kukiaq into his house, which had bright, shining windows. They walked toward the entrance, but the Moon Spirit's big dog was lying in the passageway blocking it. They had to step on the dog to get in. It growled but did nothing else. The walls of the house moved in and out, as if they were breathing or chewing. They looked like tent walls flapping in the wind.

Kukiaq got into the house safely and noticed that there were two rooms. A beautiful young woman with a child in her *amauti** sat in one room. Her lamp was burning so hot that as Kukiaq looked at the beautiful woman, the lamp scorched his neckband. The woman was the Moon Spirit's sister, the Sun. She beckoned to Kukiaq and made a space for him on her platform, but he declined her offer for fear of being burned.

"My wife, the Eater of Entrails, will come soon," said the Moon Spirit. "She will dance for us. Whatever you do, don't laugh at her. If you laugh, she will cut open your belly with her *ulu* (knife), take out your intestines, and give them to my pet ermine that lives in that little house outside. If you can't contain yourself, scratch underneath your knee with the nail of your little finger to keep from laughing."

Soon a woman entered carrying an oblong dish, in which her *ulu* lay. She put the dish on the floor and spun it around like a top. Then she began dancing. When she turned her back, Kukiaq noticed that she was hollow inside. She had no back or intestines, but only a heart and lungs. She whirled and twirled around, licking her back and making ridiculous gestures.

The Moon Spirit joined in the dance. The poses and faces that the couple made were so funny that Kukiaq could scarcely keep from laughing. At the last moment, Kukiaq remembered the Moon Spirit's warning and scratched beneath his knee with the nail of his little finger. The Eater of Entrails gave a start.

The Moon Spirit seized the Eater of Entrails and threw her down in the entryway. She went away, but a voice was heard saying, "She has left her *ulu* and her dish. If she doesn't get them, she will tear down the pillars of heaven." The Moon Spirit threw the *ulu* and dish into the entryway.

Then the Moon Spirit opened a hatch in the floor. He showed Kukiaq how he made it snow down on earth by blowing through a pipe. Snow floated from the hatch in the sky down onto the earth below.

"Now it's time to leave," said the Moon Spirit. "Don't be afraid when I push you, or you won't reach earth alive."

The Moon Spirit gave Kukiaq a shove and pushed him through the hatch. Kukiaq fainted as he fell.

When Kukiaq recovered, he heard the voice of his departed grandmother. Her spirit was taking care of him and guiding him back to earth. After he reached the surface of the earth, Kukiaq got up and went home. Nothing frightened him anymore after his adventure in the Land of the Dead. Thereafter, Kukiaq became a famous *angakok,* or shaman.

---

* Hood of the Inuit parka, designed for carrying a child.

LITTLE UNIANY*

(Evenk)

In a Siberian nomadic camp, there were many *chums*,** conical dwellings in which the Evenk lived. There, the Evenk people lived in friendship—hunting, fishing, singing, dancing, and playing in their spare time.

One day a loud noise resounded in the taiga forest. The Evenk looked up and saw an enormous and frightful winged creature flying overhead. It was the evil cannibal shaman, Korèndo. It was Korèndo's custom to don large wings and fly over the taiga, swooping down and swallowing people whenever he got hungry.

Korèndo alighted in the nomadic camp and began grabbing people. Whomever he grabbed, he swallowed alive. No one managed to get away. Korèndo grabbed everyone in his path and gobbled them up.

Only one old woman survived his attack. While Korèndo was catching people and swallowing them, she hid beneath an iron cauldron. Korèndo did not find the old woman. After disposing of everyone in the camp, Korèndo flapped his wings, rose high into the sky, and flew away.

When the whirring noise made by Korèndo's wings ceased, the old woman crawled out from under the cauldron. She went around looking into the *chums*. They were empty. Not a single person had survived.

The old woman wept. "How can I live alone without people?" she asked.

She glanced into the last *chum*. She thought that it, too, would be empty. Instead, she saw a little boy, quite small, lying there. The old woman rejoiced. She made a little cradle and began rocking the little boy. She began raising him as her own. She named the little boy Uniany.

He grew by leaps and bounds. He grew not by years, but by days. The bigger he got, the stronger he got. Soon, he began hunting and bringing home game to feed the old woman.

One day Uniany asked, "Grandmother, why are you and I the only people in camp? Where are all of our people? Did they die?"

---

* Pronounced "Oonyahny."
** Pronounced "choom."

Part 6: Spirits, Shamans, and Shapeshifters

"One night a cannibal named Korèndo swooped down on our camp and swallowed all of the people, my child. I hid under a cauldron, so the monster could not find me. It's a mystery how you managed to survive and escape the monster's notice. I fed and raised you."

"Where did the cannibal go? Tell me!"

"I would tell you, but I, myself, don't know."

Uniany became very angry. He decided to find Korèndo, the cannibal shaman, and punish him. He went into the taiga, caught a wild reindeer, and brought it to Grandmother. "Grandmother, is this the one who ate up our people?"

"No, child, no. He is not the one. This is a good animal. He is a reindeer. Take him back to the place you caught him and let him go."

Uniany obeyed. He took the wild reindeer back to the taiga and let him go. He began looking for the cannibal again. He caught sight of a wolverine. He caught it and dragged it off to Grandmother. "Grandmother, is this the one who killed our people?"

"No, child, no. That is a wolverine. She isn't guilty of anything. Take her back to the place where you caught her and let her go."

Uniany obeyed. He let the wolverine go. Next, he caught an elk* and brought it to the *chum*. "Grandmother, is this the one who ate up our people?"

"No, child, no. He is not the one. This is an elk. He doesn't eat people. Take him back to the place where you caught him and let him go."

Uniany let the elk go and caught a wolf. He brought the wolf to the *chum* and asked, "Is he the one who ate up our people?"

"No, child, no. He is not the one. This is a wolf. Let him go."

Uniany let the wolf go and caught a bear. Grandmother ordered him to let the bear go, too. Thus, Uniany dragged every animal, big and small, to Grandmother. Grandmother ordered him to take all of them back to the taiga and to let them go without hurting them.

Uniany grew melancholy. He did not know what to do. Grandmother noticed his sadness. She could not hold back. She said, "Child, don't look for the cannibal in the taiga. In appearance he looks like an enormous man. He flew to us on wings, like a bird, and then flew away. Where he is now, I don't know. I know only that he is Korèndo, the evil shaman."

Uniany stopped going to the taiga. He asked Grandmother for the lid from the big cauldron. He found a hammer and began hammering wings for himself. He sat by the fire all day forging them.[1] When he had finished, he asked Grandmother if the wings were good ones.

"No, child, they aren't very good. Korèndo's wings are larger."

* The European elk is similar to the North American moose.

Once again Uniany set to work. He began making larger wings. After he had made them, he wanted to try them out. He rose into the sky and asked Grandmother, "Grandmother, did Korèndo fly at the same height as a grouse?"

"No, child, higher!"

Uniany set about forging another pair of wings. He made the wings even larger and rose into the sky. "Grandmother, did Korèndo fly as high as a hazel hen?" he asked.

"No, child, Korèndo flew higher. He flew like you are flying now and no lower. To defeat Korèndo, you must make wings larger than his. And you must fly higher than he flies. Korèndo is big and strong."

Uniany did not grieve. He did not give up but set to work again. Without stopping to rest, he sat by the fire and began pounding with his hammer, fashioning iron wings. He made the wings yet larger. Trying them out, he rose into the sky. As he was flying, he asked, "Grandmother, tell me, did Korèndo fly higher or lower than me?"

"Now you are flying higher than Korèndo. He flew lower than you."

Uniany ascended to a great height. He rose beneath the clouds and noticed an enormous *chum* in the distance. He flew in that direction.

Uniany flew up to the *chum* and saw the place where Korèndo had descended to earth. Uniany began circling above the *chum*. As he circled, he sang:

> *Come out, Korèndo! Come into sight.*
> *I've flown to you to pick a fight.*

Uniany sang for a long time, but Korèndo did not come out. He was not there. Instead, a woman, Korèndo's wife, came out of the *chum* and sang:

> *Oh, you foolish, foolish boy.*
> *Just see who has appeared*
> *And wants to compete with Korèndo,*
> *The shaman so mighty and feared.*
> *It's impossible to defeat him,*
> *But if you don't hold your life dear,*
> *Then fly to Korèndo,*
> *Silly boy, go there.*

She indicated to Uniany the direction in which he should fly. He soared into the air and flew on. He flew for a long time.

He flew to the second *chum*. He saw the place where Korèndo had descended to earth. Singing his song, Uniany circled around the *chum*. He began challenging Korèndo to battle.

Come out, Korèndo! Come into sight.
I've flown to you to pick a fight.

Instead of Korèndo, his second wife came out of the *chum* and sang in answer:

Shaman Korèndo is mighty and feared.
It's impossible to defeat him.
But if you don't hold your life dear,
Then fly, fly to Korèndo.
Silly boy, go there.

When she had finished singing her song, she pointed out the direction in which Uniany should fly. He flapped his wings and flew away. He flew for a long time. Finally, he saw a third *chum* and a third wife and began challenging Korèndo to battle. But Korèndo was not there.

Uniany flew to a fourth *chum* and a fourth wife and did not find the cannibal there. He flew to a fifth *chum* and a fifth wife, but Korèndo was not there. He went to a sixth *chum* and found not Korèndo but Korèndo's sixth wife. He learned from her that Korèndo was living in his seventh *chum*. All of the wives with whom Uniany spoke sang one and the same song.

Shaman Korèndo is mighty and feared.
It is impossible to defeat him.
But if you don't hold your life dear,
Then, fly, fly, fly to Korèndo.
Silly boy, go there!

These words did not frighten Uniany. He flew on to Korèndo's seventh *chum*. He flew up to it and circled above the cannibal's *chum*, singing:

Come out, Korèndo! Come into sight.
I've flown to you to pick a fight.

Korèndo's seventh wife heard Uniany's singing. She came out and sang in reply:

Don't annoy, don't awaken Korèndo,
The shaman, so mighty and feared.
If I awaken Korèndo,
He'll soar on high with his winged gear
And kill you. Defenseless boy, get out of here.

But the wife did not frighten Uniany. He began circling lower and sang louder.

Korèndo destroyed my people.

I've come to avenge their deaths.

I may be small, but I am fearless.

Awaken, Korèndo! You've breathed your last breath!

Korèndo's wife went into the *chum* and awakened her husband. Afterward, she went out to Uniany and sang:

Mighty Korèndo has awakened.

Now he is donning his wings.

When he comes out of the chum,

In battle you'll suffer his sting.

Uniany began circling above Korèndo's *chum,* challenging him boldly.

Korèndo, Korèndo, Korèndo,

Come out to meet your end now!

The cannibal's coarse voice rang out in reply:

Uniany, Uniany, Uniany, just you wait.

Let me eat dinner before trying your fate.

Uniany sang:

Why must you eat, Korèndo?

You haven't long to live.

For killing my people,

Your life you must give.

Korèndo answered in a hoarse voice:

Uniany, Uniany, Uniany,

Wait till I put on my shoes.

Uniany sang:

Why must you put on your shoes?

You haven't long to live.

For killing my people,

Your life you must give.

Korèndo sang:

Uniany, Uniany, Uniany,

Wait till I put on my wings.

But Uniany would not leave the cannibal alone. He sang persistently:

Korèndo, Korèndo, Korèndo,
Why do you tarry, Korèndo?
You haven't long to live.
For killing my people,
Your life you must give.

Suddenly, the enormous, fat Korèndo flew out of the *chum* and attacked Uniany. But the light, agile Uniany soared high into the sky quickly and adroitly. Korèndo flapped his wings. He wanted to rise higher than Uniany, but Uniany kept circling above his head. He would not leave him alone.

They flew on for a long time. Uniany kept flying higher than Korèndo. Korèndo could not overtake him. He could not strike him. Korèndo began to tire and sang:

Wait, Uniany, wait!
Come down a little lower.
I can't fight when you're at a height.
It makes my head spin and ache.

Uniany burst out laughing and replied:

Korèndo, Korèndo, Korèndo,
Why does it make your head spin?
I won't come down to you.
No, I'll fight on behalf of my kin.
On behalf of my brothers and sisters,
I'll take my revenge.
I'll break your powerful wings,
And I am certain to win.

Uniany rushed at Korèndo. He circled above him.

Korèndo, Korèndo, Korèndo,
Stop swallowing my people, my friends,
Stop laying waste to my camp.
Now you must die. It's the end!

Uniany attacked Korèndo and broke his wings. Fat Korèndo fell like a stone. When he hit the earth, his belly split open. Out of his belly tumbled all of the people he had swallowed. After tumbling out of Korèndo's belly, they went home to their *chums* and their camps, where they lived happily for many years.

THE SHAMAN IN THE MOON

(Nganasan)

A shaman once went to the Moon. It happened like this. You see, the Moon is our mother. Therefore, one day when a group of women wanted to know when they would give birth, they sent the shaman to the Moon to ask. This story happened long ago when the earth was first born. After the shaman left on his journey, the women could barely await his return with the news, so anxious were they to find out when their children would be born.

When the shaman reached the Moon, the Moon ran quickly to her mother. When the Moon's mother heard about the shaman's visit, she said, "The shaman is forbidden to come here. Since he has come anyway, don't let him go home, Moon. Now he will have to become your husband."

The Moon went to the shaman, and he became her husband. The shaman bonded with the Moon, and now you can see him stuck onto her face when you look into the sky. We call him the "Man in the Moon."

The shaman had gone to the Moon seeking information about the birth of the women's children because in those days people did not know how children were born. They understood nothing about how long it took for a child to be born.

Where there is no Moon in the night sky, it means that she has gone to visit her mother. The shaman was a Nganasan man.

NANURLUK, THE POLAR BEAR

(Netsilik Inuit)

In the Arctic there are giant polar bears, the game animals of giants. They are so big that ordinary people have no hope of hunting them. However, the giant polar bears hunt people very successfully.

In spite of their size, the bears are fast runners and always attack on the run. Their jaws are so large and strong that they swallow people whole when they catch them. Then the victims die in the bear's belly, where they can't get a breath of air. The Netsilik call the giant polar bear Nanurluk.

Once Nanurluk was chasing some people who managed to slip into a cave. The entrance to the cave was so narrow that the polar bear could not squeeze his bulky body into it to reach his victims. The people thought they were safe.

However, Nanurluk stabbed at them with his long whiskers. The giant polar bear managed to pierce through the people with his whiskers, as if they were skewers. In that manner, he hauled them out of the cave and gobbled them up, one by one.

Nanurluk ate so many people that the Netsilik began to despair. They called upon a bold and powerful *angakok* to help them. The shaman went up to the polar bear and leapt into its mouth. Then he dove down into Nanurluk's stomach. There, he found all of the people whom the polar bear had swallowed.

The shaman grabbed his knife and cut open Nanurluk's stomach. Out tumbled everyone whom the polar bear had gobbled up—men, women, and children. That is how the shaman killed a giant polar bear and avenged the people the bear had eaten.

THE OLD BACHELOR WHO FLEW THROUGH THE AIR IN A KAYAK

(East Greenland Inuit)

*T*here once was a strange old bachelor who had taken a dislike to singing. Whenever he heard people singing, he put his hands over his ears and ran off in the opposite direction.

One day while he was hunting in his kayak off the coast of Greenland, he heard people singing. The song came from the crew of a boat that was sailing into the inlet against the wind. The members of the crew were sitting motionless in the boat and singing at the top of their lungs. No one was rowing, and yet the boat sailed along rapidly of its own accord.

For some reason, the old bachelor took a liking to this particular song. He went closer to the boat to hear the words of the song. He noticed that from time to time the boat rose into the air and then sank down again onto the water, all the while proceeding into the inlet, even though the crew simply rested on the oars.

Fascinated, the old bachelor said, "Oh, please take me with you."

The man at the helm said, "You may follow us if you like, but mind that you stay nearby." Then, he and the other sailors tied the bachelor's kayak to the boat.

They continued singing their magic song. "*Kangátarsa, kangátarsartigut*! (Up, up, and away!)"

No sooner had they uttered those words than boat and sailors were lifted up and taken across the land at a great speed. They rose high into the air, pulling the old bachelor in his kayak along with them.

They came to a very high mountain and struggled to get to the top. Louder and louder they sang their magic song. Finally, the old bachelor joined in, too. His added singing provided just the strength they needed to get to the top of the mountain, where they took a little rest in their respective boats.

Soon, however, they were on their way again, whipping and twirling through the air until they reached a little house. Slowly, they descended and set down beside the house. They got out of the boat. The old bachelor got out of his kayak, too, and entered the house with his companions with the intention of paying the residents a visit.

He stayed for several days with his newly found friends and came to like them very much. He learned their magic song and sang it over and over again.

After the passage of some time, the old bachelor began thinking of his mother and father and of his sisters and brothers, who must be missing him. Perhaps his old parents were shedding tears, wondering whether he was alive or dead. Finally, the old bachelor decided that he had lingered long enough and that it was time for him to return home.

His new friends filled his kayak with food and supplies. He got into the kayak and began singing the magic song. "*Kangátarsa, kangátarsartigut*! (Up, up, and away!)"

He rose high in the sky and began floating in the direction from which he had come. When he came to the high mountain, on which he and the sailors had rested, he decided to alight and rest once again on its summit. His kayak floated down like a feather and rested atop the steep peak of the mountain.

After a nice, long rest, the old bachelor decided that it was time to be on his way. He opened his mouth to sing the magic song but found that he had forgotten the words. He sat in the kayak and waited for the words to come back to him. Alas, his mind was a complete blank.

The old bachelor stood up in the kayak, in hopes that the view of the land below would inspire him so that the words would return. What a mistake that was! The kayak began rocking back and forth on the peak.

Finally, the old bachelor lost his balance, and it appeared that he was about to fall. "*Immakaja,*" he sang. "No, *kanajaja*. No, that's not it either."

The kayak tipped first to the left and then to the right. Suddenly, it tipped too far and went tumbling down the mountainside.

"Help, help!" the old bachelor cried, but there was no one to come to his rescue.

As he hurtled toward the stones and boulders at the bottom of the mountain, he suddenly remembered the words of the magic song. At the last desperate moment, he sang, "*Kangátarsa, kangátarsartigut*! (Up, up, and away!)" His kayak rose into the air just in the knick of time.

At last he looked below and saw his village and his home, where his dear parents and brothers and sisters had given him up for lost. They were seated outside when they heard a song coming from above. They looked up to see where the song was coming from and saw the old bachelor in his kayak rushing through the air.

The old bachelor steered right for the entrance of the house. The kayak came to a sudden stop on the ledge beside the house. Its nose crashed into the wall of the house.

Everyone was delighted to see the old bachelor because they had indeed given him up as lost. The old bachelor managed to repair the kayak, but he never took it through the air again. This was his first and last journey. The day came when even the words of the magic song left him forever.

THE JEALOUS UNCLE

(Dene, Kodiak, Tlingit, and Alaskan Inupiat)

A man had a beautiful wife, as well as four sisters with sons. The man was insanely jealous of any attention given his beautiful wife.

One day the man's oldest sister, her husband, and their son came to visit him. The man pretended to think highly of his nephew, but he really disliked the boy, who was very handsome. The man was afraid that his wife would notice that the nephew was handsome and would like him too much.

Instead of showing his displeasure, the uncle said, "Nephew, I am going to teach you how to fish and hunt. You'll go everywhere with me."

The man's sister was very happy that her brother thought so fondly of the boy. She and her husband went home and left their son in his uncle's care.

As soon as his sister was gone, the uncle began plotting a means of getting rid of the boy since his wife seemed fond of him.

Next morning the uncle said, "Let's go get some devilfish* to eat, Nephew. Soon the tide will be low enough to do so."

The boy was eager to please his uncle, so they set out. "Walk along that high ridge above the beach," the uncle instructed, "and I'll follow behind you."

The boy obeyed his uncle and soon saw a large object on the beach below. The object kept opening and closing. It was a giant clam. "Uncle, is that a clam? I've never seen such a creature before."

"Indeed, it is a clam, Nephew. Go to the top of the ridge and look at it from there so that you can get a better look."

The boy was eager to inspect the clam, so he went to the top of the ridge and leaned over to have a look. The clam opened, but this time it did not close. The uncle gave his nephew a push, and the boy landed inside the giant clam, which closed over him and ate him up.

* The devilfish is a cephalopod and is of the same family as the squid and octopus.

When the boy's parents found out that their son was dead, they were very suspicious, despite the fact that the uncle declared over and over again that it was an accident. The uncle even managed to weep a few insincere tears. His sister and her husband knew that the man had a jealous temperament, so they did not believe his explanation.

The man's second sister had a son who was even more handsome than the first nephew. When the uncle's wife was introduced to the young man, she commented, "How handsome your nephew is, Husband."

This comment made the man very jealous. He began thinking how he might do away with his second sister's son. "Sister," he said, "it's high time that you send one of your sons to help me. My wife and I have no children of our own, so we have no one to help out."

His second sister sent her oldest son to her brother to help him with the fishing and hunting. Shortly after the boy arrived, the uncle pushed him down into the big clam, just as he had done with the boy's cousin.

"That gets rid of another rival," the man thought. "I know that every man on earth falls in love with my wife because of her remarkable beauty."

Unwilling to stop at having caused two deaths, the jealous man sent for his third sister's son, who was older than the last two nephews he had killed. By now, the uncle was getting a reputation as a murderer. The young man knew about his cousins' fate and refused to go to his uncle for a long time. His uncle kept trying to persuade him until he finally agreed to visit.

The uncle kept close watch on the boy and his wife. He would not leave them alone together for a single moment. The wife was eager to warn the boy about her husband's intention to kill him. Her husband was afraid that she would try to warn the nephew and gave her no opportunity to do so. The woman made signs to the boy, but unfortunately he failed to understand them.

One day after the man and his nephew had left the house to go down to the beach, the young man said, "I forgot to take water with me. I must go back to the house to get some." The boy planned to go back and ask his aunt what she had meant by signaling him earlier. He thought that his uncle would wait for him, but instead his uncle followed him back to the house.

"Where's the water?" he asked his uncle's wife.

Without uttering a word, the beautiful wife fearfully pointed out the jug of water. Her husband watched suspiciously. The boy's aunt was unable to say anything in her husband's presence.

Uncle and nephew went to the ridge above the beach. Below, the enormous clam was opening and closing, opening and closing. When the boy caught sight of the clam moving, to his uncle's great disappointment, he ran past it.

The man and his nephew walked on. Suddenly the uncle said, "Nephew, do you see that hole down there?" The boy looked down and indeed there was a large hole below. "The devilfish that we are going to catch for our meal is there."

The uncle handed his nephew a pole with a hook on the end to get the devilfish. "Hook the fish," he said. "It's not hard to do."

The boy stuck the pole into the water. He poked around and felt that the fish was there. He hooked the fish and began running off with it. His uncle stood behind him. The uncle pushed the boy toward the devilfish right into its clutches. The devilfish seized the boy and dragged him into its lair beneath a big rock.

The uncle had successfully gotten rid of three nephews, but his youngest nephew, the son of his fourth sister, remained alive. The youngest nephew looked like the first nephew whom the uncle had killed. By now everyone knew what a cruel murderer the uncle was. Rumors had reached every member of the family and the village. The youngest nephew decided that he would be prepared for his uncle's tricks.

The youngest nephew's father called upon a shaman who showed the boy how to make himself look like a ball of feathers. The shaman made a bracelet of eagle down for the boy and attached a small piece of devil's club* that he had carved. "Whenever you are in danger, turn the eagle bracelet four times around your wrist," he said. "Now climb this tall tree."

The boy climbed up to the very top of the tree. The shaman climbed after him as the boy's father watched below. "Now turn your bracelet four times quickly around your wrist," yelled the shaman.

The boy did as the shaman ordered. Just as he made the fourth turn, the shaman pushed him off the tree. The father saw only a ball of eagle feathers rolling down the tree. When the ball reached the ground, it turned into the boy again. Now the boy was ready to meet his uncle. Before leaving, the shaman gave the young man an additional gift, a knife with a handle carved in the shape of the devil's club. The boy kept the knife hidden on a piece of sinew tied around his neck.

The young man's friends accompanied him to his uncle's. They stayed with him there for three days, but on the fourth day they departed for home. The uncle's wife wept bitterly to think that a boy of such tender age was left there to be killed by his uncle.

"Why are you blubbering?" asked the uncle. "You're in love again, aren't you?"

It was not the uncle's wife but the boy who answered, "You're in love with the right one this time."

"Quiet, nephew!" the uncle said angrily. "You talk too much. Come with me now. We'll catch a devilfish for our meal."

The boy and his uncle set out. Sadly thinking that she would never see the boy again, the uncle's wife watched them disappear.

* Thorny ginseng.

Part 6: Spirits, Shamans, and Shapeshifters

The young man saw the enormous clam and stood there in amazement, just as his three cousins had done. He forgot all about his eagle feather bracelet. His uncle raised his hands to give the boy a push, and the boy suddenly came to his senses. He gave his bracelet a turn. By the time he gave it a fourth turn, the boy had fallen gently into the gaping mouth of the giant clam as a ball of eagle feathers.

Meanwhile, his uncle went home humming happily, thinking that he had rid himself of the last handsome nephew. "That's the last of him," the uncle declared.

Once inside the clam, the ball of feathers changed back into a boy. The boy took the knife with the carved devil's club handle off the sinew thread around his neck and cut the muscle that kept the clam's mouth closed. He cut first one side and then the other side so that the clam opened wide. Then, the boy jumped out of the clam and onto the beach.

The pole that his uncle had given him to hook devilfish was lying on the beach. The young man picked it up and went on in search of the devilfish they were to have for a meal.

The devilfish was sitting outside its hole waiting to attack. The boy was frightened when he saw how enormous it was. Nevertheless, he decided to kill it. The boy turned his eagle bracelet around twelve times while saying, "Grow smaller and smaller, devilfish, smaller and smaller."

The devilfish began to shrink until it was so small that the boy was able to kill it easily. The nephew dragged the creature, hooked onto the pole, back to his uncle. When he reached his uncle's home, he threw the devilfish in front of his uncle. The devilfish began growing again until it was its usual size.

"Help," screamed the uncle. "Take the devilfish away, Nephew, I beg of you."

The boy made the devilfish small again and then hooked it and dragged it back to the beach. When he looked back, he noticed that once again the devilfish was enormous.

From then on the uncle pretended to think as much of the boy as his wife did. The young man stayed with them for a long time.

One day the uncle noticed his wife talking to his nephew, and once again jealousy gnawed at his heart. He decided to try to kill the boy again.

The uncle put a sharp, pointed stake in the ground beside a tree and ordered his nephew to climb to the top of the tree. The cruel uncle climbed after the boy, who knew exactly what to expect. The boy began singing and twisting his eagle bracelet. Just as he gave the bracelet the fourth turn, the uncle reached out and pushed the boy off the tree, thinking that he would be impaled on the stake below. Nothing fell to earth, however, except the ball of fluffy eagle down.

The uncle understood that it was useless to try to kill his nephew, so he treated the boy well for a long time. He watched the boy carefully and never let him out of sight.

"Your uncle is studying the situation because he can't seem to kill you," the boy's beautiful aunt said.

"It's only a ball of eagle down," the boy said mysteriously. His aunt did not know what he meant.

One day the uncle thought he would trick his wife and nephew into revealing their love for one another. He planned to catch them alone together. "Well, I'm going to the forest to hunt," he told the boy. Instead, he set out for the forest, and then he looped back to the house to spy on his wife and nephew through a hole. He listened.

The boy came over and sat down close to the uncle's wife, too close for the uncle's comfort.

"Let's run away. I'm afraid of my husband and what he might do to us," the aunt said.

"All we need is a canoe, and then we could try to run away."

"Some distance from the village there is an old abandoned canoe that we might use," said the aunt.

Furious, the uncle dashed into the house. He wanted to kill his wife, but he loved her too much to do so. The boy sat still, moving his bracelet back and forth.

That evening the uncle was very kind to his nephew. He told him stories until the boy fell asleep. This was the result the uncle had hoped for. It was not out of kindness, but out of calculation, that he told one story after another.

He tied the boy to a board. "I'll get rid of him this time," he thought. "The feathers will get wet and sink to the bottom of the sea. Then my nephew will drown, and he'll never pester me again."

The uncle took the board with the boy attached down to the beach. He waded far out to sea and set the boy adrift there.

It was a stormy night, and the waves broke over the board, nearly drowning the boy. The nephew floated for a long time, but he finally drifted onto a nice, sandy beach. It was low tide.

Suddenly he heard laughter. It was the laughter of three girls digging clams. They were sisters. The oldest girl noticed something moving on the beach and went over to it, thinking that it was a dying animal. To her surprise, it was a handsome young man. He looked at her, but he did not utter a single word.

"What happened to you? Where are you from? Why are you tied to a board?" she asked. He offered no reply.

"Sisters, come here!" she yelled.

The two sisters came running. The second sister fell in love with the young man at first glance. The youngest sister said nothing and seemed indifferent.

The oldest sister, the one who had discovered the young man, had been in love with the first nephew, whom the jealous uncle had killed. "This young man looks very much like my dead lover," the oldest sister declared. As she was speaking, eagles were gathering around him, ready to devour him.

The young man had seen the oldest girl before with his deceased cousin, so he smiled because he recognized her.

The oldest sister burst into tears. "He has my beloved's smile, but my beloved was a larger man."

"Well, I'm going to untie him and marry him," laughed the second sister.

"You two can have him," declared the youngest sister. "I'm not interested in a man who can't talk."

"If he seems normal after we have untied him, we will both be his wives," said the oldest girl. The two oldest girls set about untying the young man while the youngest sister ran off to dig clams.

"Can you speak now?" they asked.

"Yes, I can speak," came the reply.

"Then, come to our father's house with us."

Their father greeted them when they arrived home. "Who is he?" their father asked.

"We found him on the beach," the middle sister said, "and we're going to marry him."

The middle sister had the habit of being spontaneous and speaking quickly. The oldest girl was quieter and more subdued. Their father consented to their marrying the young man.[*]

Finally, the oldest girl spoke. "Father, see how much he looks like my beloved, who was killed."

The sisters were accustomed to fishing and hunting just like boys. The next morning, the youngest sister said, "I'm going out to spear a salmon this morning." Indeed, soon she came home with a salmon to cook.

The next day the two oldest sisters asked the young man to go fishing with them. To the annoyance of the middle sister, the oldest refused to leave her husband's side after he decided not to go fishing. The young man was afraid that his youngest bride would get annoyed and leave him for good, and he loved her dearly for her liveliness. In the evening, the middle sister returned with a salmon.

"Since you cling to your husband and don't go out to get anything to eat, you can live on love," the middle sister said angrily to her oldest sister.

The young man took the salmon home, and the oldest sister followed slowly. The middle sister cooked the salmon and placed it between herself and her husband. The young man passed it to his oldest wife.

"No, she isn't going to have any," protested the middle sister. "She is going to live on love."

---

[*] A man with several wives had proven that he was a successful hunter because he was capable of supporting more than one wife and her children. —Kira Van Deusen

"Let your sister have some salmon and tomorrow I'll catch another one," the young man said. It was spring, and salmon were hard to catch.

The middle sister was jealous of her oldest sister because she thought her husband loved the oldest sister more. Actually, it was the opposite. He pitied the oldest sister because of her loss and because she tried so hard to please him.

Because of the anger the younger sister felt toward the older sister and because he had unfinished business, the young man decided to leave for a while. His younger wife begged him to stay, but the older wife said nothing because he had told her his reasons for leaving.

"You must let me go," he told the younger wife. "Don't worry. I'll come back. And treat your older sister well because my cousin was in love with her."

"Which cousin are you talking about?" she asked.

"My cousin died a few years ago, and your sister was in love with him. His death was a great loss for her."

After hearing about her sister's sad loss, the younger wife finally let her husband leave. The young man had determined to kill his cruel uncle. He set out in his canoe. When he reached the vicinity of his uncle's home, the uncle spied him approaching and was frightened.

The young man spent the evening in his uncle's home. Late in the evening, he set out, presumably to return to the sisters. However, around midnight he returned to his uncle's.

"I have come to avenge the deaths of my cousins," he told his uncle. "You must pay for taking their lives, and you must pay for making me suffer."

The uncle, who had been so cruel and terrible before, now acted like the most despicable of cowards. "Please don't kill me. Spare my life, Nephew," he begged.

It was of no use. The young man marched his uncle at the prompting of a spear to the edge of the ridge high above the beach. Despite his uncle's pleas, he pushed the cruel man into the jaws of the giant clam, waiting hungrily below.

Then the young man returned to his uncle's home. "I have killed your husband," he told his beautiful aunt. "You are free now to do as you please. He has been repaid for killing my cousins and for attempting to kill me."

Afterward, the young man returned home to his wives. Let's hope that they got along much better in the future.

THE SHAPESHIFTER

(Kola Peninsula Russian)

*I*t was Granddad Aleksei who told me this tale. It is about two friends who were going to a party one evening.

The mother of one of the friends said, "Don't go to the party tonight."

"What do you mean with your 'Don't go'? It's going to be really interesting," her son replied.

The two friends got ready and set out for the affair. As they were walking along, a pig rushed to attack them. The pig kept rushing at their legs, not allowing them to pass. She attacked and broke them up.

Well, the two friends grabbed that pig and they beat her until the pig was barely alive. Then they continued on their way.

When they arrived home that night, the young man's mother, who had objected to his attending the party, was lying there groaning because she was all beat up.

"What happened to you, Mother?" the young man asked.

"What happened, indeed! You, my fine son, beat me up yourself!"

It was the young man's mother who had turned into a pig and had run about in the shape of a pig. She hadn't wanted him to go to the party, you see.

It is said that in the old days people turned into animals. Nowadays machines do everything, and people can't turn into animals anymore.

THE BLACK EWE AND THE BLUE REINDEER

(Karelian)

*T*here once lived a husband and wife. They had a daughter and son. In addition, they had a black ewe.

One day the ewe got lost. The husband and wife went into the forest and down different paths to search for the ewe. They agreed that whoever found her would call to the other.

While the woman was walking through the forest, she met Siuoiatar,* the witch. When Siuoiatar asked the woman why she was in the forest, the woman told the witch about her search for the ewe. "Spit at my legs and walk around me three times, and you'll find your black ewe," said Siuoiatar.

The woman took heart. She spat and walked around the witch three times. That is how Siuoiatar was able to turn her into a black ewe. Then Siuoiatar took on the form of the woman.

The witch called the woman's husband. "Hey, Husband dear, return. I've found your ewe," shouted Siuoiatar.

The husband came running and went home with Siuoiatar, who was disguised as his wife. The husband's daughter came out to meet them and embraced the ewe. She could tell right away who her real mother was. "This is my mother," she thought while looking at the ewe. "That one is not my mother," she thought as she inspected the witch in disguise.

They led the ewe to the shed and locked it up. The ewe was given nothing, except water and swill. The daughter brought her bread on the sly.

After several days had passed, Siuoiatar noticed that the ewe wasn't eating the swill. She said, "The ewe must be slaughtered before it becomes too thin and dies."

The husband went to slaughter the ewe, but his daughter ran after him and said, "Don't kill the ewe, Father. She is my mother. Siuoiatar turned her into a ewe."

The father did as his daughter requested. He did not slaughter the ewe. Instead, he returned to the cottage and hung the knife on a nail.

The next day, Siuoiatar said, "The ewe must be slaughtered. There's no reason to keep her."

* Pronounced "Syouyatar." In Karelian "Syöjätär."

That night when the daughter took food to her, the ewe said, "Daughter, when they come to slaughter me, eat the soup they make with my bones, but don't eat the meat, my dear. Then, gather the rest of my bones and bury them under the birch tree."

The father slaughtered the ewe, and Siuoiatar made soup. The daughter ate only a little of the soup. The others ate gluttonously.

"I must get rid of the girl," Siuoiatar decided, "since she eats nothing." Siuoiatar began plotting secretly.

Soon Siuoiatar gave birth to a daughter of her own. Siuoiatar hated her stepdaughter more than ever and made her work from dawn to dusk. The baby girl grew by leaps and bounds and quickly became an adult.

One day, the girl's father, Siuoiatar, and Siuoiatar's daughter prepared to attend a feast and ball that the tsar was throwing so that he might find a bride. Siuoiatar had used every means of persuasion to get her husband to agree to go. The couple got ready, but they did not take the man's oldest daughter with them.

Instead, Siuoiatar gave the girl work that had to be done while they were at the feast. The witch mixed together three types of grain and ordered the girl to separate the grain into three types again.

Weeping, the girl went to the birch tree, where her mother's bones were buried. "Help me, Mother," she said, "or I'll be killed, too."

"Take a twig from the tree," said the voice of the girl's mother. "Then say the following words: 'Divide into three piles as you were before.'"

The daughter did as he mother had instructed. She went into the cottage, struck the grain with the twig, and said, "Divide into three piles, grain, as you were before."

As soon as she struck the grain, it divided into three piles. She took the twig back to the tree and then walked over to her mother's grave.

"Don't you want to go to the feast and the ball, daughter?" her mother asked.

"Of course, I do, Mother, but I have nothing to wear, except this baggy *sarafan*."*

"Since I must stay down in the grave, I'll send you a horse. Wash up in one of the horse's ears and dress up in the other ear. Then ride to the ball on the horse."

The daughter stood waiting for the horse. Soon a horse came galloping. Its mane had a golden strand of hair, a silver strand, and yet another strand of indescribable color.

The girl got dressed quickly. She crawled into one of the horse's ears and came out looking so clean and beautiful that you could not find a beauty like her anywhere on earth. She crawled into the horse's other ear and came out dressed in clothing more beautiful than any clothing ever seen on earth.

---

* A *sarafan* is a peasant woman's pinafore-style dress that buttons down the front.

She mounted the horse and went to the tsar's feast. When she came to the tsar's courtyard, she tethered her horse. The tsar's servants ran out to meet her, and the guests surrounded her. "Who is she?" they asked. "She's probably the daughter of a foreign tsar."

They seated her at the best table in the best room, next to the tsarevich, the tsar's son. While sitting at the table, she noticed that Siuoiatar's daughter was under the table fighting with the dogs over some bones. The cook noticed the girl's bad behavior, too, and gave the girl such a kick that she knocked out one eye.

"Grab her! Grab her!" screamed Siuoiatar, who thought her disguised stepdaughter, who was seated nearby, had done the kicking. "Who does she think she is that she can knock out my daughter's eye?"

People rushed at the girl. They chased her and almost caught her. However, the girl threw a glove at them and got away as her pursuers were distracted in their attempt to catch the glove. The tsarevich, who had become enamored of her from the very first glance, ran after her, too, but he could not catch her.

After arriving home, the girl returned to the birch tree, beneath which her mother was buried. She gave the horse and clothing back to her mother and dressed once again in her baggy *sarafan*. She went into the cottage and pretended to be sorting grain.

Her father and Siuoiatar came home. Siuoiatar's daughter was howling as if she had been murdered because her eye had been knocked out.

"What happened to you, Sister?"

"Your sister was jumping from bed to bed and bench to bench with the tsarevich. She fell down and lost her eye," said Siuoiatar.

"There were so many people there, Sister," said Siuoiatar's daughter. "And the daughter of a foreign tsar came. What a beauty she was! Everyone admired her."

"Could I have been that girl?" asked the motherless girl.

"What a joke. You weren't that girl! Your nose is too small, and her clothes weren't like yours."

The next day they got ready to attend the second day of festivities. Siuoiatar took a jug of milk and a jug of water. She poured them into the same vessel and ordered her stepdaughter to separate the milk from the water while they were at the feast.

Weeping, the girl went to her mother's grave under the birch tree. "Now they will kill me for certain, Mama," she said. "Siuoiatar poured the milk and water together and asked me to separate them."

"Take a twig from the tree, daughter, and strike the liquid crosswise. It will be as it was before."

The daughter followed her mother's advice. She took a twig from the tree and hit the vessel crosswise. The water and milk went into separate jugs.

The girl took the twig back and placed it in the tree. Then she approached her mother's grave. Again, her mother gave her a horse and clothing. The dress was even more elegant than the previous one. The girl set out for the ball.

When she arrived, people ran to meet her. It was as if they had forgotten yesterday's incident. "The girl who was here yesterday has come," they cried, and they met her in a grand manner. Once again, they regaled her with the very best they had to offer and seated her beside the tsarevich.

She noticed that once again her stepsister was under the table vying with the dogs for food. The cook, too, noticed the girl's bad behavior and gave her a kick that broke her arm.

Again, Siuoiatar thought the disguised stepdaughter had hurt her daughter and began accusing her. The girl ran away, and the people ran after her. As she was running, she threw her ring amidst the crowd. People stopped running to catch it, thereby giving her the opportunity to escape.

She led the horse back to her mother and changed into her poor clothing. She entered the house quickly and pretended to be separating the milk from water. When the others came home, Siuoiatar's daughter was crying because her broken arm was painful.

"Your sister was playing hide-and-seek with the tsarevich when she fell and this misfortune occurred," Siuoiatar said by way of explanation. "And that beautiful stranger was there again."

"Could I have been that girl?" asked the stepdaughter.

"You weren't there. A tsar's daughter was there, and she was so beautiful that she really was something to look at. Her horse had a mane with a golden strand of hair, a silver strand, and a third strand of some indescribable color."

On the third day, the family went to the feast again and left the poor girl at home, as usual. Siuoiatar tore apart the stove before leaving and said, "When we return, if this stove is not standing as it was before I tore it down, you'll lose your head."

Once again the girl went to her mother's grave. She plucked a birch twig and took it with her. She hit the stove with the twig crosswise and said, "Take your former shape, stove."

The stove took its former shape, and the girl brought the twig back to her mother's grave. This time, too, her mother gave her a horse and clothing.

The girl set out for the tsar's. The people at the feast met her and led her to the best seat beside the tsarevich, as they had done previously. The tsarevich's affection for her grew with each new meeting.

Again, she saw her sister vying with the dogs for food. The cook noticed, too, and in exasperation kicked the stepsister so hard that she broke her leg. Once again, Siuoiatar placed the blame on the disguised beauty.

The girl ran to her horse. She threw her slipper into the crowd to distract the people who were chasing her. Thus, she was able to escape.

The girl took the horse back to her mother, changed into her old clothing, and entered the cottage. There, she began gathering clay up off the floor, as if she had just put the stove back together.

The family came home and reported that the beauty had been at the ball and had broken the stepsister's leg out of jealousy because the stepsister had been playing with the tsarevich.

"Wasn't I the beauty?" the girl asked.

"What idle talk!" declared Siuoiatar.

The tsarevich decided to marry the girl to whom the slipper, the glove, and the ring belonged. So, once again the people gathered at the tsar's palace. Everyone came to be measured.

Siuoiatar had cut off part of her daughter's feet and hands so that they would fit into the slipper and the glove. Then, Siuoiatar pared down her daughter's finger so that the ring would fit. Still, when the daughter's turn came, the items did not fit her.

"Are there still people in the kingdom who have not come to be measured?" asked the tsar's son.

"I have a daughter," said the abused girl's father, "but she wasn't at the ball."

"Let her come to be measured anyway," said the tsarevich.

"The girl is so slow-witted that we keep her at home. She hasn't been anywhere," Siuoiatar said.

Nevertheless, the girl was asked to come to be measured. Of course, everything fit just right.

"This is my bride," said the tsar's son. Turning to the poor girl, he said, "Let's travel the same roads you took to come here. Let's go to your home."

"Stay here," the girl said to him, "and I will return in a moment."

The girl left him and went to her mother's grave under the birch tree. "Now I've really gotten myself in trouble, Mama," she said. "The tsar's son wants to marry me, but I have nothing except my poor clothing."

"Take the best clothing from me, daughter. And take three horses and three carts loaded with goods, my child," her mother's voice answered.

The girl did as her mother had advised. Then she returned to the tsarevich.

Meanwhile, Siuoiatar, up to her old tricks, said to her daughter, "Accompany your sister, and when she crosses the river, push her into the water. Then take her place."

Siuoiatar's daughter followed her sister and the tsarevich. When they came to a bridge over the river, Siuoiatar's daughter tried to push her sister into the river. But the poor girl pushed her back. Siuoiatar's daughter fell into the river. Her sister rode on with the tsarevich, leaving Siuoiatar's daughter struggling in the water. The mean stepsister turned into a reed growing out of the water.

After they arrived at the tsar's palace, a wedding was held that was more magnificent than any wedding ever held before. The young couple lived happily in the tsar's palace. Soon, the tsarevich's wife gave birth to a child, a little boy.

When Siuoiatar learned that a child had been born, she prepared a gift to take to the newborn. She came to the bridge and noticed a reed growing out of the water. Thinking that it could be made into a pipe and that it would make a fine gift, she said, "I'll take this reed to my grandson."

When she pulled on the reed, it cried, "Ouch! Don't pluck me, Mama. It is I."

After learning what had happened to her daughter, Siuoiatar flew into a rage and rushed off to the tsar's palace. She arrived at the palace and screamed, "Is everyone sleeping, or are they awake?"

"They are neither sleeping, nor awake. They are ready and waiting for you, good-for-nothing," a hen's egg answered from its place in the nest.

Siuoiatar left and returned the next day. "Is everyone sleeping or awake?" she screamed again.

"They are waiting for you, and they are ready to deal with you," the hen's egg answered again.

When Siuoiatar came on the third day, the egg had rolled into a place where it was very hot, so hot that the egg was getting ready to hatch and therefore could not answer Siuoiatar's question. The witch got into the palace and sneaked into the room of the tsar's wife.

"Spit at my legs, traitor, and then walk around me three times. I'm going to turn you into a blue reindeer. If you don't spit, I'll kill you!" she ordered.

The tsar's wife had no choice. She spat and walked around Siuoiatar three times. She became a blue reindeer.

"Now I will be the tsarevich's wife," said Siuoiatar, "since my daughter wasn't able to do so."

Soon after, the baby boy's nurse took him to the bathhouse for his bath. He refused to eat. He cried without cease. The nurse did not know what to do with him. She could see that Siuoiatar, who was indifferent to the little boy, was not the woman who had given birth to the child.

Thinking that the boy would feel better in familiar surroundings, Siuoiatar took the child from the nurse and went into the palace. When she entered the palace, the servants thought it strange that the young bride's looks had been spoiled and that she no longer resembled her former self. The little boy continued to refuse food because he missed his mother very much.

Several days passed. One day the reindeer went up to an old widow and said, "Please go get my child and bring him to me so that I can feed him."

"Of course. How could I refuse your request? I'll bring him to you this very night."

The widow went to the tsarevich. "Give me your son," she said. "I'll nurse your child tonight. He is crying because he is hungry."

"Why not?" asked the desperate tsarevich. "Perhaps you will be able to comfort him."

The widow took the child and went home. When she arrived at her gate, she called:

Blue reindeer, blue reindeer,

Come feed your child.

Come out. Have no fear.

He won't eat while Siuoiatar's near.

The blue reindeer came out and shed her skin. She turned into her former self and began feeding and caring for the baby boy.

In the morning, the widow took the child back. That night the boy slept peacefully.

The next day the widow went for the child again. When she returned, she called once again:

Blue reindeer, blue reindeer,

Come feed your child.

Come out. Have no fear.

He won't eat while Siuoiatar's near.

The reindeer rushed out, took off her skin, and turned into a young woman. She went into the house with the child and took care of him that night.

On the third day, the widow went to fetch the child as the reindeer had ordered. "Give me your son to care for again," she begged the tsarevich. "This time come to pay me a visit while I'm caring for the child."

"Why not give you my son again since you take such good care of him? I'll come to see you as soon as I have taken care of some matters at the palace," said the tsarevich.

The widow took the child and went home. The tsarevich soon followed her and caught up with her on the road.

"When you visit me, you must hide," the widow told him. "A reindeer will appear in the yard after I have called her. Don't come out of hiding. When I take her into the cottage, she will throw her skin into the yard. Take the skin and burn it. After you have burned the skin, come into the cottage and say, 'You are mine, and I am yours.' You will get back your real wife. The woman living with you is Siuoiatar, the witch, and your real wife is going about disguised as a blue reindeer."

The tsarevich was amazed, but he did as the old woman had said. He hid and watched. The old woman called the reindeer out into the yard. The reindeer shed her skin and took the child into the cottage.

While his wife was feeding the baby, the tsarevich took the reindeer skin and burned it.

His wife jumped up. "Someone is burning my skin," she said. "I smell burning!"

"Who could be burning it?" asked the widow.

"I have no idea, but my skin is burning!"

The tsarevich's wife rushed to the door. The tsarevich met her at the threshold. "You are mine and I am yours," he cried. "We will live in happiness as we did before."

"I won't live with you! It would be better to run for eternity along the stony shores of the sea than to fall again into the clutches of Siuoiatar. I won't return! She killed my mother, and she almost killed me. I won't return!"

"She won't kill anyone anymore because I am going to order her to be put to death," said the tsarevich.

The tsarevich returned to the palace and ordered Siuoiatar to be burned alive. Then he went to the widow to fetch his wife and child. They lived happily every after. Moreover, the tsarevich ordered that a new home be built for the widow and that she be given a small pension for food and drink for the rest of her days.

ANARTEQ, THE SALMON BOY

(Greenland Inuit)

*T*here once was an old man who had many daughters but only one son. The son was called Anarteq. The girls were fond of going reindeer hunting with their father and brother. They often went to an inlet surrounded by steep cliffs that was located to the east from their home.

Anarteq would have his sisters go up the hill and then drive the reindeer down the hill until they came to a big lake. There, Anarteq would be waiting for them in his kayak. When the reindeer jumped into the lake, Anarteq attacked and killed them. After their *umiak* (boat) was filled with meat, Anarteq and his sisters would go home.

One day while they were out reindeer hunting as usual and the reindeer had swum out into the lake, Anarteq spotted a fawn. He caught the deer by the tail and began playing with it.

Suddenly, the fawn heaved its body above the surface of the lake and kicked Anarteq's kayak so that it turned over. Anarteq tried to right the kayak, but he failed. The kayak was full of water. At last, Anarteq managed to crawl out into the water.

His father and sisters watched him from the shore, but they could not help him. Finally, they heard him say, "Now the salmon are eating my belly."

Anarteq sank ever so slowly to the bottom of the lake. When he came to his senses, he had become a salmon.

His father and sisters had to go home without him. From then on, without a son, his father had to hunt as if he were a young man. The old man never again went back to the reindeer grounds, where his son had disappeared.

Now that Anarteq had become a salmon, he followed the other salmon in spring. After ice out, they swam down the river and out into the sea to grow fat on the abundance of food.

After the passage of many years, Anarteq's father decided to go once more to their hunting grounds. He was the leader of the hunting party. His daughters rowed the *umiak* (boat) while the old man steered with a paddle.

As they sailed into the inlet, the old man thought of his son and wept. Anarteq, the Salmon Boy, came up from the sea with the other salmon and saw the *umiak* and his weep-

---

ing father. Anarteq swam up to the *umiak* and grabbed the paddle with which his father steered.

Alarmed, the old man drew his paddle out of the water and said, "It must be Anarteq. He nearly pulled the paddle from my hand."

For a long time the old man dared not put the paddle back into the water. When at last he did so, Anarteq's father noticed that his daughters were weeping.

Once again, Anarteq, the Salmon Boy, swam up to the *umiak* and grabbed his father's paddle. When the old man tried to remove his paddle from the water, Anarteq held it so that his father could not move it. At last the old man drew the paddle slowly to the surface of the lake. This time he drew up both the paddle and his son.

From that day on, Anarteq became a man again. He hunted for many years to feed his family well.

THE JEALOUS WIFE

(Deg Hit'an/Ingalik, Ahtna, Koyukon, Aleut, Inupiat, Alaskan Yup'ik)

A man, his wife, and their two young sons lived in a small village near the mouth of a river that flowed into the sea. The man was a good hunter and provided well for his family. As soon as the spring ice broke up, he paddled up the river in his canoe looking for food. He always bagged so many animals that they could not all fit into his canoe. He had to make a raft upon which he piled his many animal skins. Every year after fishing season ended, he got into his canoe and went upriver again and repeated the entire process.

One year he paddled up the river, as was his custom, and failed to return home at the usual time. His wife began to worry about him and had difficulty sleeping at night. "Where could he be?" she wondered. The two little boys kept asking their mother where their father was.

Eventually, the man came downstream in his canoe, but this time he had very little game to show for his effort.

"Where have you been?" his wife asked angrily. "You have been gone too long. The grass is tall, and the mosquitoes are out now. And where is your raft? Don't tell me that in all that time you managed to fill just your canoe with game!"

"This time I was a poor shot. I missed most of the animals," the husband replied.

"Where are the piles of caribou and beaver skins that you used to bring home?"

"I saw them, but I kept missing the target," he replied.

Then the salmon began running and husband and wife started netting them. There were still many fish to be caught when the husband said, "I think I'll paddle up the river again."

"It is too soon to leave. Why are you in such a hurry? You usually go in autumn. And if you don't bag any more game than you did in spring, then it is hardly worth the effort."

He left anyway and was gone for a very long time. He returned when ice was forming along the shore. Once again, the canoe was full of animal skins, and once again there was no raft to be seen.

His wife rebuked him again for being gone so long and asked why there was so little game, barely enough to last them through the season. Once again, the husband made excuses.

In winter, the man got sick. He was sick but nevertheless ate well. When winter was at its coldest, his condition worsened and he seemed to be near death.

"I'm going to die," he told his wife. "After I have gone, put lots of animal skins in my canoe—wolf, otter, marten, and wolverine skins. And put the best fat in the canoe. Put my weapons, my bow and arrows, into the canoe, too. Cover the opening of the canoe with caribou hides and set it high up on poles. Then, leave it there."

The man's wife did as he had wanted. She and her two sons built a fire and wept. The woman burned her hair out of grief over the loss of her husband.

When spring arrived, the woman and her sons were still grieving over the death of husband and father. Life would be difficult for them now without a hunter to bring home food.

The birds began returning from the south, where they had flown for the winter. One morning, the woman went out before her boys had awakened. Still sad, she was weeping. She heard a bird singing in a small voice and listened attentively because she thought the bird had called her husband's name.

Sure enough! The bird spoke her husband's name again. "Your husband is married to two women who live up the river," sang the bird.

The bird's song made the woman suspicious. She went to the spot where the canoe was elevated on poles and untied the caribou hide around the opening. She lifted the hide and looked inside. The canoe was empty! Her husband's body was not there. Neither were the wolf, otter, marten, and wolverine skins. The bow and arrows were gone, too.

"The little bird didn't lie. It told me the truth," she thought. "What a mean trick my husband has played on me and our sons."

The woman got angry. She climbed up onto the cache and found a white bearskin there. She took it down from the cache and soaked it in water and stretched it until the skin got bigger. That night as the boys slept, she brought in some food for them—meat, fat, and fish. Then, the woman pulled the bearskin around her body. The claws were still attached to the paws, and the woman found some bear teeth in her workbag. She put the teeth into her mouth, and she became a bear—a very angry bear.

She rushed about in a rage and tore up trees by the roots. Tired, she came home, pushed back her hood, and took out the bear teeth. Once again, she was a woman. But she was still angry and could not sleep, so she went outside and tore down a birch tree.

When she went into the house again, she told the boys that she was going to leave, but that she would return. "Here is some food and water that I brought in for you. Don't try to fetch water yourselves, or you'll fall into the river. Don't climb up onto the food cache either. You might fall down and I won't be able to help you. Don't worry, I'll come back soon."

After giving the boys instructions, the enraged woman put the bearskin back on and set off running over hills and ravines on her journey upriver. She knocked down trees that got in her way because she was now so strong. She picked up stones and attached them on both sides of her body and onto her forehead.

Raven was up in a tree watching her. When he saw her attaching stones on her body, he laughed. "How silly you are, woman," said Raven. "Take those stones off, or people will make fun of you."

The woman removed the stones.

"That's better. Now you look beautiful again," Raven chortled.

The woman rushed on because she did not want to leave her children alone for very long. She kept running along the river until she came to a big village. She took off her bearskin and took out the teeth. She hid them beneath a tree. She came to a big *kashim*, the men's house, and saw a big house next to the *kashim*. She went into the house.

She saw two beautiful women busy cooking. They invited her in, so she sat down on the platform. Meat was boiling in the pots. The woman looked around and saw an abundance of everything—a bed made of caribou hide and fur parkas. "Where are your husbands?" she asked.

"We are married to the same man. He came here last spring after ice-out. He left in summer but returned in winter. He has been with us ever since. Just now he has gone to gather wood. He is a wonderful husband and always brings us the best meat and animal skins," the most beautiful wife explained.

It was too much for the abandoned wife to bear. She looked into the pots of boiling meat. "There is very little oil in your pots," she said.

She turned to one of the women and said, "Smile and bend over the pot."

The new wife did so and oil appeared on the top of the stew.

The woman turned to the second new wife and said, "Squint and bend over the pot."

The other new wife did as the old wife said. The abandoned old wife grabbed both of the new wives by the hair and pushed their heads into the pots, holding them there until both were dead. The old wife sat the two new wives up and positioned them so that they looked normal. One wife was smiling and the other was squinting. Then, she ran out of the house and up the hill to wait for her husband to return.

The man came paddling up the river in his canoe, towing wood on a raft. He moored the canoe and went into the house. He touched the woman who was squinting, and the skin came off her face. He touched the woman who was smiling, and the same thing happened to her.

The man ran out of the house crying, "What has happened to my wives? I bet my old wife has been here."

The villagers gathered. There was a hue and cry. "We saw a big bear on the mountain," someone shouted.

Part 6: Spirits, Shamans, and Shapeshifters

"Let's get it," another person cried. "The bear must have killed our women!"

The men grabbed their spears and weapons and headed for the mountain with the abandoned woman's husband in the lead.

The bear seized her husband and pushed back her hood to show him who she was. Then she bit off his head and tore him to shreds with her claws. "That is for abandoning your family and leaving us hungry," she roared.

The bear ran down to the village and tore down all of the houses and food caches. She attacked men, women, and children, too.

Then, the bear began thinking about her two boys and returned to her own village. When she entered her house, her sons were frightened and attacked her with sticks. The woman pushed back her hood and said, "It's only me, boys."

She went outside, took off her bearskin, and removed her teeth. She hid these items under a log. When she returned, she lifted the boys onto her lap and hugged them.

They stayed in their home that summer. When autumn came, she said, "Now we must go to another place, where we will make a new home for the winter."

It was cold, so they got dressed in bearskins. They walked up the hill until they came to a place to make their new home. They sharpened their claws by scratching on the trees and then they dug their winter home.

After they finished digging their den, the woman said, "From this day on people will see us only rarely. We will hide from them."

And that is how the story ends.

THE MAN WHO BECAME A CARIBOU

(Canadian Inuit and Alaskan Inupiat)

This story happened long ago when people could change into animals and animals could change into people.

*A*n Inuit hunter was very unhappy. He never had a successful hunt. Other hunters brought home plenty of game, but not this hunter.

One day he decided to leave home because he was of no use to his wife and two sons. "What good is a husband and father who can't provide for his family?" he asked them.

He left all his weapons at home, bid his family good-bye, and began walking inland across the barren tundra. As he walked, he thought, "I wish I were an animal, not a man. Even an animal's life must be better than that of a failure of a hunter."

He wandered on until he came to a flock of ptarmigan. They were eating some leaves and berries and making little contented sounds. They seemed happy. The hunter followed the birds all day in the hope that they would feel sorry for him and magically change him into one of them. He followed them from berry patch to berry patch until they came to the village where the ptarmigan lived. Once in the village, the ptarmigan changed into people.

The chief of the ptarmigan walked up to the hunter and asked, "Why have you been following us, hunter?"

"I have been following you because you seem happy and your life seems to be better than mine. I'm tired of being a poor hunter and would like to join you. Please use your magic to turn me into a ptarmigan."

"You are mistaken to believe that we have an easy life," said the chief. "You can't stay with us. You wouldn't like being chased by larger birds, such as the hawk or eagle, or by men like you with bows and arrows. Every moment we are at risk of losing our lives. Is that how you want to live?"

"No, it isn't," the hunter admitted, and he traveled on in his search for a better life.

After he had gone some distance, the hunter caught sight of two Arctic hares, playing among some rocks. They romped around and chased one another.

"The hares seem happy," the hunter thought. "That's the life I want to live."

The hunter followed the two hares all day. At the end of the day, the hares went into a little house dug into the bottom of a hill. The man followed them into the house. He looked around. There were no hares, but an old couple was sitting there.

"Why have you been following us?" the old man asked.

The hunter replied as he had replied to the ptarmigan. "I have been following you because you seem happy and your life seems to be better than mine. I'm tired of being a poor hunter and would like to join you. Please use your magic to turn me into a hare."

"I'm sorry," said the hare, "but you can't stay with us. Our life is not as easy as it seems. You wouldn't like being hunted by big birds or animals larger than us, such as the fox, or even by men like yourself with bows and arrows. Is that how you want to live?"

"No, it isn't," the hunter admitted, and he continued on his journey in search of a better life.

Finally, he spotted a herd of caribou. He followed them all day and observed how they ate grass and moved slowly and with dignity across the land. That evening they came to a large village. There, the caribou changed their form and became men. The men went into the meetinghouse. The hunter followed them in hopes of speaking to the caribou chief.

The caribou chief came up to the hunter and asked, "Why have you been following us all day?"

"Don't be afraid of me. I wasn't hunting you," replied the hunter. "Look, I don't have any weapons. I have been following you because you seem happy and your life seems better than mine. I'm tired of being a bad hunter and would like to join you. Please use your magic to turn me into a caribou."

The caribou chief took pity on the hunter and did as the hunter requested. He used his magic to change him into a caribou and allowed the hunter to join the herd.

It was not the life that the hunter had expected. The hunter had a hard time keeping up with the herd. He was slower than the other caribou. He did not like the food. So, unlike the other caribou, he became thin, rather than big and strong. When hunters came with bows and arrows, the Caribou Man could not sense that they were near. He was always afraid.

He was, however, very good at avoiding traps set for the caribou. He was able to sense where there were holes in the ground that he might fall into and where snares had been set to entangle his legs. Many years passed, and the Caribou Man was never caught in a trap. Perhaps it was his experience as a human hunter that helped him to detect them. Life as a caribou was far from easy, but the hunter, now very old, was resigned to caribou ways.

After the passage of many moons, the old hunter began thinking of home. He missed his wife and two sons and wanted to see them again. He went to the caribou chief with his request.

"It won't be easy," the chief said. "You know the ways of the caribou now. It will be hard to forget them and be a man again."

"I know," said the Caribou Man, "but I must see my family before I die."

"Very well, go to your family," said the caribou chief. "You have my permission."

The Caribou Man thanked the chief and set out on his long journey home. He walked on, watching carefully for traps. He avoided all of the traps until his village was in view. Then he became so excited that he forgot about the traps. Suddenly, his legs would not move. They had been caught in a snare.

As night drew near, two young men came to check their traps. They were delighted to find a caribou in their snare. The young men got ready to shoot the caribou, but to their surprise the animal spoke in a human voice. "Before you shoot me, please take your knife and cut off my skin," said the Caribou Man.[1]

At first the young men were afraid. They never had heard a caribou speak. Nevertheless, they decided to do as the caribou had asked. They took out the stitches and cut off the skin. The young men were surprised to see that a man was inside the skin.

The young men stared at the hunter in amazement. Even though he was very old, they recognized him as their father who had left home many long years before.[2]

PART 7

HEROES AND HEROINES

BLADDER-HEAD BOY BATTLES MAMMOTH

(Kaska)

A man, his wife, and their baby were traveling about in search of beavers, which they netted and ate. They wandered from lake to lake and stream to stream. They went wherever beaver were plentiful.

They came to a big lake. After crossing it, they camped on the other side. It was the woman's custom to check the nets to see if any beaver had been caught and to bring the beaver meat home on a skin toboggan.

One day she was dragging home her skin toboggan, laden with beaver meat, and carrying her baby on her back. She heard the sound of heavy stomping. Out of the corner of her eye, she noticed a large animal lumbering toward her. It was an enormous woolly mammoth.[1] The woman was frightened.

In her panic the woman scattered the beaver meat in the snow in hope that the meat would distract Mammoth until she was able to escape. She ran back to camp and in breathless excitement told her husband what had happened.

Her husband took her words lightly and refused to believe her. He laughed at her and said jokingly, "Mammoths don't exist anymore. I bet you have a lover to whom you gave the beaver meat. And now you've made up this fantastic story to cover up what you have done."

When the woman denied his accusations, the man laughed at her again. Then he left to set more beaver nets.

When the husband returned, he was very tired, so he went to bed. Soon he was asleep and snoring.

The woman was still uneasy. Before going to bed, she cut a trail through the willow brush that surrounded their camp so that she could make a hasty escape, should hungry Mammoth find them and attack. She lay down opposite her husband with the fire between them. She kept on her moccasins and clutched her baby tightly in her arms, prepared to run at a moment's notice.

While the man slept, his wife lay awake, listening. Suddenly, she heard stomp-stomp-stomp, and the earth shook. "Wake up!" she screamed to her husband.

Her husband lay without moving in a deep sleep. The woman poked him with a stick, but he just mumbled a few words and slept on.

The woman could wait no longer because Mammoth was already near. She snatched up her baby and fled.

Mammoth burst into camp and ate the unfortunate husband, who had failed to heed his wife's words and who had understood too late that his wife's story, fantastic as it may have seemed, was true.

After consuming the man, Mammoth followed the woman's trail. Mammoth made strange sounds, like a person crying. He made the ground shake with his heavy footsteps.

Exhausted, the woman came to an encampment beside a lake. She warned the people living there that huge, hungry Mammoth, who had killed her husband, was chasing her and that he was already quite near the opposite shore of the lake.

The men rushed out onto the ice on the lake and made holes in the ice on the opposite shore so that Mammoth would fall through the ice and drown long before reaching their village.

Just as they had planned, Mammoth broke through the ice because of his weight, but Mammoth did not drown. He was so big that he could walk along the bottom of the lake with his head above the ice, crunching and breaking the ice that stood in his way with his sharp tusks.

The hairy beast plodded on toward the people. Once again, the woman snatched up her baby and fled. People stood paralyzed with fear, watching helplessly as Mammoth approached. Some of them even fainted.

One boy, whom everyone abused, lived in the village. He was treated worse than a dog. Even the old women had no respect for him and stepped over him as if he were not there. The poor boy wore a moose-bladder over his head, so he looked as if he were bald. He was called Bladder-Head Boy. He was strange, but his grandmother knew that actually he had shamanic powers. She knew that he had magic trousers and magic arrows and that he was as strong and clever as the greatest warrior.

"Look!" cried the boy's grandmother. "A monster is coming!"

"Bring my trousers and arrows, Grandmother!"

Bladder-Head Boy put on his trousers and seized his bow and arrows. He jumped into the air and shook his head until the bladder burst. His long hair fell down over him.

He took an arrow and pulled back his bow. He shot the arrow right through Mammoth. Then he jumped to the other side of Mammoth and shot an arrow through Mammoth from that direction. He jumped and shot, jumped and shot, until he killed the frightful creature with his shamanic power.

The people of the village were very thankful that Bladder-Head Boy had saved their lives. As a reward, they gave him two beautiful maidens to be his wives. He selected only one maiden as his bride. In addition, the people made him their chief. Ever since that day, people have had chiefs to lead and advise the tribe.

The woman who had fled with her baby returned and began living with her new friends. Her home had been destroyed and her husband had been killed, so she could not have returned home, even if she had so desired.

YOMA AND THE TWO SISTERS

(Komi)

There once lived a man and wife who had one daughter. The wife died, and the man married a second time. He brought his new wife home, and she turned out to be an evil, shrewish woman. She had a daughter of her own, a rude lazybones whom she pampered. As for her stepdaughter, she made her work from morning to night and gave her leftovers to eat while her own daughter was given the tastiest and sweetest morsels.

One day the stepmother sent her stepdaughter to the river to rinse a skein of yarn. "Go to the river and rinse the yarn well," she said. "Never mind that the water is cold. Your hands will be warm afterward because of the work."

The girl ran to the river and began rinsing the yarn. Her fingers quickly froze and became quite numb. The skein of yarn slipped out of her numbed fingers and sank to the bottom of the river. The girl ran home in tears and told her stepmother that the yarn had "drowned."

Her stepmother struck her on the head and shouted, "Oh, you lazybones! I knew you'd "drown" the yarn. Now jump into the water and get it from the bottom of the river. Get it by any means you like, but don't return without the yarn!"

The girl burst into tears and went to the river. She went up to the riverbank, closed her eyes, and dove into the water. When she opened her eyes, she saw a green meadow. A herd of golden-maned horses was grazing there. The wind was blowing their manes about and tangling them. The girl went up to the horses and combed out the tangles in their manes with her comb.

A golden-maned mare came up to her, neighed, and began speaking in a human voice. "Go along that path," she said. "You will come to a stream of cream and then a stream of honey. Don't taste either the cream or honey because those streams belong to old Yoma, the water witch. She has your yarn. The path leads to the old witch's cottage. The cottage will be twirling in the wind. You must cry out:

> *Cottage, stop! Don't whirl or twirl.*
> *Give permission to enter to this girl.*

When the cottage stops twirling, walk boldly into it."

The girl thanked the golden-maned mare and started down the path. She came to a herd of grazing cows. Every cow had a full udder. And there was no one to milk them. The girl milked the cows.

Afterward, a brown cow began lowing and spoke in a human voice. "Listen, girl, when you come to old Yoma, she'll order you to work. As a reward for working, she'll ask you to choose between two baskets, a red one and a blue one. Choose the blue one."

The girl thanked the cow and traveled on. She came to the stream of cream. Although she was very thirsty, she did not drink the cream that belonged to old Yoma. The girl crossed the stream on a little bridge and traveled on.

She came to the stream of honey. The poor girl's mouth watered, but she did not taste the honey.

The path led to Yoma's cottage, which whirled and twirled in the wind, like a top.

The girl cried:

> *Cottage, stop! Don't whirl and twirl.*
> *Give permission to enter to this girl.*

The cottage stopped twirling immediately. The girl went in. There sat old Yoma, mistress of the watery kingdom.

"Why have you come, girl?" the old witch asked.

"My skein of yarn 'drowned,' Granny, and I've come looking for it," the girl answered.

"I have your skein of yarn," said the old witch. "But first you must do some work. Go chop some wood and heat up the bathhouse."

The girl chopped the wood and heated up the bathhouse. The old witch brought in a basket full of frogs, lizards, and water beetles.

"These are my dear children. All of them need a thorough washing and steaming so that they will be happy. Here are my swift-running lizards, naughty little froggies, and swimming beetles."

The girl washed all of the creatures carefully and gave them a good steaming so that they were happy.

The old witch brought in two baskets, a red one and a blue one. "Choose whichever one you want," she said.

The girl chose the blue basket, just as the brown cow had instructed.

"Open it when you get to the green meadow," said Yoma. "Your yarn is inside."

The girl set out for home past the streams of cream and of honey. When she came to the green meadow, she opened the basket. A big, beautiful cottage appeared. Inside was everything one might need to keep house. The girl saw the skein of yarn that had sunk to the bottom of the river there, too.

The girl was overjoyed. On the very same day she married a poor lad from her village, whom she had long loved. After the wedding ceremony, they went to live in the miraculous cottage that Yoma had given the girl.

The stepmother's fury knew no bounds. She was angrier than ever. "Why should such good fortune fall into the lap of that slovenly ne'er-do-well?" she cried. "It should have happened instead to my clever, wonderful daughter!"

The next day she sent her own daughter to the river to rinse a skein of yarn so that she, too, could receive a dowry. The daughter did not want to freeze her white hands, so she did not rinse the yarn. She just threw it into the water and let it sink to the bottom of the river.

She ran home weeping. "Mama," she whined. "I dropped the yarn accidentally, and it 'drowned' in the river."

"Oh, my darling daughter, it can't be helped. You'll have to dive into the river to get the yarn," the mother said.

The girl, who was so afraid of spoiling her white hands, dove reluctantly into the river and found herself in a green meadow. A herd of golden-maned horses was grazing there.

A mare came up to the girl and asked, "Please comb out my mane with your comb."

"I don't have time," snapped the girl, afraid to spoil her white hands. "I am looking for my skein of yarn and must hurry to Yoma's cottage for my reward, for my dowry!"

The horses said nothing. The girl ran down the path until she came to some cows.

"Please milk me, girl," one of the cows begged. "My udder is heavy and aches because it is too full."

"I don't have time," snapped the girl with the white hands. "And besides, I don't know how to milk. My father's daughter milks our cows at home. That's her job."

The girl ran on further and came to a stream of cream. "Oh, ho, drinking cream is my job," she thought.

She got down on all fours and started drinking out of the stream. She drank for a long time, then stopped to catch her breath, and started in drinking again. Finally, she got up and waddled slowly down the path.

Suddenly, she spied a stream of honey. "Oh, what a shame that I drank so much cream," she thought. "Now I don't have room for the honey. Oh, well, I'll give it a try."

Again, she got down on all fours and began eating out of the stream. She ate a bit of honey and then stopped to catch her breath. Then she began eating more honey. She just could not tear herself away from the honey, which was sweet and fragrant. Finally, she felt that there was no room for another drop. She got up with difficulty and crawled down the path.

She came to Yoma's cottage, which was whirling and twirling in the wind without cease. The girl tried to stop it with her hands and tore her white hands to shreds before she was able to. The cottage stopped whirling around, and she went in.

"Why have you come?" asked old Yoma.

"I've come for my reward and my dowry," replied the girl.

"How do you like that? She wants a reward, and yet she has done no work. Still, she goes on about a reward. Very well. Go chop some wood and heat up the bathhouse. And mind that you don't make it too smoky in there."

The girl began chopping wood, but it did not go well because she did not know how to do it. She chopped so little wood that the bathhouse was poorly heated. The water was not hot, but tepid.

Old Yoma brought the girl a basket full of frogs, lizards, and water beetles. Concerned about her white hands, the girl did not want to wash them. She just lashed them with a besom and let it go at that.

The old witch brought two baskets to her, a red one and a blue one. "Choose one of them," she said.

The girl with the white hands grabbed the red basket because it was larger and ran off without even so much as a "thank you."

Her mother was waiting for her at the door when she arrived home. "Oh, my clever girl!" she cried. "What a good girl! Now you, too, have brought good fortune to this house."

The two, mother and daughter, went into the cottage, where they opened the basket. A red fire burst out of the basket and burned their cottage to the ground.

When the father came home, he found his house and family gone. He went to live with his daughter, with whom he lived a long and happy life.

THE CHAKHKLI

(Saami)

The Chakhkli are little people who live under the ground and beneath stones. They like to run around naked. They bustle about imitating everyone they see. Although they are kind, their mischievousness gets them into trouble and sometimes harms human beings. There are many stories about their antics, and this is one of them.[1]

*N*ot far from the town of Kola, there lived an old woman and an old man.[*] They had no children. The old man hunted for a living while his wife kept house.

One day as the old man was walking through the forest, he noticed smoke rising up from the roots of an ancient fir tree. He went closer and saw a hole in the ground. He lay down on the moss and lowered his head into the hole to find out what this strange phenomenon was and what was happening in the hole.

He saw beneath the ground dwellings just like the ones the Saami have. There were little villages, some in the forest and others beside the sea. Herdsmen were tending reindeer herds, and fishermen were fishing. There were *vezhi* in the villages. *Vezhi* are cabins of rough-hewn wood, covered with birch bark and turf. They stood in two rows. People were going in and out, and children were running about in the streets. There was a woman rushing out of a *vezha*[**] and running home. She held a smoldering piece of wood in her hands, from which sparks were scattering. She had borrowed the fire from her neighbor to light the fire on her own hearth. A man was training a deer to pull a *kerezha*, or sledge. The *kerezha* was just like the Saami's *kerezha*. It looked like a boat set on a ski. Further in the distance, a herdsman was driving a herd of reindeer. Young women were rinsing clothes in the river. Everything there, under the ground, was just as it is with people on earth.

---

[*] Kola is a town south of Murmansk on Russia's Kola Peninsula.
[**] Singular form.

A man came out of his *vezha* with a rifle on his shoulder. A little dog on a leash was running behind him. The rifle was an old flintlock type that makes a great deal of noise. He was going hunting. He was very small, and his dog was even smaller. His house, too, was ever so tiny.

Some children had gathered by a tree trunk and were climbing up the trunk and out onto the earth, where the old man stood watching. He fell back and hid behind a fir tree. He waited there to see what would happen next.

The little children piled out of the hole in the ground. They had big heads and eyes that looked like cracks in birch bark. They wore large *kan'gi,* or boots, on their thin, little legs. The boots were made of white reindeer fur with toes pointed up. The children were healthy, but they had fat backsides.

"What a miracle!" thought the old man as he watched. "They are Chakhkli, who dwell beneath the earth!"

The children had already come out of the hole and were playing about. They jumped, turned somersaults, and mimicked one another. They kept laughing and giggling merrily. The children let out peals of laughter, as if someone were tickling them under their arms.

The old man was touched to see how merry and amusing the Chakhkli were. He had no children of his own, so he was happy to feast his eyes on the children of the little people. They played like little squirrels and gamboled on the moss beneath the fir tree.

As the old man watched them, he grew pensive. He returned home and said to his old wife, "Make me a big *kan'ga* (one boot with a turned-up toe), and tie a lace to it."

The old woman sewed a big boot and tied a lace to the boot. The old man added a long rope. He took the *kan'ga* and went to the spot where he had seen the Chakhkli. He threw the *kan'ga* close to the hole in the ground by the fir tree and waited to see what would happen.

It began to get dark. As soon as the sun had illuminated the treetops with its last rays, the Chakhkli children ran out of their hole in the ground and began playing. One of them saw the *kan'ga* and began fiddling with it. First, he tried it on. Then he jumped across it. Then he somersaulted over the boot. Finally, he put both feet into the *kan'ga* and wound the lace around his feet.

It was then that the old man pulled on the rope and let out a cry. The children jumped back into the hole, but the child in the *kan'ga* fell and remained lying on his side.

The old man went over to him and lifted him up. He freed him from the *kan'ga* and took him by the hands. "What is your name?" the old man asked.

The child looked into the old man's eyes and laughed. "What is your name?" he mimicked.

"Yarasim," answered the old man. "And sometimes I'm called Yarashka, too."

"Yarashka, too. Yarasim," the Chakhkli child repeated, and he burst into gales of laughter.

The old man gave his merry foundling his own name, Yarasim, and Yarashka as a nickname.

"Well, now, let's go home, Yarasim."

"Home, Yarasim. Let's go now. Well?" the Chakhkli repeated.

The old man took the boy home and said to his wife, "Since we have no children, here is a son for you."

Yarashka repeated his father's words. "Here is a son for you. Since we have no children, here is a son for you."

The old woman was happy. They began living together. Everything was fine, except for one small problem. Whatever the boy's mother or father said to him, he mimicked, laughing all the while. He laughed and burst into peals of laughter, so merry was he.

A typical conversation went like this. "Yarashka, come to dinner," the old couple would say.

"Come to dinner, Yarashka," the boy would reply.

Eventually, the old couple became used to Yarashka's ways and they lived in harmony. It was the same when Yarashka worked. He mimicked whatever someone else was doing. At times it ended badly.

Once when his mother was going to repair the fishing nets, she took Yarashka with her. She gave him a little knife and a shuttle with thread wound around it. "Cut out the torn part of the net, and weave new squares in place of the old ones," she instructed.

She showed the boy how to mend the net, and they began working together. Yarashka's mother mended the net quickly. Away with the torn net, and one, two—in two twists of the shuttle the holes of the next net were mended and it looked like a new one.

The little boy watched his mother's hands. He cut the net with his little knife in the same manner. One, two—in two twists of the shuttle there were more holes than before. He ripped up the entire net, all the while chuckling, giggling, and breaking into peals of laughter. What was he giggling about? Apparently, work was an amusement to him.

The old woman got angry and drove him away. "Take your Chakhkli and do whatever you want with him. Take him back to the hole where you found him. He has spoiled the net. Now I'll never be able to mend it," the old woman said.

Unfortunately, when his mother drove him away, Yarashka attacked her and drove her away in turn, screaming the same words at her that she had screamed at him. All the while, the Chakhkli chuckled and burst into volleys of laughter.

"She has spoiled the net!" he cried. "Take her and do whatever you want with her. Take her to the hole! Where you found her, take her. Take her and do whatever you want with her."

He kept waving his little knife and spoiling the net. Finally, he hopped up and began tickling the old woman. All the while, he kept chuckling, bursting into peals of laughter, and giggling. What was he giggling about? The old woman practically lost consciousness from all the tickling. Nevertheless, Yarashka continued to giggle and tickle the poor woman. He would not let her go.

Yarashka's father came running. The old man lectured Yarashka. He took the boy by the hand, and Yarashka held onto the old man's sleeve. They went for a walk together. The old man took a step with his left foot, and Yarashka took a step with his right foot, which was closest to the old man's foot. Thus they strode on, foot to foot, left-right, left-right. As they walked, they brushed against one another.

Yarashka had a great respect for his father and obeyed him. The old man taught his son to cut wood into boards. The work progressed quite well, and the old man hoped that soon they would be able to erect a new barn. Yarashka began cutting. He cut and cut and cut without stopping. As he cut, he chuckled and giggled. By nightfall Yarashka had cut up all of the wood.

That is how they got along. They erected the barn, and the old man was very pleased. He knew how to deal with Yarashka. For the old woman Yarashka was only destruction. He tore the fishing nets, he broke the dishes, and he smeared himself with soot. She asked the old man to take the Chakhkli to the forest and leave him there. "Let him go home and giggle there," she said.

Yarashka longed to leave. Every spring he tried to run away, but the old man looked after his son and did not let him go even one step away.

Several years passed. Yarashka grew up and became strong. He grew up to be hardy and intelligent. However, he remained the same undersized person.

Times were bad. Enemy troops, the Chuds,[*] were wandering over the lands of the Saami. The Chuds robbed the people. The Saami fled from them to the forests. There, they dug homes in the earth and lived in those dugout dwellings so that their enemies could not find them.

One spring the old man failed to keep an eye on Yarashka, and the boy left home. He ran far away. He ran over mountains and wandered through forests. He was seeking the hole under the fir tree that would lead him to his old home. He could not find it. Thus, he was wandering when he stumbled upon the Chuds.

The Chuds were sailing down the river in boats. They were fighting their way to the town of Kola.[**] They intended to plunder the town.

When they caught sight of Yarashka, they grabbed him and asked, "Where do you live?"

"You live where?" answered Yarashka, laughing.

"Who are you?"

"You are who?" Yarashka answered with a question and then gave a giggle.

"What is your name?" screamed the leader of the Chuds.

[*] A term used to refer to several Finnic tribes, especially Karelians.
[**] Oldest town of the Kola Peninsula; located in Murmansk Oblast', Russia, not far from the town of Murmansk.

"Name is what?" Yarashka asked the enemy back and giggled again "he, he, he."

No matter how they asked him, Yarashka kept answering, as he was accustomed. He answered using the same words he had been asked, only in reverse order, beginning with the last word and giggling.

The Chuds got angry. They decided to throw Yarashka into the river, straight into the waterfall below. They grabbed the boy and flung him into the water. Suddenly, the Chuds saw their own soldier flying into the river, instead of the boy adopted by the Saamis. They repeated their action, and once again they sent their own man flying into the waterfall.

"Stab him where he stands!" ordered the leader of the Chuds.

They hacked at the boy with a sword. When they looked at the results of what they had done, three of their own men, who had been standing in a row, were no longer there. Yarashka stood alive and unharmed, chuckling and sniggering.

The leader of the Chuds began to falter. He ordered the boy to lead them to his mother and father.

"If you touch one hair on the heads of my old mother and father, not one man in your detachment will make it alive to the town of Kola," said Yarashka. This time Yarashka did not laugh.

"Very well," said the leader of the Chuds. "Lead us to Kola."

Yarashka sat at the front of the boat, sailing at the vanguard. He led them down the river, across rapids, over portages, and past quiet stretches of water. They sailed on for five days and five nights. Yarashka led them to the Tuloma River,* to a high waterfall and a wide patch of ice-free water to a little island in the middle of the river.

"We'll halt here," he said. "We'll spend the night because we can't enter the town of Kola at night."

They set up camp on the island for the night. Yarashka stood guard. The Chuds slept. It was quiet. As soon as night fell, Yarashka tied all the boats together, one after another. He left just one little boat for himself. The rest he sent down into the abyss of the waterfall, where the boats were smashed to smithereens.

Yarashka crossed the river in his little boat and went home to the old couple. As for the Chuds, they were stranded on the island, and they perished there.

* One of the largest rivers in Fennoscandia, the Tuloma River originates in Finland and flows into Kola Bay.

THE DAUGHTER OF OLD KAGÈNA

(Even)

*T*here once lived a woman who was a good hunter. Her father's name was Kagè-na. He was very old and got about by leaning on two sticks. He was blind in one eye. But he was the proud owner of five reindeer and had a daughter skilled at hunting.

Riding on her father's reindeer, whose name was Khasandzhai, the young woman used to go hunting with her father. She had arrows made of mammoth bones. In just one day she could kill from ten to twenty wild reindeer. When she caught sight of wild reindeer, she would shoot arrows into the entire herd.

One day the young woman met a man while hunting. He was enormous, the size of a tree trunk. He rode on a reindeer the size of a gigantic elk. His arrows were made of strong wood.

The man did not even greet Kagèna's daughter. Seated on his riding deer, he asked, "Where are you going?"

"I'm hunting," the young woman sang. Kagèna's daughter always spoke in song, whereas the man conversed in ordinary speech.

The man stuck out his tongue and laughed. "You're just a woman. What kind of hunter could you possibly be?"

The young woman felt confused and ashamed. She was embarrassed, and so she traveled on. After traversing the distance of an arrow shot, she looked back and sang, "Why do you hurt my feelings, young man? You have insulted me, so just try to shoot an arrow into my father's deer, Khasandzhai."

After uttering these words, she led Khasandzhai aside. She grabbed the end of his reins and placed him sideways so that the young man had an easy shot.

Without hesitation, the young man climbed down from his deer and began shooting arrows into the young woman's deer. He shot thirty-five times, but not one arrow hit the woman's reindeer. Finally, he had used up all of his arrows.

"Well, now, young man, it's my turn to shoot at your reindeer," said Kagèna's daughter.

"Go ahead," the young man said confidently. He placed his deer sideways and held onto the reins.

Kagèna's daughter shot just once and shot right through the man's reindeer. The deer collapsed.

"Let's settle in the same camp, so that we can hunt together," said the young man, obviously changing his opinion of Kagèna's daughter.

"All right," the young woman agreed.

They went to live in the same place. The next day they went hunting in different directions. Kagèna's daughter killed ten wild deer, and the man killed one. They both returned in the evening.

The man went up to Kagèna's daughter to find out how successful her hunt had been. Thrusting his head into the entrance of her lodge, he asked, "How many deer did you kill?"

"I'm just a woman," she answered. "What kind of hunter could I be, anyway? I killed only ten deer." Then she asked, "How many deer did you kill?"

"I killed one."

The young woman could not believe his words. "How many did you kill? Did you say one set of ten deer?"

"No, no, no. I killed one—one deer," the young man said, and he raised his index finger to demonstrate.

"What kind of hunter are you if you have killed only one deer?" she said.

"Let's go hunting again tomorrow," the young man suggested.

"All right," Kagèna's daughter agreed.

The next day, they went hunting again. The young woman killed twenty wild reindeer, and the man killed two.

When they returned that evening, the man went to find out how many deer Kagèna's daughter had killed. Thrusting his head into the lodge entrance, he asked, "How many deer did you kill?"

"I killed two sets of ten. Tell me, how many deer did you kill?"

"I killed two."

"What kind of hunter are you? How weak you are!" Kagèna's daughter exclaimed.

Then, the young man said, "Tomorrow let's go hunting again."

The next day, they went hunting again. They saw thirty-five wild deer. They began shooting arrows. The young woman killed every reindeer she attempted to shoot. The man failed to kill even one.

The man was ashamed that Kagèna's daughter was a better hunter than he. "Tomorrow let's compare our strength," he said. "We'll have a contest and shoot at each other."

"Fine. What else can we do?" Kagèna's daughter said.

The next morning, Kagèna's daughter rose early and stood far enough away that her reindeer's antlers were not visible. "Well, hunter, you shoot first," she sang.

The man began shooting at the woman. He failed to hit her even once. He could not kill her. With her bare hands Kagèna's daughter grabbed the ends of the arrows that were flying toward her. The man shot thirty-five times. Finally, he used up all of his arrows.

"Well, hunter, take a good look at me," said Kagèna's daughter.

The embarrassed man turned aside. He began jumping from side to side, so that the young woman's arrows would not hit him. Kagèna's daughter shot just once, and the arrow went into the hunter's thigh. The so-called hunter fell, and the proud young woman left him lying there.

THE EVIL OLD WOMAN WITH THE LONG NAILS

(Alaskan Yup'ik)

A grandson once lived with his grandmother. The grandmother used to warn her grandson not to cross the river and not to go into the tall grass on the other side. "It's dangerous there," she would say. "Now, remember, Grandson, never to walk in that tall grass there."

Nevertheless, one day when the boy had gone to pick berries beside the river, he noticed some tasty berries among the tall grass on the riverbank across the way. "Those berries look bigger than these," he thought. "Surely, it won't do any harm to pick the berries near the riverbank. I'll stay away from the tall grass."

The little boy hopped into his kayak and crossed the river. He began picking the big, luscious berries on the forbidden side of the river. As he picked, the tall grass waved in the breeze temptingly. The boy watched its movement. The grass piqued his curiosity, so he wandered closer to the grass and further away from the riverbank.

Suddenly, he spied a footpath that meandered through the tall grass. He decided to follow it, to see where it led. "I won't go far," he decided, "and I'll come back soon. It won't take long."

The boy set out down the footpath. As he walked, the grass became even taller until it seemed to cover him.

Suddenly, he saw a billow of smoke flowing up to the sky. He decided to go in the direction of the mysterious smoke. Curiosity led him on. Forgetting about home and his grandmother's warning, he pressed on in search of the origin of the smoke.

Eventually, the smoke led him to a tiny house. Cautiously, he looked around the outside of the house. Seeing nobody, he climbed onto the top of the house and looked down through the smoke hole. He saw a strange, old woman sitting below. She had long nails that made a rustling sound as she played with them, flicking them this way and that.

The boy had been very quiet, but nevertheless the old woman noticed his presence. "Come down off that roof, Boy, and come in," she shouted.

The boy did as the old woman ordered and entered the house. At first the old woman seemed friendly. She served him some boiled fish. While the boy ate, the old woman continued to play with her long nails, sharpening them on a stone.

Suddenly, a small boy ran into the house and asked to eat some fish, too. "I'm hungry," he said.

The old woman refused to give him even a fishbone. "Not now!" she barked at the small boy.

The small boy began to wail and demand food. "I'm hungry! I'm hungry!" he demanded. Then he flopped down onto the ground and threw a temper tantrum.

The old woman did not relent, so the small boy ran out onto the porch. "I'll get my own food!" he shouted.

The old woman rushed after the small boy. The visiting boy heard a blood-curdling scream, followed by silence.

The old woman came back inside and sat down, acting as if nothing at all had happened.

The visiting boy was scared and began to plot his escape. "Grandma was right. I should not have crossed the river," he thought. He decided to find an excuse to go outside. Once outside, he planned to run home to his grandmother.

"I have to go to the bathroom. I have to wet," he told the old woman.

"Then wet into my palm, boy," the old woman said.

"I'd like to," the boy replied, "but I don't know how to wet into your palm."

"Then wet into my mukluk,* boy," the old woman commanded.

"I'd like to," the boy replied, "but I don't know how to wet into a mukluk."

Exasperated, the old woman said, "Then wet into my fireplace, boy."

Once again, the visiting boy said, "I'd like to, but I don't know how to wet into the fireplace."

The old woman was losing her patience. "Then go wet in front of the house, but mind that you come right back in without dawdling!"

The boy went out onto the porch. There, to his horror, he saw the hungry little boy lying dead in a big kettle. He knew that he would be the evil old woman's next victim. He tightened his belt, grabbed his pail full of berries, and fled.

The boy ran as fast as he could. While running, he heard heavy footsteps following him—stomp, stomp, stomp. He looked quickly over his shoulder and saw the old woman running like a dog after him. Her long nails were extended, coming closer and closer. He could hear the rustling sound the nails made, like many knives being sharpened.

---

* Boot.

When the boy reached the river, he saw that his kayak was gone. On the riverbank opposite, a ptarmigan was strutting about.

"Dear little ptarmigan," said the boy, "an evil old woman is chasing me. Please help me!"

The ptarmigan stretched its long legs across the river. "Walk across the river on my legs, son," the ptarmigan said.

Once on the other side of the river, the boy thanked the ptarmigan and said, "When the old woman comes, let her cross the river on your legs, too. Once she reaches the middle of the river, pull back your legs so that she falls into the water."

The ptarmigan agreed to do as the boy had requested.

When the old woman reached the river, she began screaming and wailing and shaking her long nails. "Take me across the river, ptarmigan, or I'll chop you to pieces with my long nails," she demanded.

Without uttering a word, the ptarmigan stretched out its long legs, making a bridge for the old woman. When she got to the middle of the river, the ptarmigan suddenly pulled back its long legs. The evil old woman sank to the bottom of the river and drowned.

On the spot where she sank, mice started coming to the surface of the water. They were the old woman's body lice.

The grandson ran home to his grandmother. Thereafter, he always obeyed his grandmother. From then on, the grandson was convinced that his grandmother knew what was best for him.

KIVIUQ'S ETERNAL JOURNEY

(Inuit)

Kiviuq is the Arctic's epic hero of a cycle of stories that depicts his adventures as he wanders eternally across land and sea. Kiviuq is a great shaman who is capable of battling the elements, escaping a whirlpool, and passing through an iceberg that opens and closes. He can cause a mountain or a river to appear. Sailing from adventure to adventure in his kayak, he battles Big Bee Woman, Spider Woman, a bear, sea lice, and giant caterpillars. He marries Wolf Woman, Fox Woman, and Goose Woman, for whom he searches while gliding on a salmon's tail.[1]

Kiviuq's name appears variously as Giviok, Kiviung, Kiviok, Kivioq, Kiviuk, and Qiviuq.[2] Legend records that Kiviuq killed an Inuk and could not return to his native village, so he went to the white man's land and became wealthy. It is said that now he is living the last of his many lives so that he looks so old that he is horrible to look at. He will return to his native land before his life ends.[3]

$\mathcal{T}$his is not the place to tell about Kiviuq's entire journey, but a few episodes from his adventures are in order. It is especially interesting to learn how Kiviuq happened to set out on his legendary, eternal way. Kiviuq has been on earth for a long time. He appeared soon after the world was created, at a time when humans could shape-shift into animals and animals could become human.

Kiviuq Sets Out on His Journey

There was a boy who lived with his grandmother. The two of them were all alone in the world. The grandmother had no husband, and the boy had no parents. There was no one to care for them.

They were very poor. The boy wore clothing made from the skin of birds they had snared. The boy's playmates made fun of him, and the men of the village mocked the boy and tore his clothing. Only one man, named Kiviuq, was kind to the boy and protected him from the other villagers.

When the boy came running to his grandmother in tears, she always comforted him and begged the village children and the men to stop teasing the boy and to stop tearing his clothes. Finally, the boy's grandmother could stand it no longer. She got angry and swore to avenge the boy's tormenters. Because she was a great shaman (*angakok*),[4] her threat was not an empty one.

The grandmother told her grandson to step into a puddle that had been created by the melting snow on the floor of their house. The boy obeyed his grandmother without question.

"You will emerge from the puddle by the seashore. Swim out to sea, and the bad men who teased you will chase you. Lure them farther and farther away from shore and far out to sea," the grandmother told her grandson.

As soon as he walked into the puddle, the earth opened up and the boy sank down into the bowels of the earth. He emerged near the beach in the shape of a young seal with a beautiful pelt.

When the men caught sight of the young seal, they chased it in their kayaks. The boy swam away quickly, luring the men out to sea as his grandmother had instructed. He came up for breath behind the men's kayaks so that the men could not harpoon him. Behind the kayaks, he splashed and played to lure the group on. As the group turned their kayaks to pursue the seal boy, he dove into the water and swam away. In this manner, the men failed to notice that they were being led far away from land.

Then the shaman grandmother caused a gale to rise out of the sea. The waters foamed and roared. High waves destroyed the powerless kayaks. Finally, everyone who had teased the boy and had torn his clothing was drowned. The seal boy went home, where he became an ordinary boy once again. Even his feet were no longer wet.

Only the great shaman (*angakok*) Kiviuq was spared because he had not mistreated the boy. Brave Kiviuq used his powers to battle the sea and the storm, which raged on, but he was far from land. Kiviuq drifted for many days on the open sea. Once he saw a dark mass that looked like land. His heart began beating faster. Hopeful, he paddled hard to reach it, only to find that he was rushing toward a maelstrom and not land. Twice he was deceived and thought that the dark waters of a whirlpool were land, but he managed to escape the whirlpools before being drawn down into them.

Kiviuq and Big Bee Woman

When the storm finally abated and the sea was no longer angry, Kiviuq spied land. From the water, he noticed a sod house. The house had a smoke hole, so it was open at the top.

Kiviuq pulled his kayak onto shore and left it in such a position that he could return, jump into it, and flee quickly if he had to.

He went up to the house and noticed that there were no windows. Quietly, he climbed the wall of the house and looked down the smoke hole in the roof into the house. An old sorceress named Ivigtarsuaq, Big Bee Woman, was living there.[5] She was sitting and tanning a human skin.

Kiviuq spat down upon her, and then he hid quickly. He need not have worried that Big Bee Woman would see him because when she tried to look up to see what was going on, her big, heavy eyelids flopped down over her eyes. "That's strange," she said, "my house never had a leaky roof before today."

Kiviuq spat again. This time Big Bee Woman took her crescent-shaped knife and cut off her eyelids. Kiviuq looked into a pair of eyes so horrible that they could frighten a person to death.

When she saw the intruder, Ivigtarsuaq, Big Bee Woman, came out and invited Kiviuq into her home. He followed her. To tell the truth, Big Bee Woman seemed nice enough and even offered to dry Kiviuq's wet clothes and *kamiks* (boots). She placed his wet clothes on her drying rack and invited Kiviuq to rest on the platform, which she made into a bed. Kiviuq crawled up onto the platform with a feeling of unease.

Taking her crescent-shaped knife with her, Big Bee Woman left the sod house to get fuel for the fire. Her intention was to eat Kiviuq for dinner. Before killing and cooking him, she had to fetch the fuel.

While she was gone, Kiviuq glanced around. He saw skulls everywhere. One of the heads spoke to him while rocking back and forth. It said, "Hurry! Get out of here, or you will become a skull, like us! Run!"

Kiviuq decided to take the skull's advice and run away. He reached up to grab his drying clothes, but the drying rack rose into the air out of reach. He tried several times in vain to get his clothes. Each time the rack flew into the air out of reach. Then Kiviuq called on his helping spirit, a little snow bunting. The bird swooped down and swept the clothes off the rack with its wings.

Kiviuq grabbed his clothes and ran. He rushed to his kayak and sailed out to sea hurriedly. Ivigtarsuaq, the sorceress, ran after him with her knife. She was in such a temper that Kiviuq paddled hard to get away from her.

Ivigtarsuaq saw that the situation was hopeless and that she would never catch Kiviuq, so she slashed at a huge piece of granite with her knife. The granite shattered into tiny pieces. "That's the way I would have sliced you," she cried.

Kiviuq grabbed his harpoon and harpooned a huge rock sticking up from the sea. The stone crumbed. "That's what I would have done to you," he screamed.

When Ivigtarsuaq, Big Bee Woman, saw how powerful Kiviuq was, she wanted to marry him. "Will you be my husband?" she asked.

"Never," Kiviuq replied, as he paddled away.

Big Bee Woman ranted and raved as Kiviuq paddled away. Enraged, she flung her knife after Kiviuq. It skipped over the top of the water. Everywhere that it touched turned to ice.

Thereafter, the sea began freezing over in winter, and there was no open water any-more. When the sea freezes, people say that Big Bee Woman is throwing her knife over the water to make it turn to ice. From that day on, people have had to hunt seals by listening at their breathing holes in the ice.

Kiviuq Returns Home

Kiviuq continued to roam across the Arctic. He had many more adventures. One day in his travels he came to a place that seemed familiar. Boats filled with men who had been on a whaling trip came toward him. The men were towing a big whale carcass to the village.

The young man who had killed the whale stood triumphantly in the bow. At first Kiviuq did not recognize him. He was the son whom Kiviuq had left behind as a young child. He was grown and had become a great hunter. And Kiviuq's wife had remarried.

Kiviuq wept tears of joy and pride when he realized that he was face-to-face with his son. However, he did not stay with the young man. He continued on his eternal journey and is having adventures even today. The Inuit are waiting for him to return to them again.

The rock where Kiviuq's mother waited for his return. Near Arviat, Nunavut. Photograph courtesy of Kira Van Deusen.

TAYUNE AND KINAK, THE HILL GIANT

(Canadian Inuit and Alaskan Inupiat)

*J*t was the dead of winter, and Tayune was running away from her abusive husband, who had once again beaten her bloody. As usual, her husband's rage seemed unfounded, and Tayune had no idea why he was angry and why he had beaten her. As she ran across the tundra, her husband slept. "I'll never return," she decided. "I'd rather freeze to death in the snow than continue living with him."

Tayune pushed through the snow and traveled against the cruel, Arctic wind that lashed her face. She passed several villages, but she kept away from them for fear of being discovered.

Finally, only the tundra loomed ahead. Soon Tayune's small sack of food was empty. She had to satisfy her hunger by eating fistfuls of snow.

When snow no longer sufficed to slake her hunger, Tayune stumbled upon a stash of caribou meat that she imagined some hunters had left behind. She tore off a few bites of meat to stave off starvation. "I hope the hunters won't mind my taking a small piece of meat. There is so much of it." Tayune ate part of the small piece of meat and carefully put the remainder in her sack.

Fortified, Tayune continued on her journey. She came to a strangely shaped hill that looked like a foot with five toes. She walked all day along the crest of the hill. When night drew near, she settled down in the snow between two hills that looked like two toes, and she fell asleep.

The following night, she sought refuge under a ledge. The third day, Tayune traveled higher along the ridge. At night she dug a small cave in the snow on top of a windy hill, climbed into the cave, and slept soundly.

The next day, Tayune reached a forest of tangled bushes. Fatigued at the end of the day, she nestled into the bushes and slept.

In the morning, a loud voice cried out, "Who are you? Why have you come? I am the Hill Giant, Kinak, who lies across the tundra. I have been watching you. I allowed you to sleep between my toes the first night, under my knee the second night, in my belly button the third night, and in my beard last night. As a rule, people don't visit me, so what are you doing here?"

Shaking with fear, Tayune told the story of her miserable life. "I am Tayune. I ran away from my husband because he beat me. Please forgive me. I didn't realize that I was traveling on your body."

"You may stay if you wish," Kinak said, "but mind that you stay away from my mouth. You will be blown away when I take a breath or sneeze if you get too close."

Tayune realized that for four days she had been traveling on the body of Kinak. When the young woman understood that the giant meant her no harm, she built a house of hair from Kinak's beard and began living beside the giant's nose, far from his mouth. Whenever the giant sneezed or coughed, a blizzard raged across the tundra and Tayune nestled deeply and snugly into her home.

Tayune and Kinak became good friends. The giant let Tayune use the hairs from his beard as firewood. His enormous fist made a shadow as he dropped caribou, seals, foxes, and bears down beside Tayune. She had plenty to eat and made warm clothes and rugs for her home from the animal pelts. In the coldest of weather, the giant's breath kept Tayune warm.

For many happy years, Tayune lived with the Hill Giant. From the hides of the animals that the giant brought her, she had a store of valuable furs. Nevertheless, she missed her friends and family in the village.

Kinak noticed that Tayune was sometimes sad and silent. "What is wrong?" he asked. "Why are you sad?"

"I miss home," Tayune said, "but I dare not return for fear that my husband will beat me all the harder for running away from him."

"I will protect you," said Kinak. "You have only to call my name and I will come to your rescue. Now cut the ears off all of the furs, and place them in your sack."

Tayune did as the Hill Giant instructed. He took a deep breath and blew. Tayune floated on the Arctic wind coming from the giant's mouth. She drifted through the air and floated over the tundra. When her village came into sight, she descended.

Everyone was happy to see Tayune, whom they thought had died. Even her cruel husband was delighted that she had returned and promised never again to beat her.

Tayune dumped the animal ears out of her sack and into her husband's storage shed. The next morning, each ear had become an entire animal. Tayune's husband had been made wealthy because now he possessed a large number of furs. His prestige in the community was assured, and he was grateful to Tayune.

For a while, Tayne's cruel husband did not lay a finger on her. Soon, however, he reverted to his old ways. He flew into a rage one day and beat Tayune until she was black and blue.

"Kinak, help me as you promised," cried Tayune.

The sky grew dark, like a snow sky. Immediately, it began snowing harder and harder until it became a blizzard. The Arctic wind whirled around Tayune's husband and lifted him into the sky. Tayune never saw her cruel husband again.

Kinak took pity on the mean man and protected him against the storm, just as he had protected Tayune. He let Tayune's husband live in his beard and gave him the same warning that he had given Tayune—to stay away from his mouth.

Tayune's husband refused to respect the giant's command. He decided to explore the giant's mouth in hopes of finding more fine furs.

As he clung to Kinak's beard near the giant's mouth, Kinak gave a sneeze. No matter how hard the husband clung to the hairs of Kinak's beard, he could not hold on against the Arctic wind coming from Kinak's mouth. The Hill Giant blew the cruel husband into the sky, beyond the earth and the moon, clear to the stars.

No one has seen Kinak since he blew Tayune's husband away. However, when it snows hard and the Arctic winds are more bitter than usual, the Inuit remember Kinak and his kindness to Tayune.

KAGSAGSUK, THE BOY WITH ENORMOUS NOSTRILS

(Inuit)

*O*ne day the adults of the village had gone to a song feast at the shaman's house and had left the children alone, all in one big house. The children were playing. Without adult supervision, they were making a great noise.

The tiny orphan boy, Kagsagsuk, was outside. He heard the noisy children shouting. "Sh-h-h," he said. "You're making too much noise. If you are too loud, the Fire Spirit will hear you and will come."

The children paid no attention to his words and continued to play and make noise.

Kagsagsuk noticed that the Fire Spirit was approaching. He ran into the house and said, "Lift me up onto the drying rack so that I can get my gloves." Kagsagsuk was too small to reach his gloves without help, so the children lifted him up onto the drying rack under the roof.

The Fire Spirit came hurrying into the house bearing a whip. The whip was a living ribbon seal that had long claws. The Fire Spirit cracked his seal whip and began dragging the children out through the passage with the whip. Every time he embraced a child with his fiery whip, the child began to sizzle and was burned to a crisp.

Before leaving, the Fire Spirit touched a fur that was hanging on the drying rack. It, too, turned to charcoal. However, the Fire Spirit did not see little Kagsagsuk.

After making certain that the Fire Spirit had gone, little Kagsagsuk climbed down from the drying rack and rushed to the shaman's house to tell the parents what had happened.

No one believed him. "You killed our children yourself," they cried angrily.

"If you don't believe me, make a noise like the children did and see what happens," said little Kagsagsuk.

The villagers banished Kagsagsuk and began cooking some blubber. When the oil was boiling hot and bubbling away in the pot, they began making noise and shouting loudly. They placed the pot of boiling hot oil above the entrance.

The Fire Spirit heard the commotion and came running with his live ribbon seal whip. As the Fire Spirit rushed through the entrance, the villagers poured boiling oil over his ribbon seal whip and destroyed it. Then the Fire Spirit went away.

Even though now the villagers knew that little Kagsagsuk had told them the truth, they were unkind to the boy from that day on. Perhaps he reminded them of the tragic loss of their children, or perhaps he was an outcast simply because he was an orphan. Whatever the reason, the villagers began abusing the poor orphan.

Previously, Kagsagsuk had lived in the house of Umerdlugtoq, who was a village leader. After the fire, Umerdlugtoq made the boy stay outside all the time. If Kagsagsuk tried to enter the house to dry his wet boots, the great Umerdlugtoq would grab him by the nostrils and fling him back over the threshold. This happened so may times that Kagsagsuk's nostrils grew wider and wider until they became enormous. His nostrils were the only part of him that grew. Otherwise, Kagsagsuk remained small and weak.

Little Kagsagsuk had two grandmothers. One beat him mercilessly for the smallest infraction, such as lying in the passageway. His other grandmother was kind to him and felt sorry for him because, after all, he was her daughter's son.

On the rare occasions when Umerdlugtoq and his family allowed the boy to come in, they fed him only tough walrus hide that he had to chew with the help of a stone held between his teeth. They even pulled out some of his teeth, claiming that he ate too much. If Kagsagsuk was extremely hungry, he ate the dogs' leavings. Sometimes he found a bit of walrus hide that the dogs refused to eat.

To keep warm, Kagsagsuk slept with the dogs or lay on the roof near the smoke hole. Of course, if Umerdlugtoq caught him warming himself there, he would hook his big fingers into the boy's nostrils and pull him down.

His kind grandmother gave him a pair of boots and a small bird-spear so that he might play with the children, but the children teased him cruelly They rolled him in the snow and stuffed his clothing with wet snow. The girls threw garbage at him.

As soon as spring came and Kagsagsuk was able, he wandered over the land, carefully avoiding the other children. Alone and in despair, he called, "Spirit of Strength, please enter me!"

After uttering these words, Kagsagsuk happened upon a man of enormous proportions, a giant. The giant was cutting up his catch.

"Hey, man, give me a piece of that meat," Kagsagsuk cried in a loud voice. Although the boy was shouting at the top of his voice, still the giant could not hear him.

Finally, after several attempts, the tiny sound of Kagsagsuk's voice reached the giant, who threw a little piece of meat to the boy. "Bring me luck!" said the giant, who could not see the boy and believed that he was talking to a dead person.

Young as he was, Kagsagsuk already possessed the ability of a shaman and had helping spirits that looked after him. With their help, Kagsagsuk made the little piece of meat into a big piece of meat. The boy ate his fill and hid the remainder.

Little Kagsagsuk went home and said to his kind grandmother, "I have stored away a great amount of meat. I can't stop thinking about it, so I'm going back to watch over it."

The boy went back to his hiding place, but the meat was gone. Tears began streaming down his cheeks. As he was weeping, the giant came up to him and roared, "Why are you crying?"

"I can't find the meat that I hid in this stone cairn."[*]

"Oh, I took that meat. I thought it belonged to someone else," said the giant. "Never mind, boy. Let's play and forget about it."

Little Kagsagsuk and the giant walked on together. They came to a big, heavy stone. "Let's push this stone," the giant proposed.

At first Kagsagsuk gave the stone a push and fell backward. With the giant's help, the stone twisted around.

"Again. There's another stone over there. Hurry. Do it again. And there's an even bigger stone beyond that one. Push, push," instructed the giant.

Finally, little Kagsagsuk stopped falling over backward. He was able to move the stones and twist them this way and that. Each time he managed to twirl a stone around, he chose a bigger stone the next time. He kept twisting stones until he could make the very largest stones twirl in the air.

Finally, the giant stopped him. "Now you are as strong as I am. Because you lost that piece of meat, I will repay you by helping you. I will cause three bears to come to your village. Watch for them."

Little Kagsagsuk went home and crawled up onto the roof. He lay near the smoke hole to keep warm. As usual, Udmerdlugtoq grabbed him by the nostrils and threw him onto the ground.

Afterward, Kagsagsuk went to lie with the dogs, but his mean grandmother beat him, as well as the dogs. The children teased him as they had always done. Kagsagsuk bore all of these abuses and did not reveal his newly acquired strength.

One night when everyone was asleep, little Kagsagsuk went down to the shore and hauled one of the *umiaks*[**] out of the frozen water.

In the morning, when the villagers saw what had happened, there was a great commotion.

"Someone hauled an *umiak* out of the ice!"

"There must be a strong man among us."

"Who could it be?"

[*] An inukshuk.
[**] An *umiak* is an open boat made of skins stretched over a wooden frame.

"Why, it must be little Kagsagsuk," said Umerdlugtoq, pointing mockingly at the boy.

It was shortly thereafter that three bears, a mother bear and two cubs, descended on the village, just as the giant had promised.

Kagsagsuk was inside drying his boots. Because he had no other boots, he put on his grandmother's boots and ran over the icy snow to meet the bears. He stepped with such force that he made footprints in the hard snow that resembled footprints made in soft snow.

"Is that Kagsagsuk?" the villagers asked. "Why has he come? Kick him away!"

Umerdlugtoq could scarcely believe his eyes. Kagsagsuk came running, his heels almost reaching his neck and causing the snow to sparkle and scatter in rainbow colors.

Little Kagsagsuk grabbed the largest bear with his hands, flung it against an iceberg so that it split in two, and wrung its neck. Then he grabbed the other two bears and cracked their heads together.

Little Kagsagsuk threw the big bear over his shoulder, placed the smaller bears under each arm, and went home. He skinned the bears and built a fireplace to cook the bears' meat for his grandmother. When the great Umerdlugtoq saw what was happening, he and his family disappeared.

Kagsagsuk took his mean grandmother, who used to beat him, and threw her into the fire. Everything, except her stomach, burned to a crisp. His other grandmother saw this and was about to run away.

"No, Grandmother, don't go," said Kagsagsuk. "You were kind to me. You gave me a bird-spear and boots. And you used to dry my boots for me. I won't hurt you because I love you."

After Kagsagsuk and his grandmother had eaten a meal of bear meat, he set off in pursuit of mean Umerdlugtoq. He found him encamped on the edge of a precipice.

Kagsagsuk rushed up to him and hooked him by the nostrils. He held Umerdlugtoq by the nostrils over the precipice until his nostrils burst. Then he released Umerdlugtoq, who stood holding is nose.

"Don't be afraid," said Kagsagsuk. "I won't kill you. After all, you never killed me."

Happy to be released, Umerdlugtoq fled, never to be seen again.

As for Kagsagsuk, he roamed the land showing off how strong he was. He and his deeds are known all along the coast to this day.

NOTES TO THE INTRODUCTION

After the initial citation, a shortened form or the abbreviation given in the Bibliography is used with further citations of the same work.

1. See *Athropolis. Facts: Cold, Icy Arctic*. Available at http://www.athropolis.com/arctic-facts/fact-snow-words.htm (accessed August 20, 2008). See also Edward J. Vajda, *The Ewenki*. Available at http://pandora.cii.wwu.edu/vajda/ea210/ewenkiewen.htm (accessed July 29, 2009).

2. Knud Rasmussen, *Across Arctic America, Narrative of the Fifth Thule Expedition* (New York: G. P. Putnam, 1927; reprint, New York: Greenwood Press, 1969), 223.

3. Facts about the Arctic and Subarctic were taken from *The Arctic*. Available at http://encarta.msn.com/text_761577860_0/Arctic.html (accessed March 16, 2008). Web site is no longer available.

4. *Inuit: East Greenland* (source: everyculture.com). Available at http://www.lycos.com/info/inuit—east-greenland.html?page=3 (accessed November 2, 2008).

5. *Inuit People*. Available at http://www.allthingsarctic.com/people/inuit.aspx (accessed August 20, 2008). It should be noted that the Canadian population of 30,000 Inuit consists of only 22,000 speakers of the language. See *Inuit: Quebec Inuit* (source: geocities.com). Available at http://www.lycos.com/inuit—quebec-inuit.html (accessed November 2, 2008). David Morrison places the Canadian population higher at 40,000 in *Canadian Inuit History: A Thousand-Year Odyssey*. Available at http://www.civilization.ca/educat/oracle/modules/dmorrison/page01_ (accessed August 20, 2008).

6. *Inuktitut (Eskimo/Inuit Language)*. Available at http://www.native-languages.org/inuktitut.htm (accessed February 23, 2008).

7. *Eskimo Terminology*. Available at http://en.wikipedia.org/wiki/Eskimo (accessed February 15, 2008).

8. *The Pages of Shades—Inuit. I. Introduction*. Available at http://www.angelfire.com/realm/shades/nativeamericans/inuit1.htm (accessed September 7, 2008).

9. *Inupiat*. Available at http://en.wikipedia.org/wiki/Inupiat (accessed May 23, 2008).

10. *The Indigenous Languages of Alaska and Siberia*. Available at http://www.linguatics.com/alaska.htm (accessed January 8, 2010).

11. See Robert McGhee, *Arctic History*. Available at http://www.civilization.ca/cmc/archeo/oracles/eskimos/12.htm (accessed August 20, 2008).

12. J. R. Miller, *Inuit*. Available at http://encarta.msn.com/text_761561130_0/Inuit.html (accessed March 16, 2008).

13. *Inuit*. Available at http://en.wikipedia.org/wiki/Inuits (accessed August 20, 2008).

14. *Inuvialuktun.* Available at http://en.wikipedia.org/wiki/Inuvialuktun (accessed January 4, 2009).

15. For more information, see *Inuinnaqtun.* Available at http://en.wikipedia.org/wiki/Inuinnaqtun (accessed May 17, 2009).

16. See *The Indigenous Languages of Alaska and Siberia*, op. cit., note 10.

17. For a description of Inuit life, see *Inuit. New World Encyclopedia.* Available at http://www.newworldencyclopedia.org/entry/Inuit (accessed April 10, 2009).

18. RasA, 232.

19. RasA, 225.

20. Ibid.

21. Knud Rasmussen, *The Netsilik Eskimos: Social Life and Spiritual Culture*, Report of the Fifth Thule Expedition, 1921–1924, vol. 8, no. 1–2 (Copenhagen: Gyldendalske Boghandel, Nordisk Forlag, 1931), 214.

22. RasA, 196.

23. RasN, 215.

24. RasA, 196–97.

25. RasN, 220.

26. RasN, 224.

27. RasN, 230.

28. *Groenlendinga saga.* Available at http://en.wikipedia.org/wiki/saga_of_the_Greenlanders (accessed March 1, 2008).

29. *Greenland.* Available at http://en.wikipedia.org/wiki/Greenland (accessed March 1, 2008).

30. The following history is constructed from *Inuit. New Word Encyclopedia.* Available at http://www.newworldencyclopedia.org/entry/Inuit (accessed April 10, 2009).

31. *Hudson's Bay Company.* Available at http://en.wikipedia.org/wiki/Hudson's_Bay_Company (accessed January 19, 2010).

32. *Across Arctic America* is Rasmussen's condensation of his ten-volume scientific report.

33. RasA, 232.

34. See *Inuit. New Word Encyclopedia*, op. cit., note 30.

35. RasA, 385.

36. See *The Cradle of Eskimo Civilization.* Available at http://athropolis.com/arctic-facts/fact-yupik.htm (accessed August 20, 2008).

37. Edward J. Vajda, *Siberian Yupik.* Available at http://pandora.cii.wwu.edu/vajda/ea210/aleut.htm (accessed May 23, 2009).

38. *Alaska Native Languages: Central Alaskan Yup'ik.* Available at http://www.uaf.edu/anlc/langs/cy.html (accessed February 29, 2008).

39. *The Yup'ik of Western Alaska*. Available at http://www.ucc.uconn.edu/~epsadm03/yupik.html (accessed February 29, 2008).

40. See *Alaska Native Languages*, op. cit., note 38.

41. *Yup'ik People*. Available at http://www.allthingsarctic.com/people/yupik.aspx (accessed February 29, 2008).

42. See *The Cradle of Eskimo Civilization*, op. cit., note 36.

43. *Comparative Yupik and Inuit*. Available at http://www.uaf.edu/anlc/yupik_inuit.html (accessed March 15, 2008).

44. See Vajda, *Siberian Yupik*, op. cit., note 37.

45. Anna M. Kerttula. *Antler on the Sea: The Yup'ik and Chukchi of the Russian Far East*, The Anthropology of Contemporary Issues, ed. Roger Sanjek (Ithaca and London: Cornell University Press, 2000), 108.

46. For a description of the *yaranga*, see Ibid, 56.

47. For a short summary of the Yup'ik lifestyle, see *Yup'ik People*, op. cit., note 41.

48. *Yupik*. Available at http://en.wikipedia.org/wiki/Yupik (accessed February 29, 2008).

49. *Alutiiq*. Available at http://en.wikipedia.org/wiki/Alutiiq (accessed August 26, 2008).

50. See *Yup'ik People*, op. cit., note 41.

51. Kerttula, *Antler*, 59.

52. A. Fienup-Riordan, *Eskimo Essays* (New Brunswick, NJ: Rutgers University Press, 1990). Available at http://www.ucc.uconn.edu/~epsadm03/yupik.html (accessed February 29, 2008).

53. *Siberian Yupik*. Available at http://en.wikipedia.org/wiki/Siberian_Yupik (accessed May 23, 2009).

54. The committee operated from 1924 to 1935. Denis J. B. Shaw, *Russia in the Modern World: A New Geography* (Oxford, England and Malden, MA: Blackwell Publishing, 1999), 242.

55. Kerttula, *Antler*, 12.

56. *Yupik in Siberia*. Available at http://www.connection-dte.dk/inuityupik_en.htm (accessed March 15, 2008).

57. Information from A. Fienup-Riordan, *Eskimo Essays*, op. cit., note 52.

58. See *Yup'ik People*, op. cit., note 41.

59. See *The Indigenous Languages of Alaska and Siberia*, op. cit., note 16.

60. Nikolai Vakhtin, *Transformations in Siberian Anthropology: An Insider's Perspective*. Available at http://www.scribd.com/dic/7481302/transformations-in-Siberian-Anthropology-An-Insiders-P (accessed May 30, 2009). Web site no longer available. Currently, the work is available at http://www.unc.edu/~aparicio/WAN/LibroWAN/VakhtinFinal.doc (accessed February 19, 2010).

61. Waldemar Bogoras, *The Eskimo of Siberia*, vol. 8, part 3, Memoir of the American Museum of Natural History, the Jessup North Pacific Expedition, ed. Franz Boas (Leiden and New York, 1913).

62. Although most sources give "people" as the meaning for Dene, Wikipedia translates the name as a compound word meaning "the Creator's Spirit flows through this land." Compare to *Cultures of Alaska*. Available at http://www.alaskanative.net/en/main_nav/education/culture_alaska/athabascan (accessed January 3, 2010).

63. See *The Indigenous Languages of Alaska and Siberia*, op. cit., note 10.

64. *Four Directions Institute*. Available at http://www.fourdir.com/california_na_dene.htm (accessed May 25, 2009).

65. *Alaska's Heritage: Athabaskans*. Available at http://www.akhistorycourse.org/articles/article.php?artID=150 (accessed January 2, 2010).

66. *Slavey*. Available at http://groups.msn.com/Halifaxonline/slavey.msnw (accessed August 11, 2008). The MSN Groups Service has been discontinued.

67. For the most recent updating of the Athabaskan language family tree, see *Northern Athabaskan Languages*. Available at http://en.wikipedia.org/wiki/Northern_Athabaskan_languages (accessed January 3, 2010).

68. *Cultures of Alaska*. Available at http://www.alaska.net/en/main_nav/education/culture_alaska/athabascan/ (accessed January 3, 2010). Facts about Dene life have been culled from *Alaska's Heritage*, op. cit., note 65.

69. *Tutchone*. Available at http://www.thecanadiancncyclopedia.com/index.cfm?PgNm=TCE&Params=A1ARTA0008176 (accessed May 19, 2009).

70. *Ingalik—Orientation*. Available at http://www.everyculture.com/North-America/Ingalik-Orientation.html (accessed January 2, 2010).

71. Ibid.

72. *Ingalik*. Available at http://www.mnsu.edu/emuseum/cultural/northamerica/ingalik.html (accessed January 2, 2010).

73. *Tlingit*. Available at http://www.mnh.si.edu/arctic/features/croads/tlingit.html (accessed January 2, 2010).

74. *Kaska*. Available at http://www.mnsu.edu/emuseum/cultural/northamerica/Kaska.html (accessed May 26, 2008).

75. *Kaska*. Available at http://www.everyculture.com/North-America/Kaska.html (accessed May 26, 2008).

76. Crow and Raven are used interchangeably among the Dene.

77. *Kaska*. Available at http://www.thecanadianencyclopedia.com/index.cfm?PgNm=TCE&Params=A1ARTA0004239 (accessed January 3, 2010).

78. *Tahltan*. Available at http://en.wikipedia.org/wiki/Tahltan (accessed May 29, 2008).

79. *Tahltan Indian Tribe History*. From *Handbook of American Indians*, 1906. Available at http://www.accessgenealogy.com/native/tribes/canada/tahltanindianhist.htm (accessed January 3, 2010).

80. See Tahltan, op. cit., note 78.

81. *Northern Athabaskan Languages*, op. cit., note 67.

82. Michael I. Asch, *Slavey (Slave)*. Available at http://www.thecanadianencyclopedia.com/index.cfm?PgNm=TCE&Params=A1ARTA0007450 (accessed February 19, 2010).

83. *Slavey*. Available at http://www.everyculture.com/North-America/Slavey-Orientation.html (accessed May 26, 2008).

84. *Sahtu*. Available at http://en.wikipedia.org/wiki/Sahtu (accessed May 26, 2008).

85. *Koyukon*. Available at http://www.nativewiki.org/Koyukon (accessed January 4, 2010).

86. *Ahtna*. Available at http://www.everyculture.com/North-America/Ahtna.html (accessed January 4, 2010).

87. *Ahtna*. Available at http://www.uaf.edu/anlc/langs/aa.html (accessed March 9, 2008).

88. John E. Smelcer, collected and edited by, *In the Shadow of Mountains: Ahtna Stories from the Copper River* (Glennallen, AK: The Ahtna Heritage Foundation, 1997), 5.

89. *Ingalik*. Available at http://www.historyandtheheadlines.abc-clio.com/ContentPages/ContentPage.aspx?entryID=1173735&currentsection=1161468&productid=5 (accessed January 2, 2010).

90. See Kaska, op. cit., note 74.

91. *History of Yukon First Nations People*. Available at http://www.yfnta.org/past/history.htm (accessed August 20, 2008).

92. See Slavey, op. cit., note 83.

93. For a list of explorers, see *List of Polar Explorers*. Available at http://en.wikipedia.org/wiki/Arctic_explorer (accessed February 9, 2010). Click on the explorer's name, and you will reach his biography.

94. *North-Western Territory*. Available at http://wikipedia.org/wiki/North_Western_Territory (accessed January 5, 2010).

95. *Northwest Territories*. Available at http://www.answers.com/topic/northwest-territories (accessed January 3, 2010).

96. *History of the Yukon and Its People*. Available at http://www.yukonman.com/history.asp (accessed January 3, 2010).

97. *History of Alaska*. Available at http://en.wikipedia.org/wiki/History-of-Alaska (accessed January 3, 2010).

98. See *History of the Yukon and Its People*, op. cit., note 96.

99. *Americans of North America*. Available at http://encarta.msn.com/encyclopedia_761570777/Native_Americans_of_North_America.htm (accessed March 16, 2008). MSN Encarta Encyclopedia is no longer available.

100. For a discussion of genre, see James Ruppert and John W. Bernet, editors, *Our Voices: Native Stories of Alaska and the Yukon* (Lincoln and London: University of Nebraska Press, 2001).

101. Bren Kolson, *In the Spirit of Dene Dance. Our Dene Stories*. Available at http://nativedance.ca/index.php/Dene/Our_Dance_Stories (accessed May 31, 2008). No longer available.

102. The population is given as 15,000 to 20,000 in *Innu*. Available at http://www.mongabay.com/indigenous_ethnicities/north_american/Innu.html (accessed February 29, 2008). A second site claims the population is 16,000: *The Innu*. Available at http://www.heritage.nf.ca/aboriginal/innu.html (accessed June 2, 2008). Agreement with the latter figure may be found in *Innu Nation. Nitassinan*. Available at http://www.infonet.st-johns.nf.ca/green/innul.html (accessed August 16, 2008). Access to the *Nitassinan* site is currently unavailable. The total population is close to 20,000 according to information given at *Montagnais History*. Available at http://www.dickshovel.com/mon.html (accessed March 28, 2008).

103. See *Labrador History*. Available at http://epe.lac-bac.gc.ca/100/205/301/ic/cdc/Labrador/history.html (August 11, 2008). This site is currently available at http://epe.lac-bac.gc.ca/100/205/301/ic/cdc/Labrador/default.htm (accessed February 20, 2010); *Archeological Sites of Newfoundland and Labrador*. Available at http://www.tcr.gov.nl.ca/tcr/pao/ (accessed August 25, 2008); and Lawrence Millman, *Wolverine Creates the World: Labrador Indian Tales* (Santa Barbara, CA: Capra Press, 1993), 10.

104. *Naskapi*. Available at http://en.wikipedia.org/wiki/Naskapi (accessed March 15, 2008).

105. There is some evidence that this Montagnais word has a pejorative connotation, meaning "crude and uncivilized people." See *Montagnais History*. Available at http://www.dickshovel.com/mon.html (accessed March 28, 2008).

106. Ibid.

107. *Nitassinan*. Available at http://everything2.com/e2node/Nitassinan (accessed August 16, 2008). Currently available at http://everything2.com/index.pl?node=Nitassinan&lastnode_id=124&searchy=search (accessed February 20, 2010).

108. *The Concept of Respect*. Available at http://www.innu.ca/respect.html (accessed June 2, 2008).

109. For a description of the Shaking Tent ritual, see Peter Armitage, "Religious Ideology among the Innu of Eastern Quebec and Labrador," 21–22. Available at http://www.unites.uqam.ca/religiologiques/no6/armit.pdf (accessed August 4, 2008).

110. *Naskapi Nation History*. Available at http://naskapi.ca/en/our_nation/history.htm (accessed March 28, 2008).

111. For an absorbing account of the hardships faced by the relocated Mushuau splinter band of the Innu at Davis Inlet on the Labrador coast, see Auŝra Burns, "Moving and Moving Forward: Mushuau Innu Relocation from Davis Inlet to Natuashish." Available at http://www.lib.unb.ca/Texts/Acadiensis/2006/acad35_2art04.html (accessed August 16, 2008). The group was moved first to Nutak (1948), after which they walked home to Davis Inlet (1949), then to Uitshimassits on Iluikoyak Island (1967), and finally to Natuashish (2002–2004). By the end of 2004, the Canadian government had spent $280 million to move 700 Innu.

112. *The Innu*, op. cit., note 102; *Labrador History*, op. cit., note 103.

113. Peter Armitage describes the difficulties faced by the Innu and the harm done by Europeanization in *The Innu*, op. cit., note 102.

114. John Gimlette, *Theatre of Fish: Travels through Newfoundland and Labrador* (New York: Alfred A. Knopf, 2005), 223, 226, and 255.

115. Elizabeth Penashue and Rose Gregoire, "Nitassinan: Our Land, Our Struggle," in *Peace Magazine* (August–September, 1989), 14 [online]. Available at http://archive. peacemagazine.org/v05n4p14.htm (accessed February 26, 2008).

116. *Introduction to the Innu*. Available at http://www.tipatshimuna.ca/1000_e.php. (accessed August 11, 2008).

117. This nomenclature is Peter Armitage's in "Religious Ideology among the Innu of Eastern Quebec and Labrador," 33. See op. cit., note 109.

118. The word "tundra" is a Saami word. See *An Introduction to the Sami People*. Available at http://boreale.konto.itv.se/samiengl.htm (accessed February 15, 2008).

119. "The Kola Lapps," in *The Red Book of the Peoples of the Russian Empire*. Available at http://www.eki.ee/books/redbook/kola_lapps.shtml (accessed May 23, 2009).

120. *Sami People*. Available at http://en.wikipedia.org/wiki/Sami_people (accessed July 24, 2009).

121. See *Lapland. The Columbia Encyclopedia*, 6th ed. (2007). Available at http://www. encyclopedia.com/doc/1E1-Lapland.html (accessed February 16, 2008) and "The Kola Lapps," in *The Red Book* (see op. cit., note 119).

122. See *Sami People*, op. cit., note 120.

123. Ibid.

124. See Lapland, note 121, and Elina Helander, "The Sami of Norway." Available at http:// www.reisenett.no/norway/facts/culture_science/sami.html (accessed February 15, 2008).

125. *Sami*. Available at http://www.everyculture.com/wc/Norway-to-Russia/sami.html (accessed March 28, 2009).

126. See *Sami People*, op. cit., note 120.

127. Pius Wittmann, "Lapland and Lapps," in *The Catholic Encyclopedia*, vol. 8 (New York: Robert Appleton, 1910). Available at http://www.newadvent.org/cathen/08797a.htm (February 16, 2008).

128. See *Sami People*, op. cit., note 120.

129. Sarah Andrews, "Women in Saami Society." Available at http://www.utexas.edu/ courses/sami/dieda/hist/women.htm (September 3, 2008).

130. See Sami, op. cit., note 125.

131. Ibid.

132. Ibid.

133. Doug Simms, "The Early Period of Sámi History, from the Beginnings to the 16th Century." Available at http://www.utexas.edu/courses/sami/dieda/hist/early.htm (accessed September 3, 2008).

134. See Andrews, "Women in Saami Society," op cit., note 129.

135. See Sami, op cit., note 125.

136. Information about death customs may be found in Risto Pulkkinen, "The Death and the Dead Ones," in *The Encyclopaedia of Saami Culture*. Available at http://www.helsinki.fi/~sugl_smi/senc/en/index.htm (accessed July 28, 2009).

137. See Lapland, op. cit., note 121.

138. Information about Saami deities was taken from Pulkkinen, "Pre-Christian Gods," op. cit., note 136.

139. See Helander, "The Sami of Norway," op. cit., note 124.

140. For dates and works, see Simms, "The Early Period of Sámi History," op. cit., note 133.

141. See Helander, "The Sami of Norway," op. cit., note 124.

142. See "The Kola Lapps," op. cit., note 119.

143. Ibid, and supplemented by *Sami People*, op. cit., note 120.

144. Jorn Madslien, "Russia's Sami Fight for Their Lives," *BBC News*. Available at http://news.bbc.co.uk/2/hi/business/6171701.stm (accessed February 20, 2010).

145. See Pulkkinen, "Pre-Christian Gods," op. cit., note 138.

146. For a short history of Saami folkloristics, see Hans-Herman Bartens, "Legends and Folk Tales," *The Encyclopaedia of Saami Culture*. Available at http://www.helsinki.fi/~sugl_smi/senc/en/index.htm (accessed July 28, 2009).

147. See V. I. Nemirovich-Danchenko, *Svideniia o narodnoi poezii loparei*, Izvestiia Imperatorskogo Russkogo Geograficheskogo Obshchestva, vol. 11, no. 1 (Moscow, 1875). Another respected collection of Saami stories is that of E. Ia. Patsiia, compiler, *Saamskie skazki* (Murmansk: Kn. Izd-vo, 1930).

148. See Bartens, "Legends and Folk Tales," op. cit., note 146.

149. *Siberia*. Available at http://en.wikipedia.org/wiki/Siberia (accessed January 14, 2008).

150. Ibid.

151. Michael Hammer and Tatiana Karafet, "DNA and the People of Siberia." Available at http://www.mnh.si.edu/arctic/html/peopling_siberia.html (accessed February 2, 2008).

152. *Republic of Komi. Guide to Russia*. Available at http://www.mccme.ru/putevod/11/11eng.htm (accessed January 25, 2010).

153. *Pomory. Academic Dictionaries and Encyclopedias*. Available in http://dic.academic.ru/dic.nsf/efremova/221206/ Поморы (accessed January 23, 2010). A Russian font is necessary in order to access. Go to google.ru.

154. *Komi Republic*. Available at http://www.russia-ic.com/regions/3979 (accessed January 23, 2010).

155. "Mansis," in *The Red Book of the Peoples of the Russian Empire*. Available at http://www.eki.ee/books/redbook/mansis.shtml (accessed February 20, 2010). Unless otherwise indicated, information concerning the northern people of Russia comes from *The Red Book* in this introductory article.

156. *Sakha Republic (Yakutia).* Available at http://www.hunmagyar.org/turan/yakut/index.html (accessed February 20, 2010).

157. For a map of the peoples of Russia and a listing of the ethno-linguistic groups, see "People of the Soviet Union," Supplement to *National Geographic* 149, 2 (February 1976): 144A.

158. *Russian Language.* Available at http://en.wikipedia.org/wiki/Russian_(language) (accessed January 26, 2010).

159. Information on culture and life also from *The Red Book* unless otherwise noted.

160. *Veps and Karelians.* Available at http://www.barentsinfo.org/?Deptid=15095 (accessed August 1, 2009).

161. See *Republic of* Komi, op. cit., note 152.

162. For a good narration about living among the Even "reindeer people," see Piers Vitebsky, *The Reindeer People: Living with Animals and Spirits in Siberia* (2005; reprint, Boston and New York: Houghton Mifflin, 2006).

163. Many Nenets still live in the traditional nomadic way. Nenets Oxana Kharuchi tells about her people and their life in *Nenets*. Available at http://www.siberiagym.com/siberia_pictures_nenets_oxana_kh.htm (accessed February 20, 2010).

164. *Korennye malochislennye narody Taimyra, ikh traditsii.* Available at http://www.taimyr24.ru/ (accessed July 12, 2009). This web site can be reached with a Russian font via google.ru.

165. Details about life among the "reindeer people" can be found at *Domestic Life.* Available at http://www.museum.state.il.us/exhibits/changing/journey/hunters-domest.html (accessed December 24, 2009).

166. See *Sakha* Republic, op. cit., note 156.

167. Piers Vitebsky, *Shamanism* (Norman: University of Oklahoma Press, 1995), 34. Kira Van Deusen noted that the origin is actually from the Tungus language family, of which Evenk is a branch.

168. *Mansi.* Available at http://www.raipon.org/web-Database/mansi.htm (accessed January 16, 2003).

169. *The Sacred Landscape.* Available at http://www.mnh.si.edu/arctic/html/yamalsa.html (accessed August 1, 2008).

170. Vitebsky, *Shamanism*, 36. Ordinary Chukchi and Koryak can do some shamanic things, probably having to do with the severity of the situation. Kira Van Deusen

171. *Shamanic Healing Rituals.* Available at http://www.museum.state.il/us/exhibits/changing/journey/healing.html (accessed March 29, 2008).

172. Information on the Nganasan comes from *Nganasan. Religion and Expressive Culture*. Available at http://www.everyculture.com/Russia-Eurasia-China/Nganasan-Religion-and-Expressive-Culture.html (accessed July 9, 2009).

173. In recent years, there has been a revival in shamanism. Kira Van Deusen met elder shamans in the Amur region in the 1990s. From e-mail to author, February 22, 2010.

174. Sidney Harcave, *Russia. A History* (Chicago, Philadelphia, and New York: J. B. Lippincott, 1959), 10.

175. Nicholas V. Riasanovsky, *A History of Russia*, 4th ed. (New York and Oxford: Oxford University Press, 1984), 11–17 passim; Harcave, *Russia*, 9–12.

176. Riazanovsky, *History of Russia*, 40.

177. Ibid., 152–53.

178. Information concerning the presence of newcomers to northern Russia and their effect has been culled from *The Red Book* unless otherwise indicated.

179. James Forsyth, *A History of the Peoples of Siberia: Russia's North Asian Colony, 1581–1990* (Cambridge and New York: Cambridge University Press, 1992), 38–42.

180. Information about the fate of shamans added by Kira Van Deusen. See also Anna Reid, *The Shaman's Coat: A Native History of Siberia* (New York: Walker and Co., 2002).

181. *History. The Columbia Electronic Encyclopedia*, 6th ed. (2007). Available at http://www.infoplease.com/ce6/world/A0861075.htm (accessed January 30, 2010).

182. Chukchi killed off their reindeer in protest to collectivization. Kira Van Deusen

183. For accounts about life in Siberia today, see Kerttula, *Antler,* and Reid, *The Shaman's Coat.*

184. "Priekhali," in *Russkoe ustnoe narodnoe tvorchestvo*, ed. V. P. Anikin (Moscow: "Vysshaia shkola," 2006), 1063.

NOTES TO STORIES

The abbreviations in the bibliography are used to provide information about the stories in this collection. Notes about the stories are given, as well as the names of indigenous tellers, when known.

Part 1: Tales of Daily Life

Granny Chachakan-Chachakan (Sakha/Yakut)

See Kira Van Deusen, *The Flying Tiger—Women Shamans and Storytellers of the Amur* (Montreal: McGill-Queens University Press, 2001), 102–3. Nadezhda Kimonko, Udeghe cultural worker from Khabarovsk in the Russian Far East, told me a story she had heard from her grandmother, who was a Christian. A frog was thrown onto the ice, she said. This led to a well-known folktale often called "Who Is Strongest?" The frog asks if the ice is the strongest thing in the world, and the ice says "yes." But the frog sees that the sun is stronger, because the sun can melt ice. A cloud can block the sun, Nadezhda's grandmother went on—the wind can disperse the cloud, and because the wind comes from heaven, God in heaven is strongest. On the other hand, Soviet versions usually end with man being the strongest, because he can chop the tree that breaks up the mountain with its roots. The mountain had blocked the cloud. Other versions go on to say that death is stronger than man and that a shaman is stronger than death but afraid of fire, which in turn can be put out with water. And now the story has come full circle. The earliest versions emphasize the cyclical nature of life on earth. Kira Van Deusen

The Old Woman and the Dwarfs (Netsilik Inuit)

Told by Nakasuk in RasN, 256.

Part 2: Creation Stories and Myths

Sedna, the Sea Spirit (Inuit—Arctic)

1. The story of Sedna is known throughout the Arctic in different versions. Her name varies. The Netsilik Eskimos call her Nuliajuk, for example, and the Utkuhikjalingmiut call her Putulik (RasN, 498).

2. Knud Rasmussen relates the tale about Takanaluk Arnaluk as told to him by Greenlander Aua in RasA, 27–28.

3. Knud Rasmussen tells of two destinations for the dead—one for those who died violently (People of the Day) and another for those who died of sickness (People of the Narrow Land) in RasA, 28–30.

4. Knud Rasmussen describes the shaman's difficult journey in RasA, 30–34.

There are several variations and plots involved in the Sedna myth. I chose to relate the most commonly available version with details from several others.

In some tales, Sedna is depicted as a glutton who gnaws off her father's arms. Others relate that she either willingly married or was raped by a dog and was punished by being thrown into the sea by Anguta, her father. Alaskan Yup'ik Elder Paul John describes only the marriage with a dog in his origin myth titled "How Nunivak Got Its First People," in *Stories for Future Generations. The Oratory of Yup'ik Elder Paul John*, translated by Sophie Shield (Seattle and London: Calista Elders Council, Bethel, in association with the University of Washington Press, 2003), 599–609.

In the version I selected, Sedna's bird husband is variously depicted as a raven, a fulmar, petrel (Rasmussen), a birdman, or simply a seabird. In some versions, the bird seduces her with promises and charm, and in others she goes with him against her will. Sedna either begs her father to take her away from the birdman, or her father finds her living in squalor during a visit. In some tales, the father, Anguta, kills the bird husband and is pursued by the bird's friends, or the birdman himself pursues father and daughter and creates a storm on the sea. Anguta either goes home and dies of grief after his daughter drowns or becomes a resident of Adlivun, the Underworld, with Sedna. There, he conveys dead souls to that realm.

Rasmussen notes that among the Netsilik Inuit the deity is called Nuliajuk, but before becoming the deity, the girl is called Putulik (RasN, 498).

How the Narwhal Came to Be (Inuit and North American First Nations)

1. See *Narwhal Troubles: Global Climate Change Could Hit Them the Hardest.* Available at http://www.smm.org/buzz_tags/global_climate_change (accessed July 31, 2008).

2. See *About the Tusk.* Available at http://www.narwhal.org/AboutTheTusk.html (accessed April 20, 2008).

There are several versions of the Arctic legend describing the origin of the first narwhal. The adversary is a wicked woman with a daughter and blind son, niggardly grandmother, or cruel stepmother who causes her stepson to go blind. In other versions, the antagonist is an aunt jealous of her sister's family or angered by an abusive husband. The blind boy kills a bear when his mother, sister, or grandmother, direct his aim.

A loon, or bird, cures the boy of his blindness. Sometimes both a bear and a loon appear in the same tale. When a harpoon line is tied to the waist of the wicked mother (grandmother or stepmother), she is carried into the water and becomes a narwhal with a twisted tusk. In the jealous aunt version, the nephew throws a harpoon on a line to the aunt to prevent her suicide and accidentally harpoons her lip. In the mistreated wife version, the wife falls back into the water and is rescued from her abuser by becoming a narwhal. In my retelling, I eliminated the abused wife version and combined features of the other versions.

The motif of diving into water with a loon and being granted sight is extant among the Yup'ik, Inupiat, and North American Indians (Upper Tanana, Tanaina, Eyak, and Ahtna), too, and is a common Alaskan story. One example of a First Nations version is "The Blind Man and the Loon," in Sm, 37–39.

Special note should be taken of the following versions. In Marcel Akadlaka's "A Blind Son" in Bla, 8–14, a walrus takes the place of the narwhal, and loons lick the blind boy's eyes to cause him to see. In the same collection, Thomas Kusuqaq tells a story titled "The Woman with the Long Hair," in which an abused woman is transformed into a narwhal (38–40). Paul Monroe has his own special rendition entitled "The Blind Boy and the Mulgi (Loon)" in Hall, 245–47.

Raven Steals the Light of the Sun, Moon, and Stars (Inuit and Dene)

This widely known Dene creation story is extant among many Dene groups, including the Tanaina, Tanana, Koyukuk, Deg Hit'an (Ingalik), and Ahtna. It exists, too, in Tlingit, Inuit, and Tsimshian repertoires. There are slight differences among the variants. In the Yukon Tlingit version, Crow, not Raven, is the thief. Raven/Crow may turn into a pine needle, a spruce needle, a hemlock needle, a piece of moss, cedar leaf, a small fish, or a speck of dust (Inuit). Frederica de Laguna states that Crow is really Raven, although Raven is referred to as "Crow," despite the absence of crows in interior Alaska (Lag, 77).

Versions told by indigenous storytellers include Catherine Attla's "The One Who Took Back the Sun (So Nogheełzooga)" in AttlaA, 87–106; John Dayton's "Crow Gets the Sun and the Moon" (no. 26), in Lag, 210–14; Larson Charley's "Crow Gets the Sun and Moon" (no. 25), in Lag, 201–9; Andrew Pilot's "Crow Gets the Sun and the Moon" (No. 23), in Lag 197–98; Edna Hunnicutt's "The Raven Makes Daylight" (EH6), in Hall, 83–85; *Birth of Crow. Legends Traditions, Culture*. Excerpts from *I'm Going to Tell You a Story* by Mrs. Kitty Smith. Available at LTC (accessed May 22, 2008).

Wolverine and Mink Create Earth (Innu, Eastern Cree, and Upper Yukon Dene)

1. *High Country News: The Perils of Secrecy.* Available at http://www.hen.org/ articles/17093 (accessed August 11, 2008).

2. Turn, 163.

3. The *Mishtapeuat* were giants who inhabited *Tshishtashkamuku*, the land of giants, which was connected to earth by a land bridge. Anyone who attempted to cross to *Tshishtashkamuku* by sea ran the risk of being sucked down into an enormous whirlpool. The shaman used to consult with the *Mishtapeu* chief in the shaking tent and interpret his words. The chief of the giants was good to man and was his helping spirit. It was thanks

to Wolverine and Mink that earth and the bridge that connected it to *Tshishtashkamuku* existed at all. It is Wolverine who created the earth that became man's home.

Innu and Eastern Cree creation myths are very similar. Mink or Muskrat is said to be Wolverine's helper in creating earth, depending upon the source. Both storyteller John Poker of Davis Inlet (once Utshimassit and now Natuashish) and Eastern Cree storyteller Job Kawapit of Whapmagoostui (Great Whale River) designated Mink as Wolverine's helper. However, Muskrat figures in Lawrence Millman's "Wolverine Creates the World" (MillW, 22–23). An Alaskan Athabaskan (Dene) version has Man and Muskrat as the main characters (Jud, 81).

Sources not listed above: *Massu Re-creates the World*, narrated by Job Kawapit. Translated by Luci Bobbish-Salt. Commentary by Marguerite MacKenzie, 2006. Available at http://www.eastcree.org (accessed August 11, 2008); *To the End of the Road: Québec's Côté-Nord*, by Christopher Frey. Available at http://brokenatlas.wordpress.com/archives/to-the-end-of-the-road-quebecs-cote-nord (accessed August 12, 2008).

How the Seasons Were Created (MacKenzie River Slavey)

A version in which people, rather than animals, search for the bag of warmth and battle the bear exists as well. "Dene—Creation of Seasons." Available at CM (accessed April 19, 2009).

Toy People (Chukchi)

Based on a story told in 1948 by Uvatygyn, an inhabitant of Uèlen in Chukotka. P. Ia. Skorik recorded the tale and translated it into Russian (Gl, 47).

The Creation of Caribou (Netsilik and Caribou Inuit)

The Netsilik Inuit Nâlungiaq told about the marriage of the mountain spirit and the fox and about fishing dried meat out of the earth (RasN, 212). The Caribou Inuit Kibjarjuk told of the appearance of caribou from a hole in the earth in "An Inuit Legend about the Origin of the Caribou," *Observations on the Intellectual Culture of the Caribou Eskimos* by Knud Rasmussen, Report of the Fifth Thule Expedition, 1921–1924, vol. 7, no. 2 (Copenhagen, Gyldendalske Boghandel, 1930). Available at http://www.climatechangenorth. ca/section-BG/pdf/BG-08E-print.pdf (accessed February 28, 2009). A longer version of the tale gives an explanation for the existence of caribou and for their having flat heads due to being kicked in the head by a spirit. See OMF (accessed February 2, 2009). In the Upper Yukon Dene version titled "The Camp Robber" (Jud, 128–29), Canada Jay is the creator and not the Inuit Mountain Spirit.

The Ingrates (Chukchi)

Based on a tale told in 1945 by Aritval', who lived at the mouth of the Khatyrka River. Recorded by O. E. Baboshina. Translated into Russian by Aukiki (Gl, 47).

Sister Sun and Brother Moon (Inuit, Aleut, and Deg Hit'an/Ingalik)

1. The kissing motif and blackened mouth motif is taken from Knud Rasmussen's version collected from the Utkuhikjalingmiut (RasN, 526).

2. In the Deg Hit'an/Ingalik version, the young woman puts feathers in her brother's hair. Most versions represent the encounter between brother and sister as a rape.

This story chronicling the origin of the Moon Spirit and his Sun Sister is part of a trilogy that includes the stories of the blind boy and the loon and the origin of the narwhal.

Hare Rescues the Sun (Chukchi)

Told by Rike'wgi, a Maritime Chukchi man at Mariinsky Post in October 1900 ("The Hare Tale," no. 2, in BogrCM, 155). The latter part of the story, in which the *kele* is flown to a great height and is dropped can be found in Kira Van Deusen's work on storytelling in Chukotka (DeuR, 41 and 121–22). In "Raven, Kelye, and Hare," as told by Margarita Takakava (Chukchi), the kele flies on the back of Raven. In Gleb Nakazik's Yupik version, titled "Reindeer, Crow, and Evil Spirit," Crow makes the flight.

Part 3: Tricksters and Fools

Raven Kills Whale (Dene and Alaskan Inupiat)

1. Raven is often referred to as Crow in English, despite the fact that there are no crows in the interior of Alaska.

In Catherine Attla's version (AttlaS, 119–35), there are many more episodes. A soup is made of Raven's intestines. He stuffs mittens into his rear end, where his intestines once were, and there is a great flood of soup when Raven's child sees the mittens and extracts them.

The Copper River Ahtnas tell a different tale, in which Raven tricks Whale into letting him enter his mouth. From inside Whale, Raven gradually consumes Whale's insides until Whale dies (Sm, 15–17).

The Inupiat version has much in common with the Ahtna. See Hall, 117.

Wolverine and the Brant (Innu)

1. The brant is a goose with a short neck. In the past, there were sufficient migrating brant to provide feasts for the Innu. Today both the brant and the wolverine have disappeared. The brant changed their migratory route when the feeding beds of eelgrass were destroyed by a fungus. For more information, see *The Story of the Disappearing Apishtiss (Brant)*. Available at http://www.innu.ca/brant.html (accessed March 28, 2008).

2. Lucien Turner explains that when the Innu see a flock of birds, they make a loud noise. The birds are so frightened that they fall to the ground and are killed (Turn, 163).

The retelling here is a combination of two versions of the tale from four sources. The version told by John Peastitute of Schefferville and Joseph, Edward, and Charlotte Rich of North West River, as translated by Joseph Peastitute and Matthew Rich, has Wolverine killing the two old women who defecate on him. See *Episode 5—Wolverine and the Geese*. Available at http://www.wolverinecom.nf.ca/wolverinemyth5.html (accessed March 5, 2008) and Des, 85–87. The Lucien Turner version has an old woman disemboweling Wolverine. See Turn, 163.

A Tale About a Silly Old Man (Even)

The Yukaghir have a similar tale, in which the old wife survives.

Part 4: Legends and *Pourquoi* Tales

The Origin of the Ptarmigan (Inuit)

1. Information about the ptarmigan may be found at *Aqiggiq—(Willow and Rock) Ptarmigan*. Available at http://www.polarlife.ca/Traditional/traditional/animals/ptarmigan.htm (accessed March 12, 2009).

Sources not listed above: *Origin of the Ptarmigan. Bayat Gallery: Legends of the North*. Available at http://www.inuitgallery.com/origins.shtml (accessed October 2, 2008—no longer available); *Inuit Legends—Origin of Ptarmigan*. Available at http://soapstonecarvings.blogspot.com/2004_07_01_archive.html (accessed February 27, 2009).

Inukshuk (Arctic)

1. Inukshuk is the English spelling. *Inuksuk* and *inutsuk* are Inuit spellings.

2. *Inukshuk*. Available at http://en.wikipedia.org/wiki/Inukshuk (accessed March 12, 2009) and *Legends. The Inukshuk*. Available at http://www.inuitartofcanada.com/english/legends/inukshuk.htm (accessed May 26, 2008).

3. Peter Irniq, *What Is an Inukshuk?* Available at http://www.youtube.com/watch?y= NKQ97rOwBHO (accessed March 12, 2009).

4. See "The First Inutsuk," from a collection gathered in the 1980s for the Torngasok Cultural Center in Nain, Labrador (Bla, 25–31).

5. In the Labrador legend, *inutsut* is the spelling rendered to reflect a minor variation in pronunciation.

Toadman Takes a Wife (Innu)

1. See *Kushhapatshikan: The Shaking Tent.* Available at Innu (accessed February 15, 2008).

2. In an interview with Mary Madeline Nuna of Sheshatshiu, she relates that the girls were picking bake apples. See *Mary Madeline Nuna Talks about Shaking Tents and Anikunapeu (the Toadman).* Available at Innu (accessed March 28, 2008).

3. A detail from Mary Madeline Nuna's version. See note 2 above.

4. In Mary Madeline Nuna's version, the axe failed to cut through Toadman's hand because his hand was like steel.

5. The legend of Toadman (Anikunapeu) explains the existence of Petshikapushkau Mountain, Toadman's home. This retelling was constructed from six sources. Most of the sources repeated the same 1967 version of the tale as told by Sébastien (Ishpashtien) Nuna and Pasteen Nuna of North West River. The original is in Laboratoire d'anthropologie amérindienne in Montreal.

Raven and Owl (Inuit and Upper Yukon Dene)

The Netsilik have a similar tale that Knud Rasmussen recorded from Manêlaq titled "The Raven and the Loon Who Tattooed Each Other" (RasN, 399), in which the loon plays the role of the owl. This version is found, too, as "The Loon and the Raven" as told in 1950 by Thomas Kusuqaq of Aivilik (Repulse Bay) in Bla, 35 and 37.

The etiological tale is extant, too, among the North American Indians. In a lovely Ahtna tale, Raven paints a necklace around Loon's neck. Loon replaces Owl in the Ahtna version by Mary Smelcer-Wood and Morrie Secondchief (Sm, 23–25).

The Giant Cannibal Dog (Greenland Inuit)

1. Inuit tales from Greenland bear witness to a hostility that existed between people living on the coast and people living inland.

2. It used to be customary to kill girls at birth, unless they were already promised in marriage because they were not as necessary to the survival of the group as were boys, who hunted for food. Consequently, there was a shortage of wives and women to do the domestic work, such as processing hides, cooking, and sewing. Kidnapping of women to obtain wives was not uncommon. See RasA, 225.

How Mosquitoes Came to Be (Tlingit)

Another Inuit version tells of two starving old women who eat their body lice and thrive while others die. Suspected of cannibalism, their stomachs are cut open, and the consumed lice take wing as mosquitoes. This tale was on OMF, an MSN group that is no longer available.

Two Brothers and a Giant (Kaska)

This story is one episode of a longer story chronicling the brothers' adventures. See Teit (accessed August 27, 2009).

Why Raven's Beak Is Crooked (Yukon River Dene)

Sources not listed above: *How Raven Lost His Beak. Raven.* Available at http://www. velcrohead.com/gecko/raven.html#HowRavenLostHis (accessed August 18, 2009) and *Raven's Great Adventure* by Glenn Welker. Available at http://www.indigenouspeople. net/ravenadv.htm (accessed August 18, 2009).

Beaver and Porcupine (Dene, Tlingit, and Tahltan)

Source not listed above: Teit, James A. "Two Tahltan Traditions." *The Journal of American Folk-Lore.* Vol. 32. No. 124. 1919: 226. Also on the following website: *Tales Online-Full Text.* Available at http://www.talesunlimited.com/fulltext.asp?taleid=1399&search_criteria= (accessed May 26, 2008). Requires membership.

The Origin of Fog (Greenland and Canadian Inuit)

1. See *Dorset Culture.* Available at http://en.wikipedia.org/wiki/Dorset_culture (accessed October 2, 2008).

2. Singular form also spelled Tuneq.

This retelling has elements of four versions. Rasmussen's villain is a Mountain Spirit (RasE, accessed July 27, 2008), and Millman's is a Glutton Spirit (MillK, 24–25). At OMF (accessed August 7, 2008) and at *Origin of Fog. Bayat Gallery.* Available at http://www. inuitgallery.com/origins.shtml (accessed October 2, 2008), there are references to a Tuniq and a Giant as villains. Rasmussen's Inuit heroes (RasE and RasN) place two barriers in the path of the Giantess. Rasmussen's Netsilik version (RasN, 375–76) is part of the Kiviuq cycle, and the villain is a bear. In the Netsilik version, the mountain ridge that Kiviuq created is the ridge that runs through the Adelaide Peninsula, and the river that Kiviuq created is the New River. In this instance, the explanatory tale gives the origin of geographic formations, as well as the origin of fog.

Part 5: Stories About Animals and Marriages with Animals

Who Shall I Be? (Siberian Yupik)

Told by Kivagmè and recorded by K. Sergeeva.

The Woman Who Adopted a Polar Bear (Greenland Inuit)

The Greenland version is based on "The Woman Who Had a Bear as a Foster-Son" in RasE (accessed September 1, 2008). A Netsilik version exists in which people's actions necessitate the bear's leaving. However, the bear continues to provide the old woman with meat and fish ("The Old Woman with a Bear as Foster-Child," told by Nakasuk, in RasN, 407–8).

The Owl and the Siksik (Canadian Inuit and Alaskan Inupiat)

1. *Artic Ground Squirrel. Natural History Notebooks.* Available at http://www.nature.ca/notebooks/english/grndsqur.htm (accessed March 1, 2009).

The Bold Little Mouse (Nenets)

1. Compare this story, in which Ice bests the boastful Mouse, to "Granny Chachakan-Chachakan" (Part I), in which Earth proves stronger than Ice. Kira Van Deusen

The Man Who Married a Seagull (Inuit)

This tale shares many traits with the European tale of the Swan Maiden (subtype of Type 400—Type 400A in N. P. Andreev, *Ukazatel' skazochnykh siuzhetov po sisteme Aarne* [Leningrad, 1929]). My retelling is based largely on Dr. Henry Rink's "The Man Who Mated Himself to a Sea-Fowl" in Rink, 145–48. A few details have been added involving the Salmon Man from the Netsilik version as told by Kuvliutsoq in his narration of the epic journey of Kiviuq in RasN, 374. This version appears to be the basis of renditions of "The Goose Wife," as told by Samson Quinangnaq, Bibianne Nivinvak, and Therese Kimmalidjuk as part of Kiviuq's journey. See *Kiviuq's Journey.* Available at http://www.unipka.ca/Stories/Goose_Wife.html (accessed January 24, 2009). Samson Quinangnaq's version is unique in that the birds leave their socks, rather than clothes, on the ground while swimming. It is also interesting that Kiviuq slurps two of the four eggs that the couple bore, thereby eating two potential offspring.

An Alaskan version as told in the 1920s by Fred, an Eskimo of Nome, demonstrates features of retelling that add interest to the narrative, somewhat at the expense of authenticity. See Jen (accessed July 20, 2008). In European style with its emphasis on the number three, there are three men that the husband encounters. His helper is a fox, rather than a

---

salmon. The ending is happy, rather than tragic. The husband stays in duck land for quite some time and finally returns home with his wife and new baby son, leaving behind the two older children.

The Fox Wife (Inuit)

This story is often told as part of the Arctic hero Kiviuq cycle. My retelling is based on the version in Thom, 161–62, which is from Lucien M. Turner's *Report of the Bureau of American Ethnology*, xi, 264.

A fox wife appears, too, in RasE (accessed January 24, 2009). This story involves a man who swapped his fox wife for a hare wife. The hare's husband insulted the fox because of her smell, so she left to stay with a worm. The husband loses interest in his wife.

In Dr. Henry Rink's "The Faithless Wife" (Rink, 143–45), the hero kills his first, unfaithful wife and lives with his new fox wife until one day jealousy causes him to comment on her odor. She leaves him. He pursues her and burns her alive in a fit of madness.

The most beautifully told version provides motivation and lays the blame for the fox woman's departure not on the hero but on the interference of covetous men living in the camp. It is from a collection gathered in the 1980s for the Torngasok Cultural Center in Nain, Labrador. See "Makusie, the Blind Boy," in Bla, 20–24.

Part 6: Spirits, Shamans, and Shapeshifters

Tshakapesh, the Moon Spirit (Innu)

1. Folktales indicate that in prehistoric times mammoths inhabited the Arctic. For more on woolly mammoths and the discovery of an intact baby mammoth found on Siberia's Yamal Peninsula by Nenets reindeer herder, Yuri Khudi, see Tom Mueller, "Ice Baby," in *The National Geographic*, vol. 215, no. 5 (May 2009): 30–55.

Members of the Rich family (Joseph, Philip, Uinipapeu, and Jean-Baptiste) have told versions of this tale, as well as Tshinish Pasteen. See Des, 55–58; MillW, 126–29; Innu (accessed February 29, 2008); and NorN, 209–11.

Fart Man (Innu)

1. For more about Fart Man, see Arm (accessed August 10, 2008).

The Forest Spirit (Khant)

Story recorded in 1973 on the Pim River from teller Fedos'ia Danilovna Vandymova, who was born in 1948 on the Liamin River. The story comes from the latter river area— "Lesnoi dukh" (no. 77), NovM (accessed August 8, 2009).

The Girl and the Moon Spirit (Chukchi)

This tale is extant among the Nganasan, too. See "Devushka i luna," SNS (accessed July 13, 2009) and "Devushka i luna," SSS (accessed July 12, 2009).

Flying to the Moon (Greenland and Canadian Inuit)

In the version collected by Dr. Henry Rink, Kanak is the hero's name ("The Moon—Kanak," no. 91 in Rink, 440–41).

Little Uniany (Evenk)

When Uniany gets to work forging wings, he is showing us the connection between shamans and blacksmiths, which is strong not only in Siberia but among the Celts and other peoples as well. Kira Van Deusen

The Shaman in the Moon (Nganasan)

This story was based on one told by Turdagin Nganduo, also known as Montuku (1879–1950). His brother was a shaman. He suffered from tuberculosis and in 1948 lived with an unmarried daughter in Avamskii Region. His repertoire of sixty texts shows the influence of the Enets and Nenets, with whom he spent time. See Novik (accessed July 16, 2009).

Nanurluk, the Polar Bear (Netsilik Inuit)

I have reordered the episodes of this story to give it continuity. It is based on a tale told by Manêlaq in RasN, 254.

The Jealous Uncle (Dene, Kodiak, Tlingit, and Alaskan Inupiat)

The most elaborate version can be found in Thom, 87–93. The retelling here is closer to John Swanton's "The Jealous Uncle" (no. 52), in SW, 198–203.

The Shapeshifter (Kola Peninsula Russian)

This story was originally told by fifty-five-year-old Mikhail Mikhailovich Kozhin in 1961. Irin'ia Andreevna Kozhina, who was seventy-three years old at the time, added the ending paragraph by way of explanation. See "Oboroten'," in Bal, 355.

The Black Ewe and the Blue Reindeer (Karelian)

Based on "Chernaia ovtsa" (no. 28), in Kon, 180–85. Considerable reworking had to be done to add motivation and to rid the tale of illogical narrative. A better told version is "Golubaia vazhenka." Available at SSS (accessed July 12, 2009).

The Jealous Wife (Deg Hit'an/Ingalik, Ahtna, Koyukon, Aleut, Inupiat, Alaskan Yup'ik)

The Reverend John W. Chapman's texts were my main reference in retelling this story of love and betrayal. See "The Jealous Wife," in Chap, 123–36, and "The Injured Wife's Revenge," in Kari, 168–72. Although the story is widely told throughout Alaska and Canada, there are variations. In the Ahtna version ("The Man with Too Many Wives," in Sm, 73–74), the hunter has two wives and encounters a pretty single woman, the reverse of the Chapman text. Moreover, the man returns to his first two wives in the Smelcer version. In Catherine Attla's Koyukuk version, the hunter survives and turns into a lynx ("Lynx," in AttlaA, 77–86).

The Man Who Became a Caribou (Canadian Inuit and Alaskan Inupiak)

1. In the Alaskan versions told by Edna Hunnicutt (EH2) and Paul Monroe as told by Frank Burns (PM109) in Hall's *Eskimo Storyteller,* the caribou man takes off his hood upon meeting his sons.

2. In the two versions mentioned in note 1, the caribou man starves to death because he is unused to human food.

"The Caribou Man" (no. 28), in Jen, 58A–59A, is told by a woman of Cape Prince of Wales. Yet another version is Qaqortingneq's "The Soul That Lets Itself Be Born Again in All the Animals of the Earth," in RasN, 217.

Part 7: Heroes and Heroines

Bladder-Head Boy Battles Mammoth (Kaska)

1. The woolly, or tundra, mammoth is an extinct species that disappeared 10,000 years ago. For more information, see National Geographic websites: *Woolly Mammoth Resurrection, "Jurassic Park," Planned.* Available at http://news.nationalgeographic.com/news/2005/04/0408_woollymammoth.html, *Woolly Mammoth DNA Reveals Elephant Family Tree.* Available at http://news.nationalgeographic.com/news/2005/12/1220_051220_mammoth.html, and *Waking the Baby Mammoth.* Available at http://channel.nationalgeographic.com/episode/waking-the-baby-mammoth-3630/overview (accessed December 17, 2009).

Yoma and the Two Sisters (Komi)

Source not listed above: *Starukha Ioma i dve devushki. Skazka naroda Komi.* Available at http://www.nskazki.nm.ru/komm.html (accessed July 31, 2009).

The Chakhkli (Saami)

1. This story is largely based on a tale told by Kalina Ivanovich Arkhipov. Arkhipov (1864 to approximately 1957) was a guide on geological expeditions. He founded the village of Monchegorsk, and he knew many stories, which he told in Saami and in Russian. See Kalina Ivanovich Arkhipov, told by, "Chakhkli," in *Saamskie skazki* (Moscow: Khudozestvennaia lit-ra, 1962), 162–68. Available at Bib (accessed March 28, 2009). Other sources include A. I. Gerasimov, told by, "Smert'chakhkli" (no. 76), recorded and translated into Russian by V. K. Alymov, Notozero Village, 1931, in *Saamskie skazki* (Murmansk: knizhnoe izd-vo, 1961), 77. Available at http://skazmurman. narod.ru/library/ssk80076.htm (accessed March 28, 2009); and S. P. Dmitriev, told by, "Chaklingi," (no. 77), recorded and translated into Russian by V. K. Alymov, in *Saamskie skazki* (Murmansk: knizhnoe izd-vo, 1961), 77–78 (accessed March 28, 2009).

The Evil Old Woman with the Long Nails (Alaskan Yup'ik)

"Long Nails" is a commonly known Yup'ik story. Three versions of the tale (in Yup'ik, in bilingual format and in a translation made by the sixth grade students of David Miller and Sophie Enoch at the Lewis Angapak Memorial School of Tuntutuliak, Alaska) were housed on *Long Nails*. Available at http://www.lksd.org/Tuntutuliak/htm/pages/longnailtranslation.html (accessed February 29, 2008). The text but not the source of the version in Yup'ik was given. The bilingual version of "Long Nails" (Cetugpak) was translated into English by Anna W. Jacobson, *Yup'ik Stories Read Aloud (Yugcetun Qulirat Naaqumalriit Erinairissuutmun)* (Fairbanks, AL: Alaska Native Language Center, 1998), 9–17. The school web page is no longer available, but the students' translation may be found as *Long Nails*. Available at http://breadnet.middlebury.edu/%7Edavid_Miller/html-pages/longnailtranslation.htm (accessed August 16, 2009). The students' translation also may be found on You Tube—*Traditional Yup'ik Story—"Long Nails"* (recommended for children). Available at http://www.youtube.com/watch?v=_Z2D8EacET8 (accessed August 16, 2009).

Kiviuq's Eternal Journey (Inuit)

1. "The Origin of Fog," "The Fox Wife," and "The Man Who Married a Seagull" are stories that appear both as part of the Kiviuq cycle and independently. Early recorders of the cycle were Henry Rink, Franz Boas, and Knud Rasmussen. Rasmussen's version is the most complete one.

2. For additional spellings, see *Children's Books About Kivioq*. Available at http://epe.lac-bac.gc.ca/100/200/301/nlc-bnc/heroes_lore_yore_can_hero-ef/2001/h6-216-e.html (accessed August 1, 2008).

3. See RasN, 376–77. Today some elders say that Kiviuq may still be living in the south and was seen as recently as the 1940s with a lichen-covered face. "When he dies, there will be no more air to breathe and life on earth will end." See *Kiviuq's Journey*. Available at http://www.uipka.ca/Kiviuq_story.html (accessed January 24, 2009). This site offers several stories from the cycle in versions told by Inuit elders.

4. The modern Nunavut spelling is *angakkuq*. Kira Van Deusen

5. Rasmussen refers to the Bee Woman as Invigtarsuaq (RasN, 366), but Boas names her Arnaitiang (Boas, 215).

Tayune and Kinak, the Hill Giant (Canadian Inuit and Alaskan Inupiat)

One version of the Kinak tale originated in the Northwest Territories, north of the Horton River. Another version comes from the Bering Strait Inupiat in Alaska. There are many similarities between the two. However, the Alaskan tale, the heroine of which is named Taku, has a continuation of the story chronicling the birth of the heroine's son, whom Taku names Kinak after the giant. The son inherits many of the cruel husband's traits and is similarly punished.

Kagsagsuk, the Boy with Enormous Nostrils (Inuit)

Kagsagsuk's name is variously rendered as Kagssagssuk or Kagsagssuk, Kautyayuq or Kautyayuk, Quadjaq, and Kaassassuk, to list just a few. Kagsagsuk's helping spirit is variously a giant, an *amarok* (wolf), Moon Man, and the star Uvdloriasugssuk (perhaps Venus in Rasmussen's Itquilik version).

GLOSSARY

Note: N = Spelling currently used in Nunavut, if different from what appears in the story.

amauti—A woman's parka with a large pouch on the back for carrying a baby. (Inuit)

angakok (N: angakkuq)—Shaman (Inuit)

brant—A type of wild goose

chum—A portable dwelling with a cone-shaped frame made of small trees and covered with hides or birchbark (Siberian)

inukshuk (N: inuksuk)—A large stone figure, often made in the shape of a person; used as a landmark, and also in hunting caribou

kak—Deerskin bed blanket (Inuit)

kashim—Men's gathering house (Alaska)

kelet, plural (or kele, singular)—Evil spirit(s) (Paleo-Asiatic Siberian)

kerezha—Sledge (Saami)

kukhlianka—Parka (Paleo-Asiatic Siberian)

Nanorluk (N: Nanurluk)—A great polar bear, often helping spirit of shamans (Inuit)

sazhen—A measure of length equal to 2.13 m or 7 feet (Russian)

shaman—A spiritual healer, diviner, and leader (from the Tungus language family, Siberia)

siksik—Arctic ground squirrel (Inuit)

taiga—A zone of coniferous forest generally located south of the tundra (from the Turkic language family, in which it refers to a forested mountain)

torbasa—Boots (Siberian)

tundra—Treeless Arctic plain, generally located just south of the sea ice

ulu (alternate spelling, ulo)—A crescent-shaped knife used by women (Inuit)

umiak—A skin-covered boat (used from Alaska to Greenland)

urasa—a cone-shaped tent covered with hides, birch bark, or sod chunks. (Siberian)

vezha—A tent covered with twigs and moss (Russian)

yaranga—An arctic dwelling. A circle of tripods is topped with a tipi-shaped roof. Covered with reindeer hides or, today, canvas (Paleo-Asiatic Siberian)

yurt—A portable dwelling with a lattice frame and covered with felt; used by Asian steppe peoples (The word has spread widely via the Russian language and is now sometimes used to refer to any aboriginal dwelling; from the Turkic language family)

BIBLIOGRAPHY OF MAJOR SOURCES

Books and Articles

Additional sources referred to only once or rarely are given in full in the notes to the Introduction and the stories.

Arm   Armitage, Peter. "Religious Ideology Among the Innu of Eastern Quebec and Labrador." Available: http://www.unites.uqam.ca/religiologiques/no6/armit.pdf (accessed October 22, 2009).

AttlaA   Attla, Catherine. *As My Grandfather Told It: Traditional Stories from Koyukuk* (Sitsiy yugh noholnik ts'in'). Translated by Eliza Jones and Melissa Axelrod. Koyukuk, AK: Yukon-Koyukuk School District, 1983.

AttlaS   Attla, Catherine. *Stories We Live By: Traditional Koyukon Athabaskan Stories* (Bekk'aatugh Ts'uhuney). Translated by Eliza Jones and Chad Thompson. 1989. Revised Edition. Fairbanks, AK: Yukon-Koyukuk School District and Alaska Native Language Center, 2001.

Bal   Balashov, D. M. *Skazki Terskogo berega Belogo moria.* Akademiia nauk SSSR. Karel'skii filial. Institut iazyka, literatury i istorii. Leningrad: "Nauka," 1970.

Bay   Bayliss, Clara Kern. *A Treasury of Eskimo Tales.* New York: Thomas Y. Crowell, 1922. Available: http://www.gutenberg.org/ebooks/24569 (accessed September 28, 2008).

Bier   Bierhorst, John, edited by. *The Dancing Fox: Arctic Folktales.* New York: William Morrow and Co., 1997.

Bla   Blake, Dale, compiled by. *Inuit Life Writings and Oral Traditions: Inuit Myths.* St. John's, Canada: Educational Resource Development Co-operative, 2001.

Boas   Boas, Franz. *The Central Eskimo.* Sixth Annual Report of the Bureau of Ethnology. Washington, D.C.: Smithsonian Institution, 1888. Reprint. Lincoln: University of Nebraska Press, 1964. Available: http://www.canadiana.org/view/53177/0253 (accessed October 20, 2009).

BoglKh   Bogoliubskaia, M. K., and A. L. Tabenkina, compiled by. *Khrestomatiia po detskoi literature: Uchebnoe posobie dlia doshkol'nykh pedagogicheskikh uchilishch.* 5th ed. Moscow: "Prosveshchenie," 1968.

BoglNS   Bogoliubskaia, M. K., and A. L. Tabenkina, compiled by. *Nashi skazki i pesenki narodov SSSR*. Vol. 2. Bibliotechka detskogo sada. Moscow: "Detskaia literatura," 1966.

BogrCM   Bogoras, Waldemar. *Chukchee Mythology: Part 1*. Edited by Franz Boas. The Jessup North Pacific Expedition. Memoir of the American Museum of Natural History. Vol. 8. Leiden and New York, 1910. Available: http://www.sacred-texts.com/asia/cm/cm00.htm (accessed October 21, 2009).

BogrES   Bogoras, Waldemar. *The Eskimo of Siberia: Part 3*. The Jessup North Pacific Expedition. Memoir of the American Museum of Natural History. Vol. 8. Leiden and New York, 1913. Available: http://www.sacred-texts.com/nam/inu/eos/index.htm (accessed January 20, 2008).

BogrKT   Bogoras, Waldemar. *Koryak Texts*. Edited by Franz Boas. Publications of the American Ethnological Society. Vol. 5. Leiden and New York: E. J. Brill, 1917. Available: http://www.sacred-texts.com/asia/kort/kort00.htm (accessed January 20, 2008).

BogrTYL   Bogoras, Waldemar. *Tales of Yukaghir, Lamut, and Russianized Natives of Eastern Siberia*. Anthropological Papers of the American Museum of Natural History. Vol. 20. Part 1. New York, 1918. Available: http://sacred-texts.com/asia/tes/tes00.htm (accessed July 15, 2009).

BR   Bruner, Jerome, adapted by, and Knud Rasmussen, collected by. *The Many Lives of Kiviok: Traditional Tales of the Netsilik Eskimos*. Cambridge, UK: Education Development Centre, 1968.

Bul   Bulatov, M., retold by. *Khoziain vetrov: Skazki narodov RSFSR. Shkol'naia biblioteka dlia nerusskikh shkol*. Moscow: "Detskaia Literatura," 1960.

Chap   Chapman, Rev. John W. *Ten'a Texts and Tales from Anvik, Alaska*. Publications of the American Ethnological Society. Vol. 6. Leiden: E. J. Brill, 1914.

Des   Desbarats, Peter, editor. *What They Used to Tell About: Indian Legends from Labrador*. Toronto: McClelland and Stewart, 1969.

DeuK   Deusen, *Kira Van. Kiviuq—An Inuit Hero and His Siberian Cousins*. Montreal: McGill University Press, 2009.

DeuR   Deusen, Kira Van. *Raven and the Rock: Storytelling in Chukotka*. Seattle and London: University of Washington Press, 1999.

Erd   Erdoes, Richard, and Alfonso Ortiz, selected and edited by. *American Indian Myths and Legends*. New York: Pantheon, 1985.

Fed   Fedorenko, P., compiled by. *Bol'shaia khrestomatiia liubimykh skazok*. Moscow: "Planeta detstva," 2001.

FR   Fienup-Riordan, Ann, edited by. *Stories for Future Generations: The Oratory of Yup'ik Elder Paul John* (Qulirat Qanemcit-llu Kinguvarcimalriit). Translated by Sophie Shield. Seattle and London: University of Washington Press, 2003.

Ge   Gesse, N., and Z. Zadunaiskaia, retold by. *Zhuravlinnoe pero: Skazki narodov Severa*. Leningrad: "Detskaia literatura," 1968.

Gi   Ginsburg, Mirra, translated by. *The Master of the Winds and Other Tales from Siberia*. New York: Crown, 1970.

Gl   Glotser, Vladimir, and Gennadii Snegirëv, retold by. *Chudak Pakaika: Skazki Chukotki*. Moscow: "Detskaia literatura," 1983.

Go   Goretskii, V. G., L. F. Klimanova, L. K. Piskunova, and L. S. Gillershtein, compiled by. *Kniga dlia chteniia: Uchebnik dlia uchashchikhsia 3 klassa trëkhletnei nachal'noi shkoly*. 4th ed. Vol. 1. Moscow: "Prosveshchenie," 1990.

Grib   Gribova, L. I., compiled by. *Voron Kutkha: Skazki narodov Severa*. 2nd ed. Moscow: "Malysh," 1976.

Grin   Grinblat, M. Ia., and A. I. Gurskii, compiled by. *Skazki narodov SSSR*. Minsk: "Narodnaia Asveta," 1970.

Hall   Hall, Edwin S. *The Eskimo Storyteller: Folktales from Noatak, Alaska*. Knoxville: University of Tennessee Press, 1998.

Jac   Jacobson, Anna W. *Yup'ik Stories Read Aloud* (Yugcetun Qulirat Naaqumalriit Erinairissuutmun). Fairbanks, AK: Alaska Native Language Center, 1998.

Jen   Jenness, Diamond. *Eskimo Folk-Lore: Myths and Traditions from Northern Alaska, the MacKenzie Delta and Coronation Gulf*. Part A. Report of the Canadian Arctic Expedition, 1913–18. Vol. 13. Ottawa: The King's Printer, 1924. Reprint. Honolulu, HI: University Press of the Pacific, 2002. Also, nine stories from Jenness's collection are included in Traditional Eskimo Tales from Alaska and MacKenzie River. Available: http://enargea.org/tales/Eskimo/Inuitlist.html (accessed April 20, 2008).

Jud   Judson, Katherine Berry, selected and edited by. *Myths and Legends of Alaska*. Chicago: A. C. McClurg and Co., 1911. Originally accessed at http://www.archive.org/stream/mythslegendsalasoojudsrich/mythslegendsalasoojudsrich_djvu.txt (accessed May 2, 2009; no longer available). Available: http://openlibrary.org/works/OL108556W/Myths_And_Legends_Of_Alaska (accessed January 1, 2010).

Kari   Kari, James, retranscribed and edited by. *Athabaskan Stories from Anvik: Rev. John W. Chapman's "Ten'a Texts and Tales."* From material originally published in Ten'a Texts and Tales from Anvik, Alaska. Publications of the American Ethnological Society. Vol. 6. 1914. Fairbanks: University of Alaska (Alaska Native Language Center), 1981.

Kon	Konkka, U.S., ed. *Karel'skie narodnye skazki.* Academiia nauk SSSR: Karel'skii filial. Institut iazyka, literatury i istorii. Moscow: Akademiia nauk SSSR, 1963.
Lag	Laguna, Frederica de, edited by. *Tales from the Dena: Indian Stories from the Tanana, Koyukuk, and Yukon Rivers.* Seattle and London: University of Washington Press, 1995. Tales recorded in 1935.
Mann	Manning, Eve, translated by. *The Daughter of the Moon and the Son of the Sun.* Moscow: Progress Publishers, 1976.
Mc	McClellan, Catherine. *My Old People's Stories: A Legacy for Yukon First Nations.* Occasional Papers in Yukon History. Vol. 5. No. 3. Yukon, Canada: Cultural Services Branches, 2007.
MillK	Millman, Lawrence, collected and retold by. *A Kayak Full of Ghosts: Eskimo Folk Tales.* Northampton, MA: Interlink Books, 2004.
MillW	Millman, Lawrence, collected and retold by. *Wolverine Creates the World: Labrador Indian Tales.* Santa Barbara, CA: Capra Press, 1993.
NorG	Norman, Howard, edited and told by. *The Girl Who Dreamed Geese and Other Tales of the Far North.* San Diego, New York, and London: Harcourt Brace and Company (Gulliver Books), 1997.
NorN	Norman, Howard, selected and edited by. *Northern Tales: Traditional Stories of Eskimo and Indian Peoples.* Pantheon Fairy Tale and Folklore Series. New York: Pantheon Books, 1990; Lincoln: University of Nebraska Press (Bison Books), 2008.
NovM	Novik, E. S., compiled by. *Mifologicheskaia proza malykh narodov Sibiri i Dal'nego Vostoka.* Available: http://www.ruthenia.ru/folklore/novik/index.htm (accessed October 21, 2009).
Pats	Patsiia, E. Ia. *Saamskie skazki.* Murmansk: Kn. Izd-vo, 1961.
Ples	Plesovskii, Fëdor Vasil'evich, comp. *Komi narodnye skazki. Syktyvkar': Komi knizhnoe izdatel'stvo,* 1975. Available: http://www.pechora-portal.ru/biblio/komibook/komiskazki/ex.html?/biblio/komibook/komiskazki/komis-kazki001.htm (accessed July 31, 2009).
Pom	Pomerantseva, È. V., adapted by. *Mordovskie skazki.* Moscow: "Detskaia literatura," 1973.
RasA	Rasmussen, Knud. *Across Arctic America. Narrative of the Fifth Thule Expedition.* New York: G. P. Putnam, 1927. Reprint. New York: Greenwood Press, 1969.
RasE	Rasmussen, Knud. collected by. *Eskimo Folk-Tales.* Translated and edited by W. Worster. London, 1921. Available: http://www.sacred-texts.com/nam/inu/eft/index.htm (accessed July 27, 2008).
RasN	Rasmussen, Knud. *The Netsilik Eskimos: Social Life and Spiritual Culture.* Report of the Fifth Thule Expedition, 1921–1924. Vol. 8. No. 1–2. Copenhagen: Gyldendalske Boghandel, Nordisk Forlag, 1931. Reprint. New York: AMS Press, 1976.

Rink Rink, Dr. Henry. *Tales and Traditions of the Eskimo with a Sketch of Their Habits, Religion, Language and Other Peculiarities.* Translated by Author from Danish. Edited by Dr. Robert Brown. Edinburgh and London: William Blackwood & Sons, 1875. Reprint. Mineola, NY: Dover Publications, 1997. Available: http://www.sacred-texts.com/nam/inu/tte/tte2-015.htm (accessed August 2, 2008).

RioP Riordan, James, collected by. *The Songs My Paddle Sings: Native American Legends.* London: Pavilion Books, 1997.

RioS Riordan, James, collected and translated by. *The Sun Maiden and the Crescent Moon: Siberian Folk Tales.* Edinburgh: Canongate Publishing Limited, 1989; New York: Interlink Books, 1991.

Rup Ruppert, James, and John W. Bernet, edited by. *Our Voices: Native Stories of Alaska and the Yukon.* Lincoln and London: University of Nebraska Press (Bison Books), 2001.

Sh Shartse, Olga, translated by. *Folk Tales from Russia.* Moscow: "Detskaia literatura," 1983; Moscow: Raduga Publishers, 1990.

Sm Smelcer, John E., collected and edited by. *In the Shadows of Mountains: Ahtna Stories from the Copper River.* Glennallen, AK: The Ahtna Heritage Foundation, 1997.

SW Swanton, John R., recorded by. *Tlingit Myths and Texts.* Smithsonian Institution. Bureau of American Ethnology. Bulletin 39. Washington, DC: Government Printing Office, 1909. Available: http://www.sacred-texts.com/nam/nw/tmt/tmt000.htm (accessed August 27, 2009).

Teit Teit, James A. "Kaska Tales." *The Journal of American Folk-Lore.* Vol. 30. No. 118. 1917. Also archived on the following web sites: Canadian Libraries. Available: http://www.archive.org/details/kaskatales00teituoft (accessed October 25, 2009) and Available: Internet Archives. http://www.archive.org/stream/kaskatales00teituoft/kaskatales00teituoft_djva.txt (accessed October 25, 2009).

Thom Thompson, Stith, selected and annotated by. *Tales of the North American Indians.* Bloomington: Indiana University Press, 1929. Reprint. Bloomington and London: Indiana University Press (First Midland Book Edition), 1966.

Turn Turner, Lucien M. *Ethnology of the Ungava District, Hudson Bay Territory: Indians and Eskimos in the Quebec-Labrador Peninsula.* Eleventh Report of the Bureau of Ethnology. Smithsonian Institution, 1889–90. Washington, DC: Government Printing Office, 1894: 165–350. Reprint. E/SPACES. Vol. 2. Inuksiutiit Association Inc. Quebec, Canada: Presses Coméditex, 1979.

Wolf Wolfson, Evelyn. *Inuit Mythology.* Berkeley Heights, NJ: Enslow Publishers, 2001.

Web Sites

The Internet is an ever-changing medium. There is no guarantee that the following websites remain at the same location to date. However, they were at the location indicated on the dates given. Some of the sites with which I worked have been archived. Others have a change of address, and still others have been removed.

Am   *American Folklore.* Available: http://www.americanfolklore.net (accessed February 18, 2010).

Bib   *Biblioteka.* Available: http://rodon.org/lib (accessed October 25, 2009).

Ca   *Canada's Arctic. Mythology.* Available: http://www.arctic.uoguelph.ca/cpl/Traditional/sidemyth.htm (accessed February 18, 2010).

CM   *Canada's First Nations. A. Native Creation Myths.* Available: http://www.native-languages.org.chipewyan-legends.htm (accessed April 19, 2008).

Dene   *The Dene World View.* Available: http://www.sicc.sk.ca/heritage/ethnography/dene/beliefs/worldview.html (accessed May 31, 2008).

ECO   *Early Canadiana Online.* Available: http://www.canadiana.org/ECO (accessed October 29, 2009).

FPL   *First People—The Legends.* Available: http://www.firstpeople.us/FP-Html-Legends/Legends-AB.html (accessed October 20, 2009).

IndPL   *Indigenous People's Literature.* Compiled by Glenn Welker. Available: http://www.indians.org/Resource/natlit/natlit.html (accessed October 20, 2009).

Innu   *Innu Nation.* Available: http://www.innu.ca/ (accessed October 25, 2009).

IntA   *Internet Archive.* Available: http://web.archive.org/collections/web.html (accessed October 25, 2009).

InuitL   *Inuit Legend.* Available: http://www.narwhal.org/IntuitLegend.html (accessed April 20, 2008).

InuM   *Inuit Mythology.* Available: http://www.windows.ucar.edu/cgi-bin/tour_def/mythology/inuit_culture.html (accessed October 20, 2009).

InuML   *Inuit Myths & Legends.* Available: http://www.inuitmyths.com/traditional.htm (accessed October 20, 2009).

Kiv   *Kiviuq's Journey.* Available: http://www.unipka.ca/Index.html (accessed February 18, 2010).

Kras   *Moi Krasnoiarsk (narodnaia èntsiklopediia). Skazki naroda Severa.* Available: http://region.krasu.ru/node/82 (accessed February 18, 2010).

LA   *Legend Categories: North America/Arctic Area*. Available: http://www.ucan-online.org/legends_list.asp?category=11 (accessed October 25, 2009).

Leagle   *Like a Searching Eagle Viewing Our Earth: Native American Lore*. Available: http://web.archive.org/web/2004108010118/home.online.no/~arnfin/native/lore/index0.htm (accessed October 20, 2009).

LS   *Legend Categories: North America/Subarctic Area*. Available: http://www.ucan-online.org/legends_list.asp?category=11 (accessed January 21, 2010).

LTC   *Legends, Traditions, Culture*. Available: http://www.yfnta.org/past/legend/htm (accessed January 21, 2010).

MLNM   *Mify i legendy narodov mira*. Available: http://www.ckazka.com/myth/myth.html (accessed October 21, 2009).

Myth   *Myth Encyclopedia: Myths and Legends of the World*. Available: http://www.mythencyclopedia.com/ (accessed January 21, 2010).

NAL   *Native American Lore*. Available: http://www.geocities.com/gbritt/lor213.htm (accessed October 25, 2009).

NaM   *Native Creation Myths*. Available: http://www.ucalgary.ca/applied_history/tutor/firstnations/world.html (accessed March 26, 2008).

NLA   *Native Languages of the Americas: Native American Indian Legends and Folklore*. Available: http://www.native-languages.org/legends.htm (accessed October 25, 2009).

OMF   *ONEOFMANYFEATHERS*. Available: http://oneofmanyfeathers.com (accessed October 20, 2009).

PM   *Pyramid Mesa*. Available: http://pyramidmesa.com/home.htm (accessed January 21, 2010).

Sedna   *Sedna*. Excerpts from *Goddesses and Heroines* by Patricia Monaghan. Available: http://www.hranajanto.com/goddessgallery/sedna.htm (accessed January 21, 2010).

SednaI   *Sedna, Inuit Goddess of the Deep Sea*. Available: http://www.goddessgift.com/goddess-myths/Inuit-goddess-Sedna.htm (accessed March 21, 2008).

SednaM   *Sedna Mythology*. Available: http://www.karmastrology.com/NewPlanets/Sedna-myth.shtml (accessed March 24, 2008).

SedW   *Sedna (mythology)*. Available: http://en.wikipedia.org/wiki/Sedna_(mythology) (accessed March 21, 2008).

SeS   *Severnye skazki*. Available: http://vto.org.ua/skazki/ (accessed October 22, 2009).

SK   *Skazki*. Available: http://fairy-tales.su/ (accessed October 21, 2009).

SNS   *Skazki narodov Severa.* Available: http://www.skazkisevera.ru (accessed February 1, 2010).

SSS   *Skazki: Severnye skazki.* Available: http://teremok.in/narodn_skazki/Severnie_ckazki.htm (accessed October 21, 2009).

ST   *Sacred Texts.* Available: http://www.sacred-texts.com (accessed February 18, 2010).

Story   *Storytelling: Oral Tradition.* From *Tales from the Igloo* by Maurice Metayer. Available: http://www.virtualmuseum.ca/Exhibitions/Holman/english/storytelling/index.php3 (accessed January 21, 2010).

SW   *Story Lovers World.* Available: http://www.story-lovers.com/index.html (accessed October 25, 2009).

TH   *Toy's House: Skazki.* Available: http://www.toys-house.ru/skazki.php (accessed October 21, 2009).

INDEX

Gimlette, John, xxxvi. *See also Theatre of Fish*

"Girl and the Moon Spirit, The" (Chukchi), l, 162–64, 257n

Gold. *See also* Gold Rush
  Alaska and Yukon, xxxi, xxxii, xxxiii
  Russia, xlvi, xlix

Gold Rush, xxxi, xxxii, xxxiii

Golden Horde, xlviii. *See also* Mongols

Goose Bay, xxxvi

Grandmother. *See* "Bladder-Head Boy Battles Mammoth"; "Evil Old Woman with the Long Nails, The"; "Kagsagsuk, the Boy with Enormous Nostrils"; "Kiviuq's Eternal Journey: Kiviuq Sets Out on His Journey"; "Little Uniany"; "Sergevan', the Hunter"

Grandson. *See* Grandmother

"Granny Chachakan–Chachakan" (Sakha/Yakut), 3–4, 247n

Great Slave Lake, xxxi

Greenland, xviii, xix, xxi–xxvi *passim*

Ground squirrel, xix, xxx, 126. *See also* ""Owl and the *Siksik*, The"; "Who Shall I Be?"

Guillemot, xix. *See also* "Guillemots"

"Guillemots" (Eastern Inuit), xxv, 112–13

Gwitchen, xxx

Han, xxx

Hare. *See* "Hare Rescues the Sun"; "Man Who Became a Caribou, The." *See also* rabbit

"Hare Rescues the Sun" (Chukchi), l, 46–47, 251n

Hearne, Samuel, xxxii

Helping spirits, xxiii, xxxvi

Heroes and Heroines, xviii, xxvi
  "Bladder-Head Boy Battles Mammoth" (Kaska), 207–209
  "Chakhkli, The" (Saami), 214–18
  "Daughter of Old Kagèna, The" (Even), 219–21
  "Evil Old Woman with the Long Nails, The" (Alaskan Yup'ik), 222–24

"Kagsagsuk, the Boy with Enormous Nostrils" (Inuit), 232–35

"Kiviuq's Eternal Journey" (Inuit), 225–28

"Tayune and Kinak, the Hill Giant" (Canadian Inuit and Alaskan Inupiat), 229–31

"Yoma and the Two Sisters" (Komi), 210–13

Historia Norvegiae, xl

Högström, Pehr, xli

Holikachuk, xxx

Homes
  chum, xlvi, 11–14, 41–42, 41n, 48, 97, 115–16, 165–67, 170–75
  barabaras, xxvii
  ena, xxvii
  igloo, xxiii
  kata, xxxviii
  lavvu, xxxviii
  log cabins, xxx
  modern homes, xx, xxxv
  qasgiq, xxvii
  tipi, 32
  urasa, 5, 76–78, 138–46 *passim*, 161
  vezha, xxxviii, 261
  yaranga, xviii, xx, xxvii, 38–39, 163–64, 261

Horse. *See* "Black Ewe and the Blue Reindeer, The"; "Yoma and the Two Sisters"

"How Mosquitoes Came to Be" (Tlingit), xix, xxxiv, 105–106, 254n

"How Reindeer Reconciled Tui–Niamy, Mother Fire, and Mou–Niamy, Mother Earth" (Nganasan), l, 48

"How the Narwhal Came to Be" (Inuit and North American First Nations), xxv, 24–25, 248–49n

"How the Seasons Were Created" (MacKenzie River Slavey), xxix, xxxiv, 32–34, 250n

Hudson, Henry, xxxii

Hudson Bay, xxi

ABOUT THE AUTHOR

BONNIE C. MARSHALL—prize-winning author, teacher, storyteller, translator, and folklorist—is a museum teacher at the New Hampshire Historical Society's Museum and is working on stories to include in a family audio guide for the Museum of Russian Icons in Clinton, Massachusetts. A native of New Hampshire Dr. Marshall received her education from Boston University, Assumption College, and the University of North Carolina, as well as from institutions of higher learning in Russia—Moscow State University, Leningrad State University, and the Herzen Institute.

Dr. Marshall established Russian programs at Davidson College and at Johnson C. Smith University, where she served as Adjunct Associate Professor of Russian and Curriculum Coordinator of the Russian Program. Her diverse career has encompassed teaching Russian language and literature and English in high schools and universities throughout the United States and Russia. She taught Russian at the University of Montana, the University of South Alabama, and the College of the Holy Cross, among others. She taught English in St. Petersburg and Moscow at the School for Global Education and the American Academy of Foreign Languages.

Her publications include several collections of folktales. They are *Baba Yaga's Geese and Other Russian Stories* (Indiana University Press, 1973), *Tales from the Heart of the Balkans* (Libraries Unlimited, 2001), *The Snow Maiden and Other Russian Tales* (Libraries Unlimited, 2004), and *The Flower of Paradise and Other Armenian Tales* (Libraries Unlimited, 2007).

ABOUT THE EDITOR

Photograph by Jasmin Dzin.

KIRA VAN DEUSEN is a professional storyteller and researcher. She has traveled widely in Siberia and the Canadian north recording indigenous tales and epics. She is the author of *Kiviuq—an Inuit Hero and His Siberian Cousins*, *Singing Story Healing Drum—Shamans and Storytellers of Turkic Siberia*, *The Flying Tiger—Women Shamans and Storytellers of the Amur*, and *Raven and the Rock—Storytelling in Chukotka*. www.kiravan.com

Recent Titles in the
World Folklore Series

Mongolian Folktales
Retold by Dashdondog Jamba and Borolzoi Dashdondog; Edited by Anne Pellowski

Polish Folktales and Folklore
Retold by Michał Malinowski; Edited by Anne Pellowski

The Singing Top: Tales from Malaysia, Singapore, and Brunei
Retold and Edited by Margaret Read MacDonald

Princess Peacock: Tales from the Other Peoples of China
Retold by Haiwang Yuan

Lao Folktales
Kongdeuane Nettavong, Wajuppa Tossa; Edited by Margaret Read MacDonald

A Fire in My Heart: Kurdish Tales
Retold by Diane Edgecomb; with Contributions by Mohammed M.A. Ahmed and Çeto Ozel

The Flying Dutchman and Other Folktales from the Netherlands
Theo Meder

Folktales from the Japanese Countryside
As told by Hiroko Fujita; Edited by Fran Stallings with Harold Wright and Miki Sakurai

Mayan Folktales; Cuentos Folklricos Mayas
Retold and Edited by Susan Conklin Thompson, Keith Thompson, and Lidia López de López

The Flower of Paradise and Other Armenian Tales
Translated and Retold by Bonnie C. Marshall; Edited and with a Foreword by Virginia Tashjian

The Magic Lotus Lantern and Other Tales from the Han Chinese
Haiwang Yuan

Brazilian Folktales
Livia de Almeida and Ana Portella; Edited by Margaret Read MacDonald

Additional titles in this series can be found at www.lu.com